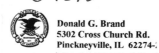

HUNTERS OF THE REICH VOL I

NIGHT FIGHTERS

David P. Williams

SPELLMOUNT

Cover illustration from a painting by Robert Taylor.
Reproduced courtesy of the Military Gallery, Bath, England.

First published in 2001
This paperback edition published in 2011 by Spellmount,
an imprint of The History Press
The Mill, Brimscombe Port
Stroud, Gloucestershire, GL5 2QG
www.thehistorypress.co.uk

British Library Cataloguing in Publication Data.
A catalogue record for this book is available from the British Library.

ISBN 978 0 7524 5961 5

Typesetting and origination by The History Press
Printed in Great Britain
Manufacturing managed by Jellyfish Print Solutions Ltd

Contents

Foreword by Anton Weiler

More than fifty years after the end of the Second World War, this fatal event still stirs the souls of many people on this earth. Renowned historians are trying to understand and fathom the cause of this bloodshed that extinguished the lives of over fifty million human beings.

Evidently, many years must go by before an unbiased examination of this dramatic conflict is possible in Europe. Especially the German point of view, which up to now has suffered from a remarkable abundance of prejudices.

However, a change has been initiated. It was, above all, British and American men who contributed to this change. Unphased by the terrible occurrences of the time, neither their view of people, nor of their feelings and personal achievements were obscured. We were filled with gratitude and pride when soon after the end of the war, British and American airmen reached out to their former enemies and even joined the German Fighter Pilot's Association.

David Williams' book can certainly be regarded as a fine example in the line of critical reconciliation of nations, for it looks after those who, having been driven into this war, many times against their will, neither gave up on their feelings nor neglected their virtues.

Anton Weiler
President
German Fighter Pilot's Association

Introduction

The question I have been most frequently asked while researching and writing this book is why I have chosen to write about German night fighter pilots. The answer is easy!

Over the past four years, since I first became a member the German Fighter Pilot's Association (*Gemeinschaft der Jagdflieger*), I have had the honour of meeting and corresponding with a large number of former pilots from the night fighter force – known as the *Nachtjagd*. Through my affiliation with this organization I have also had many opportunities to come into contact with former members of Bomber Command.

When you see these two groups of ex-servicemen, most of whom are now in their late seventies or early eighties, talking to each other it is hard to imagine that almost sixty years ago they were trying to kill one another in a brutal and deadly air war, which raged in the night skies over mainland Europe for almost five years.

It is a great testimony to these men that after such a bitter struggle, which saw many thousands of aircrew and civilians killed during the night offensive against Germany, that they are now able to put the horrors of the past behind them. Subsequently, over the post-war years, many of these former adversaries have met at reunions and lectures, with the result that many firm friendships have been formed. It was with this spirit of reconciliation in mind that I decided to write this book.

As the night air war progressed the art of night fighting became more and more sophisticated with both protagonists finding themselves using technology which, in its time, was on the cutting edge of modern science and warfare. I have purposely refrained from delving too deeply into the methods and technicalities of night fighting, so as not to detract from the real subject of the book – the pilots themselves.

During the war, these young German men, and hundreds like them, flew primarily to protect their families and their homeland from a sustained and devastating bombing campaign. They did so bravely, honourably and as many former Bomber Command personnel will testify, very effectively. Sadly, in Germany today, a country that is still struggling to come to terms with its own past, their wartime exploits and sacrifices are conveniently forgotten.

As I began to learn more about this subject I discovered that there were very few books available that detailed, in any depth, the lives and careers of these pilots and their crews. I surmised that this was probably due to the fact that, as defeated combatants, many of them at the end of the war preferred to forget the past and simply slipped quietly away into obscurity.

Over the years my correspondence with them grew and so did my knowledge about their careers. Having read their accounts it soon became clear to me that these individuals had fought as determinedly and bravely as our own RAF aircrews. Unfortunately though the German public has not afforded the same recognition to the former members of the *Nachtjagd*, as the British public has to the men and women of Bomber Command.

At the end of the war British airmen were quite rightly accorded the acclaim they deserved. In Germany it was a completely different story – its former combatants were neglected and stigmatised. It is for this reason that I felt compelled to attempt, in a small way, to redress this imbalance. I have selected five former night fighter pilots, each of whom played their part in defending Germany, and who were the epitome of many hundreds of similar young men.

In the last two years or so, since I first started researching and writing about this topic, much of my spare time has been spent letter writing or visiting each of the subjects in their homes. As a result I have had some wonderful visits to Germany and Austria where I have been welcomed with open arms and treated as if I were a member of the family. To have stayed as a guest in their homes, and to have been in the presence of these men while they recounted their wartime exploits, during many hours of interviews, has been a truly unique experience for me.

As well as these interviews each of the participants has contributed dozens, and in some cases, hundreds of pages of correspondence. The end result of all of this hard work is a book that not only accurately depicts the lives and careers of each of these men, but also gives an insight into the everyday dangers that they and their fellow airmen faced throughout the war. However, despite their valiant efforts they were unable to prevent Germany's defeat. By combining their personal recollections and private photographs, most of which have never been published before, it is my aim to show that brave men are not only found on the side of the victors. This is their story.

David P. Williams

Acknowledgements

In undertaking this project I have needed the help and support of a great many people, without whose generous assistance this book would never have been written. If for some unknown reason I have omitted to include someone, I not only offer them my heartfelt thanks but also my sincere apologies for doing so.

I would like to thank the following:

Horst Amberg, Robert Becker, Chaz Bowyer, Richard Brandon, Monica Brodie, Douglas Cooper, Bridget Cox, Frank Diamond, Bill Evans, Ben Fourmy, Ted Gardener, Peter Heinrich, Vincent Hemmings, Ian Herbert, Hazel Hughes, Roy James, Werner Kock, Gunther Lauser, Jill Lucas, Martin Middlebrook, Peter Millington, Joanne Moore, Gert Overhoff, Brian Pillinger, William Sparks, Don and Barbara Thomsett, Raymond Toliver, Anton Weiler, Graham White, Christine Wilson, and Geoffrey Wilson.

There are two people to whom I would like to say particular thanks because without their constant encouragement and advice I feel sure this project would have fallen by the wayside long ago. The first of these is Martyn Ford-Jones, an established author in his own right and the official historian for XV Squadron based at Mildenhall in Suffolk. When I was first introduced to Martyn some three years ago he was extremely busy completing one of his own books. Nevertheless, he still took time out of his busy schedule to help and advise me, as well as introducing me to people who could help with my own project. His knowledge of Bomber Command, combined with his very large and extensive archive, has proved invaluable over the years. I value the friendship that has grown from our association, and I sincerely thank him and his wife, Valerie, for their tireless support.

The second person to whom I owe a great deal is Peter Hinchliffe, a remarkable man blessed with an enormous spirit of generosity. During the war Peter was a navigator with 51 Squadron and was himself shot down over Belgium by a German night fighter on 4/5 November 1944. Since our first meeting at his home in 1997, Peter has assisted me greatly, by translating the large amounts of correspondence I have received from each of the participating pilots and by providing information concerning certain aspects of the battle. Through his own books about the night offensive against Germany and Heinz Schnaufer, the leading German night fighter, Peter has befriended a great number of former night fighter pilots and is well respected within their veterans organisation. Without his continued support and friendship, supplemented by one of his many early morning cooked breakfasts, this book simply would not have been written. My heartfelt thanks to you Peter.

In addition I should also like to convey my gratitude to my wife, Sarah. Having poured through an almost endless amount of reference material, I have discovered that behind every book is a long-suffering wife or partner, and my wife is no exception to this rule. From the very beginning of this project she has had to endure many an evening on her own when I have had to spend time away from home interviewing or carrying out research on this subject. In recent months she has even accompanied me across Germany and Austria, ably assisting me with the map as we covered over 2,000 miles on visits to each of the subjects covered in this book.

Last, and by no means least, my thanks go out to Wolf Falck, Georg Greiner, Werner Hoffmann, Peter Spoden and Paul Zorner, as well as to their wives, for their friendship and wonderful hospitality over the last three years. Thank you for your patience and trust, as well as all of your hard work. I hope I have been able to do justice to your remarkable lives and careers.

This book is dedicated to the airmen from both sides of the conflict, to those who survived, and to the memory of those who did not.

1

Oberst Wolfgang Falck

Running hard, heart thumping and pulse racing, Wolf Falck threw himself into the nearest muddy slit trench and covered his head with his hands. As he did so a series of explosions tore up the airfield, throwing large plumes of earth and smoke high into the air. The staccato rattle of machine-gun fire filled the damp, dawn air as the RAF intruders harried the fleeing pilots and ground crews into their air-raid shelters. It was April 1940 and the airfield was Aalborg in Denmark, situated to the northern end of the Jutland Peninsula.

Nuisance attacks, by this time, had become an all too common occurrence that had infuriated and frustrated Falck to the point of despair. As a result of this, and in close co-operation with selected personnel, he began to formulate a plan to counter these nightly sorties by RAF bombers. In a relatively short time the theory for such a plan was devised. Operators from a coastal radar station, situated close to the airfield, would inform

Formal portrait of Major and Geschwader-kommodore, Wolfgang Falck, c.October 1940. (Falck)

Oberst a.D. Wolfgang Falck, at home in the Tyrol. (author's collection)

Gruppenkommandeur of I./ZG 1, *Hauptmann* Falck, greets *General der Flieger*, Albert Kesselring in May 1940. By this time, Falck had already penned his theories on night fighting, and Kesselring was one of those who showed an early interest in the concept. (Falck)

Falck by telephone of any incoming enemy aircraft. The type of radar being used at this time was called *Freya*, which had a range of 100km and could detect aircraft flying up to a maximum altitude of 10,000ft. As well as working closely with the radar station, assistance was also sought from the local flak and searchlight units. The final part of the plan involved dividing up a large-scale map of the area around Aalborg into a series of rectangular grid squares called *Planquadrates*. Each *Planquadrat* was then allocated two specific letters that identified its position on the map.

In theory it was hoped that incoming bombers would be detected by radar at an early stage, at which time Falck and aircraft from his unit, I./ZG 1, would be directed to the *Planquadrat* in which the bomber had first been located. However, this system failed to yield any success and a re-think was urgently required. The next step was to have the Bf110 twin-engined fighters standing by in a pre-arranged holding area, flying at a pre-arranged height and in constant radio contact with the radar station. Unfortunately this new method also failed to bring any successes, however, it did provide the *Zerstörer* pilots with a clear insight into the difficulties of flying at night, as well as providing them with experience that would prove invaluable later on.

After a further raid by the RAF on Falck's airfield on the night of 30 April/1 May 1940, he took off, along with three of his most experienced pilots, (*Oberleutnant* Streib, *Oberleutnant* Radusch and *Feldwebel* Their) and pursued the British bombers across the North Sea. Here he recounts the operation which, in just a few short months,

Hauptmann Werner Streib (left), along with Falck, Radusch and Their, was involved on 30 April/1 May 1940 in the first attempt to intercept bombers at night from Aalborg in Denmark. *Generalleutnant* Josef Kammhuber is pictured on the far right. (author's collection)

would act as the catalyst for the formation of a night fighter force that would become known as the *Nachtjagd*.

> The RAF came back from Germany travelling very slowly and dropped their bombs on our airfield and aircraft. This was the very early part of the morning when it was just getting light. So I said to the other crews, which I had selected to examine the possibility of using the Me110 as a night fighter, 'Lets Go!' We were in the aircraft and took off. We were also very lucky, as there were holes on the airfield that we hadn't seen and the four of us were fortunate that nobody crashed! Each of us saw one aircraft even though we had no contact with the ground stations. One or two of us shot at them but they flew down over the sea where there is always a light fog, and they disappeared. One of us (Radusch) also received some hits on his aircraft but he was able to make it home. It was the first time that we could show that with reorganisation and training of the crews, it would be possible to engage the bombers.

Filled with a resurgence of hope and determination, Wolf Falck sat down and proceeded to write a comprehensive report detailing his thoughts, findings and objectives before sending it to the Air Ministry. This thesis created a great deal of interest among the powers that be, bringing him to the attention of the Luftwaffe's highest ranking and most influential officers.

However, some twenty-three years before *Hauptmann* Falck had penned his new and innovative ideas, the basic theory of night fighting had already been put into practice during the final years of the First World War. Its origins can be traced right back to 1916 when air warfare in general was still in its infancy. The first night time confrontation took place between units of the Imperial German Air Force and the Royal Flying Corp, who were increasingly targeting the German's airfields and their infrastructure.

As can be expected without up-to-date information on the bombers course and location, and without close co-operation from the searchlight units, success was always going to be 'hit and miss' in the early stages. The first recorded night time victory between two aircraft took place a little after midnight on 6 April 1917, when the Royal Flying Corp attacked the German airfield at Douai in Northern France. *Leutnant* Wilhelm Frankl of Jasta 4 took off after the raiders and succeeded in shooting down a British B.E. 2b bomber from 100 Squadron. Frankl, a holder of the prestigious *Pour le Merite*, didn't live long enough to contemplate the significance of his victory as he was killed in action two days later.

Others quickly followed this success, but it wasn't until May 1918 that a system of co-operation between the fighters, flak units, listening posts and searchlight units was implemented. This system, using a single fighter aircraft in a pre-specified 'standby zone', was not dissimilar to that of the *Himmelbett* system used by the *Nachtjagd* in 1941. Although there were initial teething problems this close co-operation quickly paid dividends. On the night of 22/23 May 1918, three Allied aircraft were shot down while four others were forced to jettison their bomb loads prior to reaching their targets. Similar successes were to follow using this method.

During the inter-war years much of what had been learned about night fighting was forgotten. This was certainly the case in Germany where the country underwent almost complete disarmament. Under the directives of the Treaty of Versaille however, the new German State known as the *Weimar* Republic, was allowed to maintain an army restricted to 100,000 long-term volunteers. It was within this small, but select military force, known as the *Reichswehr*, that Wolfgang Falck began his military career when he joined its ranks in April 1931. However, this remarkable man's life story began some twenty years before in the halcyon period leading up to the outbreak of the First World War.

Wolf, the son of a priest, was born in Berlin on 19 August 1910, although many generations of the Falck family had lived in what was then West Prussia, but is now in Poland, in the area of Graudenz/Danzig. He grew up during turbulent times in Germany and experienced the many changes that took place, both politically and socially.

> My father was a priest and moved to Berlin shortly before my birth, together with my mother and their two daughters (my sister, Else twelve years older, and my other sister Irmgard). In Berlin my father became a priest at the Melanchton Church in south-west Berlin. In this way I experienced various aspects of the Kaiser period and the First World War, and also the revolution, the civil war and the Weimar Republic. In 1917 my parents moved to Berlin-Treptow, where I spent all my school life from the first day to the last, finishing with my Abitur. We lived next to Treptow Park, where I spent the majority of my free time. In addition I played a lot of sport, particularly rowing, athletics, swimming as well as skating on the lake in the park in winter.
>
> In Berlin the final years of the war were bad. There was a great shortage of food. As a child I fainted from the lack of it on two occasions. But my father, as a result of his strict

Right: At home with his two older sisters, Irmgard and Ilse. (Falck)

Below: A relaxed Falck poses with his former history and Latin teacher, Georg Neuendorf. (Falck)

Below right: A very happy Falck, with an equally jubilant looking gamekeeper, displays a hare he has shot while on his brother-in-law's farm. As was typical of most fighter pilots, Wolf Falck was a gifted marksman. (Falck)

On his brother-in-law's farm at Treuhofen (now in Poland), this time with his best friend, Günther Lützow. Lützow went on to become one of the Luftwaffe's most outstanding fighter pilots and respected *Geschwaderkommodoren*. He was reported missing in action on 24 April 1945, near Donauwörth in Southern Germany, while flying a Messerschmitt 262 jet. (Falck)

Easter 1929. During a break in his studies for the Abitur, Wolf Falck took a short holiday in the Spreewald, located to the south of Berlin, where he spent most of his time rowing. (Falck)

Also at the Spreewald, this time eating with friends at the camp. (Falck)

Prussian upbringing, would have nothing to do with black market dealings. Inflation was also bad. Sometimes my father came home with a thick purse of money, and my mother and we children would rush out immediately and go shopping as the money would be worth nothing the following day.

From the time of his earliest childhood Wolf was interested in soldiering, a passion he sustained by reading countless books on the First World War and its combatants. Both of his brothers-in-law were officers, and it was his great wish to follow their example and become an officer himself. It was during his time at school that he first became fascinated in flying and all that it involved. One of the teachers at his school was a pilot and he did his very best to get the students interested in aviation. Many workshops took place in the basement of the school where the scholars spent hours participating in making models of aircraft.

In April 1931, having just passed the *Abitur*, he joined the *Reichswehr* and was selected as one of its thirty most promising candidates to go to the *Deutsche Verkehrsfliegerschule* at Schleissheim near Munich. It was here that he would get his first opportunity to fly. Unlike the other pilots covered in this book who gained their first flying experiences at a relatively young age, either with the Hitler Youth or with civilian gliding clubs, Wolf Falck had to wait until he was twenty-one before he took to the air for the first time. This maiden flight took place in a *Klemm* 25 and the event left him 'deeply impressed'.

Of the thirty candidates, ten were selected to go on to receive fighter pilot training in Russia, more specifically at Lipetsk, located approximately 300 miles south-east of Moscow. Clandestine pilot training of German personnel had been taking place at Lipetsk since 1925. A treaty signed on 15 April 1925 allowed Germany to secretly train its pilots using Russian facilities and, in exchange, the Russians received technical data acquired as a result of the training programmes. One of those fortunate enough to be selected to go to Russia was Wolf Falck, who began his training in April 1932. Among the nine other successful candidates were young men who would go on to become some of the finest pilots and leaders the Luftwaffe ever produced. Men such as Günther Lützow, Günther Radusch and Hannes Trautloft. Each candidate was issued with a new passport and, as part of the illusion, given a false occupation to conceal the purpose of their trip. In Wolf's case he was listed as being an electrician even though he knew next to nothing about electricity. Dressed appropriately in civilian clothing, so as not to raise suspicion, the would-be fighter pilots left for Russia. The training was inevitably tough and the living conditions were hard but, on the whole, it was an enjoyable experience.

At first we had to learn to fly the Fokker D XIII, which was very different to the aircraft we had flown before, more power and much more temperamental. The first days were spent flying curves, acrobatics and so on in order to show that we could handle this aircraft in all situations.

Then we started with the fighter pilot training. Formation flying in a Kette of three aircraft, single fighter attacks and then shooting at targets on the ground and in the air. Every day we were either shooting with pistols, rifles or machine-guns or taking part in sport – it was a wonderful time!

On the base, which was a huge airfield with a smaller one next to it, was a Russian bomber squadron. There was a Russian commanding officer and all of his people, the pilots, guards,

The Officer's Mess situated on the airfield. (Falck)

One of the Fokker D XIII fighter aircraft used at Lipetsk. Fitted with a Napier-Lion engine it was highly thought of by the men who flew it in Russia. (Falck)

crews and so on, but we had our own barracks. We had no contact with them at the barracks and we had our own commanding officer and instructors at the airfield. On the airfield there was an Oberwerkmeister who was responsible for our aircraft which were lined up, all very exact and Prussian like. In the workshops the [technicians] were German and all the labourers were Russian.

The ten of us who were there in 1932 loved Russia. We loved the Russian people, the Russian culture as well as its traditions and music. It was one of the best times of my life!

After six exhilarating months in Russia he returned to Germany and joined his Regiment at Schweidnitz, completing fourteen weeks of basic army training in the process. From 1 February 1933, until the time of his promotion to *Leutnant* on 1 October 1934, Wolf attended the Infantry School at Dresden, where he received all the necessary training to become an officer.

When this period of instruction had finished, on 30 September 1934, not only had he qualified as an officer but he was now also fully qualified as both a pilot and instructor. However, as the Luftwaffe's existence had yet to be revealed, a fact that would remain undisclosed until March 1935, Wolf was ordered to write a letter to the Minister of War requesting that he be retired from the Regiment. The letter was in fact a clever ploy, which, having been accepted, enabled him to join the *Deutsche Verkehrsfliegerschule* at Schleissheim as a *Kettenführer* or pilot instructor. As one of the instructors at this school it was his responsibility to select pilots, according to their flying abilities, for the different branches of what was to become the Luftwaffe:

We had to decide during the training which [students] were capable of becoming fighter pilots and which were not. Those that didn't became reconnaissance, transport or bomber pilots. To be a fighter pilot under normal circumstances – though later in the war it changed – you had to be born to it. You can learn it, but you could never be a good fighter pilot – it has to be in your blood! A bomber pilot for example speaks another language than we, it is just very, very different.

On 1 April 1936 he was simultaneously promoted to *Oberleutnant* and transferred to the 5th *Staffel* of *Jagdgeschwader 132* 'Richtofen', based at Jüterbog-Damm, some 70km south of Berlin. *Hauptmann* Galshe, the *Staffelkapitän* of the 5th *Staffel*, used Wolf Falck's experience to train the new pilots that came fresh from the flying schools. This extra instruction played a very important role in the development of these young airmen, as it had been recognised that newly qualified pilots from the schools lacked the necessary flying skills and experience that would be required to fly effectively in combat. These could only be gained with an operational unit and Falck's involvement in their training proved invaluable as it redressed this imbalance. It not only enhanced their flying and tactical ability, but additionally improved their overall performance.

After spending about a year as an instructor, his hard work was finally rewarded when he was selected to become the *Kommodore's* adjutant. Even though this was a prestigious position for any pilot to hold it wasn't long before Wolf became bored, and he began to look for an opportunity which would release him from his desk job, and allow him to take to the air once more.

Wolf Falck (back row, far right) with some of the other pilots who went to Lipetsk with him in April 1932. Directly in front of him is Günther Radusch, to Falck's immediate left is Hannes Trautloft, and on the far left of the back row is Günther Lützow. (Falck)

Following a heavy drinking session, the young German airmen decided to shave their heads. The following morning the results of their do-it-yourself haircuts can clearly be seen. (Falck)

On returning from Russia, Wolf Falck joined his Regiment at Schweidnitz. Pictured are the officers of the 15th Company in the autumn of 1932. From left to right, back row: Eichart, Schütt, Najork, Falck, Steinhardt, Koschmieder. Front (sitting): Unteroffizier Billermann and Gefreiter Glassmann. (Falck)

While at Schweidnitz, Falck underwent fourteen weeks of basic army training, these two formal portraits were taken at about this time. (Falck)

Fahnenjunker Falck takes a well-earned break from field manoeuvres. (Falck)

Falck is a member of this machine-gun crew waiting for orders during a field exercise. (Falck)

Infantry training at Dresden, between February 1933 and October 1934. Falck, Lützow and Trautloft take time out to share a private joke. (Falck)

Finding a quiet moment to study for his final officer's exams. (Falck)

Oberfähnrich Falck is pictured shortly after he had successfully qualified as an officer. On 1 October 1934 he was promoted to Leutnant. (Falck)

Falck (back row, second from the right) with other officer cadets at Dresden. From left to right, front row: Trost, Hartmann, Guillaume, Oberleutnant Danke, Heinig, Holzapfel, Toop. Middle row: Michael, Scharffenberg, Kuckein, von Plehwe, von D-Sode, Weniger, Adler. Back row: Kling, Schmidt, von Bonin, von Manteufel, Herbert, Falck, Bernecker. (Falck)

The Falck family, Christmas 1933. Falck's parents are to his immediate left. To his immediate right are his sister, Ilse, and her husband, Günther. The little girl on the right is Wolf's niece, Rosemarie. (Falck)

A visit to the Deutsche Verkehrsfliegerschule at Schleissheim by Herrmann Göring in the autumn of 1934. (Falck)

An appropriate opening presented itself on 1 July 1938, when the *Geschwader* added a third *Gruppe* to its growing establishment. Without a moment's hesitation, and eager to get operational again, he applied to become a *Staffelkapitän* in the new unit. The application was quickly approved and *Oberleutnant* Falck took command of the 8th *Staffel* which, along with the rest of the *Gruppe*, was transferred to Fürstenwalde near Berlin.

This was a period of great transition for this particular unit, which began to receive a new type of aircraft to replace its existing Messerschmitt 109s. Göring himself had championed the development of this new aircraft that was designated the Messerschmitt 110, a twin-engined fighter capable, it was hoped, of escorting bombers deep into enemy territory. In a speech he made while visiting *Jagdgeschwader* Richtofen, Göring said he hoped the new fighter would become the spearhead of the Luftwaffe, a force comparable to that of Cromwell's 'Ironsides'.

With the political situation in Europe becoming more and more tense the *Gruppe* was transferred to Olmütz where the programme for re-training crews on this new machine was immediately implemented. Radios were installed and blind flying was included in the schedule, as well as this the fighter pilots had to contend with the fact that they now had a second crew member in the aircraft with them. This was all very unfamiliar to men who, up to now, had been used to flying single-engined, single-manned fighters. The unit was re-designated I./ZG 76 and was one of the first *Zerstörer Gruppes* to be formed.

In August 1939, as war loomed ominously on the horizon, I./ZG 76 was transferred to a small airfield at Ohlau in Upper Silesia, close to the Polish border. When the *Wehrmacht* invaded Poland on 1 September 1939, *Oberleutnant* Falck, *Staffelkapitän* of 2./ZG 76, took off with his *Staffel* and flew towards Krakow. Much to their disappointment the flight was totally uneventful – no enemy aircraft were seen at all. The highlight of the day for them was watching the early morning sun light up the golden roofs of this beautiful Polish city.

On 5 September he had his first contact with the Polish Air Force in the area around Lodz. At the briefing that morning it was decided that I./ZG 76 would lead the mission, and the remaining two *Staffeln* would follow behind in support. The main target would be the airfield at Dalikow, about 28km north-west of Lodz. As the early morning mist drifted slowly across the airfield, and the sun began to rise in the east, the aircraft of the second *Staffel* took off. On reaching Dalikow the airfield was pinpointed, and the Polish aircraft parked on its runway were systematically strafed and destroyed. At 06.40 hours, after the attack on the airfield, Wolf scored his first aerial victory against the Poles.

I climbed to 1,500m, signalled to the Staffel to regroup, [in order] to look for further action. What was that flickering in front of us? It looked suspicious to me and I dived towards it. It was a PZL P-23 bomber, flying towards me at a lower altitude. I slammed the throttles open, pulled the aircraft around and dived. I could clearly make out the red and white checkerboard and the Polish cockades on its wings and fin. The Polish observer was already firing at me, but he aimed poorly. His tracers flashed past us. At the same time I got him in my sights. A small correction – now! I pushed the button and my machine-guns hammered away. A flame shot out and he exploded. As I roared away above him he disappeared below as a sinking ball of fire, before finally crashing in a freshly sown field.

Wolf Falck stands in front of an Arado 65, which is parked on a grass airstrip at Nuremburg. Falck, along with other instructors, was part of a special Staffel used to protect parades held in the Bavarian City. (Falck)

During the opening days of the Polish campaign Oberleutnant Falck and his Staffel, 2./ZG 76, were based at Ohlau in Upper Silesia. (Falck)

Award certificate for the Iron Cross Second
Class, awarded to Hauptmann Falck on 13
September 1939. (Falck)

Barely a week later, on 11 September, he shot down a Fokker F IX and a single-engined reconnaissance aircraft in the space of five minutes, taking his total of aerial victories to three. When the Polish campaign finished I./ZG 76 was moved back to Nellingen, near Stuttgart, for rest and re-equipping. The months that followed were quiet, with the boredom broken only by the occasional patrol flight along the Rhine.

On 17 December 1939, a beautiful winter's day, I./ZG 76 was transferred to Jever on the North Sea coast. The crews were immediately issued with all the necessary sea-rescue equipment such as life jackets, dinghies and pouches of yellow marker dye. The following day was to be a memorable one for *Hauptmann* Falck, the events of which would result in his name and face becoming well known to the German public. The air battle that took place over the Heligoland Bight on 18 December 1939, was well reported in the press on both sides of the Channel. The RAF dispatched twenty-four Wellington bombers to attack shipping docked at Wilhelmshaven. Weather conditions were perfect over the port, and twenty-two of the bombers that reached the target bombed from an altitude of 13,000ft. Accurate flak caused the Wellingtons to break from their formation and they were subsequently attacked by fighters as they left the target area. In the running battle that followed twelve of the RAF aircraft were shot down. Wolf Falck recalls his personal contribution to the battle in which he gained his fourth aerial victory.

> It was a clear, cloudless day, and we were given orders to make a practice flight over the sea to the north of the Friesian Isles to accustom ourselves to flying over water, which until then we had no experience of.

On 17 December 1939, I./ZG 76 was transferred to Jever where it carried out operations over the North Sea against the RAF. Here, Wolf Falck can be seen discussing tactics with Oberleutnant Helmut Woltersdorf (later Woltersdorf became a night fighter and was killed in action on 6 June 1942). (Falck)

A sketch by a German war artist Wolfgang Willrich of Falck with his Bordfunker, Alfred Walz, at Jever in January 1940. (Falck)

I took off with my Schwarm with Unteroffizier Fresia, Leutnant Graeff and Leutnant Fahlbusch. As radio operator I had with me Unteroffizier Alfred Walz, who had acquitted himself well in Poland. We first flew towards the west at an altitude of about 1,500m until we were a short distance from the Dutch island of Texel, and then on a westerly course over the sea to the north of the islands. When we were in the approximate latitude of Juist we had an R/T message from the Geschwader Operations Room at Jever to the effect that a formation of English bombers were making an attack on Wilhelmshaven, and that I should try to intercept the enemy formation. So, full throttle and head towards Heligoland in order to cut off the path of the British. We soon saw puffs of flak in the sky, and shortly afterwards the retreating bombers, which were already under attack by Me109s. We could also see bombers already going down in flames. The bombers were flying at about 3,500m, so that we had to climb rapidly.

When we got nearer I could see that the bombers were Wellingtons. The formation was, however, already somewhat spread out and the aircraft were flying homeward to the north-west individually or in small groups. When we reached the bombers I gave the signal to attack. I myself approached a Wellington obliquely from astern and with a slight height advantage. Immediately on doing so I came under defensive fire from the rear gunner. But, right after my first attack the starboard engine began to burn and the aircraft went down in a shallow dive. As we were already more or less at the limit of our endurance I didn't wait to see it hit the sea, but looked for a second target. Once again I attacked from astern, got in close to him and fired with all my guns. There were hardly any visible results from this first attack, so I immediately decided on a second attack, and I went in closer to the Wellington. Now the Wellington began to burn at once and dived straight into the sea. However, in the course of my second attack the rear gunner had shot excellently. My starboard engine stopped immediately and out of the fuselage in front of me, where the ammunition boxes for the four machine-guns were located, thick smoke was coming into the cabin, making me want to cough. I had no sooner got over the shock than my port engine stopped. There was complete silence, and for the first time in my life I was flying a glider. My first reaction was, 'Bale out!' but we were to the west of Heligoland and below us was the North Sea, which was scattered with ice-floes. By now the fire had apparently extinguished itself, but the petrol was flowing from the bullet-holes in the tanks and wings. I decided to get as close as I could to the coast, and sent an emergency message by radio in the hope that after we had ditched they would come and fish us out of the sea as soon as possible. On this day Walz and I had not just one guardian angel, but a whole Geschwader of them. We did succeed in reaching the airfield on the island of Wangerooge thanks to the fact that we were already at the end of our flying time and what remained of the petrol had leaked out. In addition, the majority of our ammunition had been used up, the wind was favourably inclined and we still had sufficient height. I therefore lowered the flaps and undercarriage with compressed air and landed smoothly, coming to rest about 30m in front of the flying control building. It was one of the luckiest moments of my life. The whole time Unteroffizier Fresia had accompanied me like a faithful hound. He now flew back to Jever, dropped his Funker off, took on a little more fuel and picked us up a short time later. There was naturally much jubilation when I got back to our Staffel, on the one hand because of the outstanding success of our Schwarm in terms of kills and on the other hand because of our safe home-coming.

A second Schwarm from our Staffel had been scrambled and also enjoyed success. From these crews one machine had been hit, but only by one bullet. This bullet had pierced the cabin roof, passed through the shoulder of the pilot, Leutnant Üllenbeck, and then hit the back of his Funker's left hand, Unteroffizier Dombrowski! That same evening I visited both of them in sick quarters, but both wounds were innocuous, and so we could look back with pride and gratitude. And our Staffel badge, the red ladybird with seven black dots, had fully proved itself once again!

In conclusion I should point out that the first Wellington that I attacked was not confirmed as a kill by the German Ministry, because the impact with the sea was not witnessed. That's how strict the rules were!

Following the raid on Wilhelmshaven, one of a number that went badly for the RAF in the months after the outbreak of the war, Bomber Command was forced to re-think its strategy. A change in policy followed, which resulted in future bombing operations over German airspace being switched to take place during the hours of darkness. A decision that would, over the next four years or so, result in the most bloody and prolonged air battle in history.

Through January 1940 the RAF carried out a number of sorties over the North Sea in its determination to find and destroy German warships. One such mission took place on 10 January, but before its Blenheims were able to locate any enemy shipping they were intercepted by a formation of Messerschmitt 110s led by *Hauptmann* Falck. In the battle that followed one of the Blenheims was shot down and two more were badly damaged. Flight Lieutenant Douglas Cooper was piloting one of the nine Blenheims involved and he recounts the events of that day:

This saga started on 10 January 1940 when I was stationed with 110 Squadron at RAF Wattisham in Suffolk where we flew Mk IV Blenheims – a lovely aircraft to fly but woefully vulnerable to attack from below.

On that date nine of us were dispatched to carry out a reconnaissance over the North Sea in search of German shipping. We were led in three flights of three by Squadron Leader Ken Doran who had already gained the first DFC of the war by leading an attack on Wilhelmshaven the day after war was declared.

We were well out over the North Sea flying at about 2,000ft, and not expecting any trouble, when four German Me110s suddenly appeared and promptly attacked us. Regrettably one of our Blenheims was shot down in this first attack after which Doran led us in a steep dive down to sea level, thus making further attacks from below impossible. The Me110s were able to fly rings around us and the engagement lasted about ten or fifteen minutes. The No. 2 in my flight got badly shot up and had to return to the nearest landing ground in England. Once the scrap was over we continued with the shipping recce but did not sight any German shipping before returning to base. My guardian angel, as usual, was working overtime and made sure that my plane didn't have a single bullet hole!

The damaged Blenheim in Douglas Cooper's flight that was badly shot up in the ensuing battle, limped back across the North Sea and crash-landed back at Wattisham where it was declared beyond economical repair. One of the members of this crew was Sgt Bill Evans:

Squadron Leader Doran dived down to sea level, jinking left and right so that we, in No. 2 position, lost close formation position. I was flying with Pilot Officer Arderne and

Flight Lieutenant Douglas Cooper was flying one of nine Blenheims that encountered 2./ZG 76 over the North Sea on 10 January 1940. At the conclusion of the air battle one Blenheim was shot down, and Falck claimed it as his fifth victory. (Douglas Cooper)

One of the other participants in the air battle of 10 January 1940 was Sgt Bill Evans. He was the wireless operator on board Blenheim N6213 piloted by P/O P.V. Arderne, which crash-landed on its return to Wattisham in Suffolk. (Bill Evans)

Leading Aircraftsman Tippett. I saw a pall of smoke where Sgts Hanne and Williams, and Aircraftsman First Class Vick had gone into the sea. I saw a 110 shoot past our starboard side and then we got a pounding – I still remember the first smell of cordite! We were badly damaged in a running fight over the sea and on return to base we crashed when the port undercarriage collapsed.

Having spotted the formation of nine Blenheims, *Hauptmann* Falck had led his Second *Staffel* down through the RAF bombers, as a result of which he left one of its number trailing a banner of yellow smoke from its starboard engine. This Blenheim was probably N6203 VE – piloted by Pilot Officer G.H. Pemberton, which later crash-landed at Manby in Lincolnshire. Then, during a second attack, a withering burst of fire tore through a Blenheim piloted by Sgt Hannes causing it to explode just metres above the water. Debris and a small oil slick marked the final resting-place of Falck's fifth victory.

His next aerial success followed on the afternoon of 17 February 1940 following a short engagement with a lone Blenheim carrying out a reconnaissance flight over the North Sea. The two-engined bomber, which was flying at an altitude of approximately 500m, stood little chance in the engagement that followed. With his superior height and speed Wolf attacked his intended victim from above and behind. The dorsal turret gunner from the bomber opened fire on the German fighter at a range of 500m; simultaneously the Blenheim pilot put his aircraft into a dive in an attempt to escape into surrounding cloud cover. The cloud, however, was rather scattered and had large holes in its formation. Wolf calculated where he thought the bomber would emerge and waited. His patience and cunning were rewarded within a very short space of time, the bomber appearing exactly where he predicted it would do. A withering hail of gunfire from the Messerschmitt's nose-mounted guns met it as re-appeared. This devastating combination of cannon and machine-gun fire ripped through the unfortunate bomber, which immediately reared up out of control and plunged, burning into the cold waters below. On checking through Bomber Command's losses for that day only one such aircraft was reported lost. This was a Blenheim from 110 Squadron, serial No. N6211 VE-, piloted by Sgt F. Bigg and tasked to reconnoitre Heligoland and Borkum. This was one of only four Blenheims lost by the RAF between 14 February and 1 April 1940 during 250 shipping missions over the North Sea.

Just two days after achieving his sixth confirmed kill, Wolf Falck was transferred from ZG 76 and made *Gruppenkommandeur* of I./ZG 1. At that time the *Gruppe* was based at Düsseldorf, however, at the beginning of April it was ordered to Barth on the Baltic Coast. And it was from here, on 9 April 1940, that his *Gruppe* took off and assisted in the invasion of Denmark. This short, but decisive campaign, code named '*Weseruebung*' or 'Weser Exercise' was to witness Wolf's seventh and final aerial victory of the war:

We received the order just as German troops were to cross the border at six o'clock in the morning, and at seven o'clock German bombers would fly over Copenhagen. This was more or less a demonstration flight because they told us that the Danish people would be surprised that we were coming and would welcome us.

At that time I was Gruppenkommandeur of I./ZG 1 and I received the order to fly with my Gruppe to Vaerlöse/Copenhagen, which was the centre of the Danish Air Force. We knew that there were recce and many fighter aircraft located there [such as] the Dutch Fokker D-21. They were excellent aircraft at lower altitude, much better than we were, but at higher altitudes they were not. We received our orders and were told that if someone was to take off and fight we were to destroy them. I decided with my Staffelkapitän, the night before, that we would have to fly low, a few metres above the sea, so that they couldn't detect us with radar. Then, at an exact point on the coast, we would have to increase altitude to 1,500m. Then, from here, we would be able to see the airfield in front of us.

The next morning we flew exactly as planned. Looking at the airfield we saw two or three rows of aircraft. Unfortunately the first recce aircraft on the right hand side took off. What else was I to do? So, by the time he reached the end of the airfield he was burning on the ground. We then received [enemy] machine-gun fire from a little wood on the edge of the airfield. I told my people to attack, but we couldn't see where the gunfire was coming from. We attacked two or three times. All of a sudden there was a bang and my left engine stopped. I got a kick in the backside and struck my head against the roof of the cockpit. I told my radio operator to tell one of my Staffelkapitän to take over the command and to fly on to Aalborg as it was quiet there. I decided to fly back. I knew which roads the German Army were using in order to occupy Denmark and I intended to make a forced landing just at the head of the German troops. When I couldn't find any troops I decided to fly back across the sea to Barth on one engine. It's astonishing how the distance changed. On the way to Vaerlöse it was not so very far but now, with one engine and being wounded, it was a very, very long way. We didn't fly low as I tried to get a little bit of altitude in case we had to make a forced landing or parachute out. When we came back to Barth I jumped out of the aircraft and asked Walz to look at my backside – but there was nothing! I had a look under the airframe of my aircraft and saw, just under the cockpit, a hole! I went back to my seat – nothing! All of a sudden I saw the stick [control column], which was covered in leather, was torn. When I took my parachute from the seat there was a hole and the metal was twisted. I took the parachute and in it was also a black hole. There were fifty-four layers of silk and in the fifty-second layer was the bullet. I was convinced from that time that the parachute was very important for the crews, not just for jumping – but to protect them also!

The Danish campaign was over almost as quickly as it had begun. With Denmark's main airfield having been knocked out in a pre-dawn raid, the Luftwaffe roamed over Copenhagen completely unmolested. At one stage, in a show of unabridged aerial mastery, even the Royal Palace was buzzed by German aircraft. At the same time as this was happening, the *Kriegsmarine* had seized Copenhagen harbour and German troops had driven far into the small, flat peninsula of Jutland. Due to its geographical make-up, it was almost impossible for this small country to effect any type of resistance or successfully defend itself. By 8.34a.m. it was all over. The Danish government accepted the inevitable and what little resistance had been put up came to an end.

Weseruebung had been a combined operation, involving not only the invasion of Denmark, but also the simultaneous invasion of Norway. But, unlike the Danes, the Norwegians refused to accept the German ultimatum and continued to fight. So, in support of the *Wehrmacht's* continuing campaign in Norway, I./ZG 1 flew missions from their newly acquired airfield at Aalborg in Denmark. While stationed here, and as a direct result of nuisance raids carried out by the RAF on his base, Wolf Falck began to formulate theories for countering the threat of British bombers operating at night.

On completing this thesis it was submitted through the usual channels to the Luftwaffe's High Command. The report had an almost immediate effect on the powers that be. In a little over a week *Generaloberst* Milch visited Wolf at Aalborg where he question him extensively about the possibilities of night fighting. However, other events were to overshadow the report, and plans to develop Falck's ideas were shelved when the Battle of France commenced on 10 May 1940.

However, it was during the French campaign that Wolf was ordered by Kesselring to return to Düsseldorf with part of his *Gruppe*, which at the time was operating from Le Havre on the Channel Coast, so that it could commence night fighting trials. Although many of his pilots were more than competent when it came to flying the Bf110, few of them had received the level of instrument training required to fly at night. The enormity of the task before him was almost bewildering and, inevitably, there were more questions than answers:

> You receive an order to do something without any advice, no programme and no material. It's a similar situation to the one I would put you in at night, in a big hall without lights, and tell you 'Now go and catch the flies!' I had nothing. No aircraft [specifically designed] for this purpose, no crews or organizational assistance. Only one thing existed and that was a Flakscheinwerfer battery commanded by Oberstleutnant Fichter, and under his command was IV. Gruppe of Jagdgeschwader Richtofen, which was led by Major Blumensaat. He had been my shooting instructor at Lipetsk and his most experienced Staffelkapitän was Johannes Steinhoff. They had worked together with no success but had experienced some losses. These fighter pilots were under the direction of a searchlight officer who decided when they had to fly – he had no idea about flying – it was criminal!

Just four days after the *Gruppes'* transfer to Düsseldorf, on 26 June 1940, *Hauptmann* Falck was summoned to a top-level meeting at Wassenaar in Holland. The conference was held at *General* Christiansen's headquarters and was chaired by Göring and attended by some of the most prominent figures in the Luftwaffe. These included *General* Karl Bodenschatz, Göring's Chief of Staff, *General* Kastner, Head of Personnel of the Luftwaffe as well as Udet, Kesselring and Bruno Loerzer.

During the course of the meeting Göring made a lengthy speech concerning the progress of the war. He explained to those in attendance that the war would be won, but that the night attacks by the RAF were causing annoyance and embarrassment. As a result of this he announced that he was setting up the *Nachtjagd*, and that Falck, with his practical experience, would become the *Kommodore* of the first night fighter *Geschwader* – *Nachtjagdgeschwader* 1.

This sudden announcement came as a bolt out of the blue to Wolf who, as a humble *Hauptmann*, was probably the lowest ranking officer at the conference. Usually, the position

Wolf Falck (centre), Kommandeur of I./ZG 1, with officers from his Gruppe during the French campaign. (Falck)

of *Geschwaderkommodore* was held by an *Oberst* or, at the very least, an *Oberstleutnant*. Göring made it clear that this was to be the first of many such promotions with other junior officers following Falck's example. In the months that followed the older *Geschwaderkommodoren* were steadily replaced by a succession of younger, battle-hardened pilots such as Mölders, Galland, Lützow and Wick.

At the conclusion of the conference Wolf Falck returned to Düsseldorf, still somewhat stunned by his good fortune, and immediately set about the difficult task of building up his new command.

The first of many changes saw his former *Gruppe*, I./ZG 1, being re-designated I./NJG 1. Next, the new *Geschwaderkommodore* introduced a new crest to the unit in order to give it a unique identity. This crest would become synonymous with the *Nachtjagd* and could be seen emblazoned on all of its aircraft:

> When, in spring 1940, I was appointed Kommandeur of the I. Gruppe of Zerstörergeschwader 1, then stationed in Düsseldorf, it was rapidly apparent to me that much needed to be done to form the Gruppe into a homogeneous unit, filled with 'èsprit de corps', and equal to the tasks they would have to perform.
>
> In addition to organizational, personnel and training measures I had already, as Staffelkapitän of my 'Ladybird Staffel', recognised that a badge, an emblem, can not only be an external symbol of the solidarity of a unit but can also be of great value and worth in terms of psychological training. With this realisation in mind I put a call out to all members of I./ZG 1 to submit to me suggestions for a badge for the Gruppe. Of

the various designs the one I liked the best was one by the then Oberleutnant Victor Mölders, brother of the later well-known and successful General der Jagdflieger, Werner Mölders.

The badge, which was in the shape of a shield, showed a segment of the globe covering our operational area, from Norway through Denmark and Germany to the French Atlantic coast, including England, on which was a white falcon – taken from my family coat-of-arms – diving down on England with behind it, a red flash of lightning, the point of which terminated in southern England. This was symbolic of our operational role, because at that time the RAF was our sole opponent. The background to the segments in the shape of the above-named countries was light blue.

I had only just decided upon this badge when, at Wassenar on 26 June 1940, I was ordered by the then Generalfeldmarschall Göring to form Nachtjagdgeschwader 1 from my Gruppe plus a fighter Gruppe, stationed in the Rhineland and equipped with the Me109, and as a lowly Hauptmann I was appointed Kommodore of the Geschwader.

For this new function the Gruppe badge that had just been chosen had to be altered to conform to the new circumstances. The solution was simple; the sky became black and the outlining white. Now the badge was exactly as I wanted. As I always tended to be conservative in my basic concept I had chosen the colours black, red and white combined with the white falcon from my family coat-of-arms and the red flash of lightning, symbolising our operational role and our readiness for action. In the eyes of the gentleman from the Party it was a symbol of victory, and so the design was introduced without any objection.

The badge was painted not only on the aircraft but also on the vehicles of the Geschwader. In addition I had small badges with pins made, and every member of the Geschwader was officially permitted to wear this emblem. This fact, too, had a value that was not to be overlooked. When someone new was posted to the unit, after a few weeks probation the badge was awarded to him and pinned on his uniform in front of the unit on parade, and so he was formally accepted as a member. In the event of any breaches of discipline the first action was to remove the badge from the culprit because he had damaged the unit's good name.

As the Nachtjagd continued to grow new Geschwader were set up within the Division and later the XII Fliegerkorps. A number of flak, searchlight and signals regiments were also added to it and this badge remained the norm for all other units, with slight symbolic changes according to their function.

Each Geschwader had the same badge, but NJG 1 had a white outline, while that of NJG 2 was red, that of NJG 3 yellow, and so on. For the searchlight regiments a symbolic cone of searchlights was introduced, while that of the air-signals regiments had their signals emblem. Additionally the Division, and later the Fliegerkorps, adopted it, adding the symbol of their particular Headquarters. When the war came to an end in 1945 it was the final stroke – for the time being – for the Luftwaffe and thus for the Nachtjagd and its badge.

Following the implementation of the unit's crest, his next problem was the unenviable task of informing *Major* Blumensaat, the *Kommandeur* of IV./JG 2, that he was not only relieved of his command, but that he should return home to await further orders. Even though this had come directly from Göring himself, Wolf still found it difficult and somewhat embarrassing telling a superior officer that he was sacked. Things didn't get any easier. Next he had to tell *Oberstleutnant* Fichter, the officer commanding the *Flakscheinwerfer* battery, that IV./JG 2 was now no longer under his command, but was to be transferred forthwith to the *Nachtjagd* and re-designated II./NJG 1. This too didn't go down well with Fichter, but realising he was powerless to do anything about it, he accepted the decision with the good grace befitting an officer of his rank.

It soon became clear to Wolf that creating an efficient night fighter force was not going to be an easy task. To acquire the support and co-operation of the many facets that made up the existing defensive system, such as flak, searchlight and ground radar units, was going to be beyond the capabilities of just one man – even for a man with Falck's enthusiasm and drive.

In order to remedy this problem a night fighter division or *Nachtjagddivision* was created on 17 July 1940, and placed under the command of *Oberst* Josef Kammhuber. From his headquarters at Zeist in Holland, Kammhuber's principle role was to oversee the enlargement and development of the night fighter force. It was well known that he had no previous experience of this type of aerial warfare, but this hadn't been an important consideration when the High Command had been looking for a suitable candidate for the job. Before the war his superiors had noted that he was a gifted organiser, and it was these very skills that were now needed to expand the *Nachtjagd*.

To begin with a completely new programme of training was required to convert existing pilots. Entirely new night fighter schools had to be created because at this time training was being carried out at blind flying schools such as Schleissheim. There were no guidelines,

With the formation of the *Nachtjagd* in June 1940, Wolf Falck introduced a crest to represent the unit. It was initially designed by Viktor Mölders for I./ZG 1, and then later adapted for the Night Fighters. It can be seen here on a Bf110 at Deelen. (Falck)

everything had to be learnt from the experiences of others and much of the training was completed once the new crews arrived at their operational units.

A further problem was the aircraft at the *Nachtjagd*'s disposal. It operated at this time with the standard designed Messerschmitt 110. These machines did not differ from their daytime variants in any respect other than the all over black paint scheme that had been introduced in July 1940. Modifications were made including fitting flame dampers to the engine exhausts and changing the aircraft's internal lighting. There were many other problems to overcome but they were gradually ironed out.

In the meantime, working with only limited resources and with such a large front to protect, Wolf Falck carefully selected an area from which he could not only defend the industrial heartland of the Ruhr, but also Berlin. His first decision was to move I./NJG 1 to Gütersloh, some 40km to the east of Münster, although his own headquarters remained at Düsseldorf. After doing this he established a belt of searchlights and sound detectors that formed an illuminated belt to the north-east of Münster.

It was hoped that when enemy aircraft had been detected, the night fighters would take off after being alerted with the code word *Fasan*. Once airborne they would patrol to the east of the searchlights so that their engine noise would not interfere with nor impede the effectiveness of the listening posts. They would then wait in standby zones at an altitude higher than that of the expected bombers, hoping that one of them would be caught in the glare of the searchlights. As soon as a bomber had been caught in the beam of a searchlight the prowling night fighter would then attempt to intercept it and shoot it down. The fighter pilot would usually have no more than about three minutes to do so before the bomber had cleared the searchlight belt. This type of night fighting became known as *Helle Nachtjagd* or 'illuminated' night fighting. *Oberleutnant* Werner Streib claimed the first victory using this method on the night of 20 July 1940. However, the accolade for the first night time kill is given to *Oberfeldwebel* Paul Förster of 8./JG 1 who, on 9 July 1940, shot down a Whitley bomber near the island of Heligoland.

The RAF were, however, quick to discover the existence of this searchlight belt and took the only sensible course left open to them – they simply flew around it. To counter this problem Kammhuber fought strenuously for further searchlights in order to extend the length of the existing defensive system. This turned out to be a mammoth undertaking which, when completed, stretched almost 900km from Schleswig-Holstein to Liege, and was some 30km in depth. A second line was constructed to protect the German capital and this ran from Güstrow (south of Rostock) to Gardelegen (east of Braunschweig). At about the same time as this was happening the Germans regained the initiative from the British by implementing the use of radar in their defensive system.

Since the outbreak of the war in 1939 a signals officer, *Leutnant* Hermann Diehl, had been carrying out experiments using *Freya* radar. His idea was to use *Freya* in conjunction with ground stations to direct individual fighters, by means of radio, against individual bombers. In June 1940, at the time of his transfer to Düsseldorf to set up the night fighters, Wolf had the good sense to take Diehl with him. Two months later, in August, both men went to Kammhuber and during a lengthy meeting outlined the theory behind this innovative idea.

Operational trials were duly authorised by Kammhuber and these began in September. After careful consideration, a *Freya* installation was erected in the village of Nunspeet in Holland, situated between Utrecht and Zwolle. This was an ideal location, offering the Germans the best possible chance of success as the RAF regularly crossed this area en route to Germany. By 2 October 1940 the *Nachtjagd* had its first close-controlled radar success. On that night *Leutnant* Ludwig Becker of 4./NJG 1, while being controlled from the ground by Diehl, intercepted and shot down a twin-engined bomber to gain the first radar-controlled victory at night.

This method of night fighting was to become known as *Dunkle Nachtjagd* or 'Dark' night-fighting. Following this initial success, similar installations were set up along the Dutch and German coastlines. These were placed in front of the searchlight belt and these zones became known as *Dunkelnachtjagdräume* or radar night interception areas. Slowly but surely further technological advances were to follow. Towards the end of 1940 *Freya* was being used to control the searchlights and, at about the same time, a new type of radar known as *Würzburg* was introduced. *Würzburg* had been designed with the sole purpose of controlling anti-aircraft guns, however, with its greater versatility and accuracy it was later used with the searchlights. By the end of 1940 the *Nachtjagd* could boast forty-two victories. This was not a huge number admittedly when compared with the RAF's losses over the next four years, but it was a move in the right direction.

As the fledgling night fighter organization slowly expanded and began to establish itself as a force to be reckoned with, Wolf was to spend the next two-and-a-half years working closely with Josef Kammhuber:

> I was, for almost three years, the best horse in his stable. If there was anything that needed doing – anywhere – Crete, Russia, France, I did it because I was now no longer flying missions.
>
> A short time after he became the Divisional Commander he called me just as I was preparing for a flight. He said 'From today no more missions, others can do what you are doing, I need you for organising, training and so on'. On one hand, all the orders I got to carry out were very interesting but, on the other, I lost the connection with my Geschwader, with the men and the crews. I was no longer a pilot – I was now the Geschwaderkommodore of a flying unit responsible for building and organising.

On 1 October 1940, in recognition of his seven aerial victories, as well as his outstanding leadership and organizational skills, *Major* Falck was awarded the Knight's Cross. *Reichsmarschall* Göring himself personally bestowed this much-coveted medal upon him, only a very small number of which had been awarded by this stage of the war.

With Wolf's drive and vision, combined with Kammhuber's mastery of organization, the *Nachtjagd* slowly began to find its feet. From the time of their first association in July 1940, until they parted company in July 1943, both men played an important role in the development and expansion of the night fighter force and all that it entailed.

One of the main problems facing them had been the availability of suitable aircraft for the role of night fighting. One way to overcome this had been to use other aircraft such as the Junkers 88, the Dornier 217 and Heinkel 219, all of which had been converted, or were being developed and tested, to be used in such a role.

On 7 October 1940 Falck attended the Air Ministry in Berlin where he received the Knight's Cross from Göring himself. Here he is helped on with the medal by Major von Brauchitsch, Göring's adjutant. (Falck)

Vorläufiges Besitzzeugnis

✠

Der Führer
und Oberste Befehlshaber
der Wehrmacht

hat

dem Major Wolfgang Falck

das Ritterkreuz
des Eisernen Kreuzes
am 1.Oktober 1940 verliehen.

Hauptquartier d.Ob.d.L., den 7. Oktober 1940
Der Chef des Luftwaffenpersonalamts

Generalleutnant

The official award certificate that accompanied the Knight's Cross. (Falck)

Additionally, a new type of airborne radar had evolved in the form of the *FuG 202 Lichtenstein B/C* that had its first successful use in the early hours of 9 August 1941. This first airborne interception 'kill' using *Lichtenstein* was credited to *Oberleutnant* Ludwig Becker, the same man who, less than ten months earlier, had been credited with the first radar-controlled night victory. It is also interesting to note that Becker, known within night fighter circles as the 'Professor', also introduced a method of attacking bombers that would soon become standard practice among other *Nachtjagd* pilots. He was able, over a period of time, to develop a set of sound tactics that enabled him to approach and shoot down enemy bombers without being seen. It was simple and deadly in its effectiveness.

Once airborne, Becker would climb to an altitude higher than that of the expected bomber stream, and there he would wait, prowling the dark night sky until a target appeared on the *Lichtenstein*. Having located one he would then position his own aircraft behind that of his intended victim, shove the control column forward and dive earthwards with the aim of levelling out some 500m below it. It was then hoped that the RAF machine would be silhouetted against the night sky, thus making it easier to manoeuvre the fighter until it was just a matter of metres beneath the bomber. Pulling up the nose of his Dornier 215, Becker would then open fire, letting his victim fly through a long burst of 7.9mm rounds and 20mm cannon shells. The main advantage to this type of attack was that it more often than not concealed the German fighter from the prying eyes of the bomber's gunners – who posed the biggest threat to any attacking night fighter.

With the continued advance in radar technology, specifically the introduction of the *Würzburg-Riese* or Würzburg Giant, a highly successful system of night fighting known as *Himmelbett* was developed. The *Würzburg-Riese* had a greater range than its predecessor and was more versatile with a 360° rotation. The most important improvement though was the inclusion of a built-in height-finding capability, an essential addition that would ultimately make the interception of enemy bombers easier.

Himmelbett was operated in the *Dunkelnachtjagdräume*, which were situated in front of the searchlight belt, and required the use of two *Würzburg-Riese* radars, one to track the course of the bomber, and the other to show the position of the fighter. The course of both aircraft were then plotted by hand on to a plotting table in chinagraph pencil, red for the bomber and blue for the fighter. The table on which both aircraft's positions were marked was basically a map of the area covered by the *Würzburg*, which had a range of approximately 60km.

This method of using chinagraph pencils to mark the course of the aircraft was later replaced with a clever system of appropriately coloured lights (blue was replaced with green) that were then projected on to a ground-glass situation map from below. This particular plotting table was known as the *Seeburg-Tisch*.

From constantly updated information on the bomber's movements, the fighter-control officer was then able to guide the night fighter slowly towards its quarry. This improved system of night fighting immediately began to pay dividends for the *Nachtjagd*, by the end of 1941 they had accounted for 421 of the 756 aircraft lost by the RAF.

With the widening of the defensive network, nicknamed 'The Kammhuber Line' by the British, the number of victories scored by the night fighters increased steadily throughout 1942 and 1943.

Berlin, 28 November 1941. The funeral of General der Jagdflieger, Oberst Werner Mölders. The four officers nearest the camera are Adolf Galland, Wolf Falck, Herbert Kaminski and Karl-Gottfried Nordmann. Following at the rear of the casket is Reichsmarschall Hermann Göring. (author's collection)

As well as having to cope with night time raids in the west, the Germans were also experiencing a similar problem on the Eastern Front. It was in this theatre of the war that Wolf found himself in August 1942. At this time there were no night fighter units operating on the Eastern Front, and the only defence available was provided by a few individual crews who attempted to improvise with what little resources they had available. In his quest to help bolster the pitiful situation, he travelled along the entire front to get a clearer idea of what needed to be done in order to help remedy the problem. Well aware that the *Nachtjagd* was barely able to hold its own in the west, he was adamant that there would not be a transfer of resources from west to east. He therefore proposed that the Luftwaffe units in the east would have to either re-train or re-equip some of their own *Zerstörer Staffeln*. As a result of Wolf Falck's proposals suitable pilots from bomber, reconnaissance and *Zerstörer* units were selected and then transferred to Wiener Neustadt for night fighter training.

Unfortunately, due to Soviet offensives around Stalingrad and the Donets, many of these newly trained crews were used, not for combating Russian bombers at night, but in ground support missions against Russian supply columns during the day. Consequently, due to the speed of the Russian advance, some of the aircraft had to be blown up by their own crews in order to stop them falling into the hands of the advancing Red Army. Sadly, within just a few short weeks, this fledgling night fighter unit was disbanded.

On 1 July 1943, Wolf Falck was promoted to *Oberst* and transferred to the *Generalstab* as Kammhuber's permanent representative at the Luftwaffe*nführungsstab*. However, as a result of this promotion, he was forced to give up the command of his beloved *Geschwader*. For just over three years Wolf Falck had led the largest and most successful *Geschwader* in the *Nachtjagd*. Some of the highest scoring night fighter pilots, such as Heinz Schnaufer, Helmut Lent, Manfred Meurer and many others all served under his command. The only consolation in losing his command was that Werner Streib, a close personal friend and experienced night fighter pilot himself (with approximately fifty-seven victories under his belt at the time), replaced him as the *Geschwaderkommodore*.

At the same time as this was happening the relationship between Falck and Kammhuber was becoming more and more strained. The sheer effort of building up the *Nachtjagd*, its subsequent enlargement, combined with the continual fight for resources and the growing ferocity of Bomber Command's offensive were all beginning to take their toll on the relationship. To compound their already sizeable problems, both men had different opinions on how to overcome them. Wolf describes his relationship with Kammhuber and the circumstances that led to the break up of their partnership:

> We had a very good relationship. Sometimes though you have a different point of view, but it did not affect our personal relationship. He attempted to make the Nachtjagd bigger and bigger, which was correct and necessary. His policy was to divide the [existing] units, to build new Staffeln, Gruppen and Geschwader, and he asked for more aircraft and personnel. My opinion was also to make the Nachtjagd larger in order to fulfil our task, but I preferred a concentration, which meant less administration and more aircraft in a unit – not many units with only a few aircraft!

Following his promotion to Oberst on 1st July 1943, Wolf Falck became Kammhuber's permanent staff representative on the Luftwaffe's High Command (Luftwaffenführungsstab). He is seen here with his friend, and one of the pioneers of early night-fighting, Werner Streib. (Falck)

On 1 July [1943] I became Oberst on the General Staff, and the third man in his staff. I received an order from Kammhuber to go to Schleissheim to build up the Headquarters of the new 7th Jagddivision and the night fighter school. Oberst Heinrich Wittmer (Kammhuber's Chief of Staff) called me there and told me that the General was being transferred to Norway to become Chief of Luftlotte 5 Scandinavia and that General 'Beppo' Schmid would be his successor. He (Kammhuber) was to take with him three or four key personnel from our staff who had been with us from the very first day. They knew everything and did outstanding work. He took these key people from his own staff so that he had his friends with him – this made me mad! If this was true I told Wittmer then I would be against it.

I do not know what happened, but a few days later Kammhuber came to Schleissheim to visit my staff and to see what we had done. He arrived and I reported to him. He then proceeded to tell me, word for word, what I had said to my friend Wittmer. He told me 'You're fired – I don't need you any more!' There were two possibilities, either Kammhuber was listening on the telephone or Wittmer went to the General. Two or three days later I got an order to say that I was to be transferred to Luftwaffenbefehlshaber Mitte in Berlin. This later became Luftflotte Reich and its Gefechtsstand was in a small bunker at the Reichsportsfeld where the 1936 Olympics had been held.

In September 1943 *Oberst* Falck took over his new command as *Einsatzleiter Nachtjagd*, or 'Head' of Operations. His headquarters were, as already mentioned, based in Berlin, and it was from here that the night fighter defence of the *Reich* was directed.

On one of his many whirlwind tours of the Eastern Front, Oberstleutnant Falck speaks briefly with Hauptmann Hoppe before leaving Bucharest. (Falck)

From September 1943 Wolf Falck became Head of Operations for the Nachtjagd with responsibility for the night-fighter defence of the Reich, which he directed from his headquarters in Berlin. From here he was constantly updated by telephone as to the position of the incoming bombers. Behind him can be seen a map of the Reich, which was divided into a system of grid squares called Planquadrates (see Appendix VIII). (Falck)

On 5 February 1944 Luftwaffen*befehlshaber Mitte* was re-designated, becoming *Luftflotte Reich*, with *Generalmajor* Freiherr von Falkenstein becoming its first Chief of Staff. He was replaced, just three months later, by *Generalmajor* Andreas Nielsen, who was fortunate enough to have Wolf Falck as his Operations Officer. From their bunker at Berlin-Wannsee they were able to evaluate all the available information concerning the strength and direction of any incoming bomber stream, and direct the German night defences, particularly the night fighters, accordingly.

As a result of the political situation in Berlin following the assassination attempt on Hitler in July 1944, Wolf went to see his close friend, *General der Jagdflieger*, Adolf Galland. He listened sympathetically to Falck's concerns and agreed to help him leave the German capital. Galland appointed him *Jagdflieger-Führer* for the Balkans, with its headquarters located in Pancevo near Belgrade. An elated Falck took up the new position in August, but his new command was not destined to last long. The war in the east was not going at all well for Germany and, to compound its problems further, Rumania and Bulgaria changed allegiance and joined the Russians. These defections, combined with reports of advancing Russian and Titoist forces, threatened the very stability of his Balkan command and so he transferred its headquarters to Vienna. Shortly after his arrival in the Austrian capital he again found himself on the move, this time being transferred to Potsdam in October 1944:

> I became Chief of Staff for the General Flieger-Ausbildung, which meant that this headquarters was responsible for all of the Luftwaffe training schools. There were, I do not know how many schools for young pilots, for bombing training, fighters, Night Fighters, wireless training and so on. It was an immense organisation that we had under our command.

In March 1945, with the war drawing towards its inevitable conclusion, Wolf found himself in the Düsseldorf/Cologne region of Western Germany. His orders, with the Allies expected to cross the Rhine River at any moment, were to identify possible landing sites for their troops and then report back with possible ideas on how to prevent them. However, the reality of Germany's hopeless position quickly hit home. There were too many possible landing sites and resources, such as ground troops and anti-aircraft guns to protect them all, were few and far between. The situation was grave and the war was lost.

Towards the end of April, with the fall of the *Reich* imminent, he found himself on a small airfield at Bad Aibling in Southern Bavaria, along with 5,000 other military personnel and refugees. When he learned that the American Army would be at the airfield within hours, he drove to a nearby castle owned by a family acquaintance and awaited the inevitable. Early on the morning of 2 May 1945 an American soldier entered the castle, where much to his surprise, he was greeted by a smiling Luftwaffe officer. The German officer, wearing the uniform of an *Oberst*, handed over his pistol and resignedly walked into captivity. After more than five years of war Wolf Falck was now officially an American prisoner of war.

Upon his release from captivity on 7 June 1945, no one would employ a former *Oberst* from the General Staff of the Luftwaffe, and so he was forced to work as a manual worker on a farm in Hessen for a measly twenty *pfennigs* an hour.

After almost six years of continual war Wolf Falck begins to enjoy the peace. (Falck)

Over the next few years he was employed in a variety of jobs, ranging from construction of primitive motor vehicles for farming to working in a pharmaceutical company. One of the jobs he held during this time was even given to him by the British Army who were looking for someone with good administrative skills, and more importantly, someone they could trust and rely upon. He was immediately offered, and accepted, the position of Civil Officer at the stores section of the 47th Royal Engineers.

Although delighted at his good fortune, Wolf soon realised that in order to build a brighter and more prosperous future for himself, he would have to broaden his horizons and look for a job with better prospects. One way in which he was able to do this was by studying business at night school. His hard work, and subsequent qualifications, soon paid dividends.

A newly established playing card company, the only one in West Germany at that time, offered him the position of sales representative. In 1961, having risen to become the manager of the company he was approached by North American Aviation who persuaded him to become a consultant for them. Five years later, in 1966, he became a consultant for another aviation company, this time for McDonnell Douglas.

In 1986, at the grand age of seventy-six, Wolf Falck finally retired after more than fifty-five years of almost continual employment. Throughout his life, those people who have had an opportunity to meet Wolf Falck, whether it was during the war or after it, have spoken of his decency and sense of fair play. During the course of the war he had occasion to meet various downed British airmen who benefited from his

Squadron Leader Peter Tomlinson with Hauptmann von Sreve of NJG 1, after Tomlinson's forced landing at Deelen on 22 September 1941. After being wined and dined by his German captives, he was flown to the Frankfurt in Falck's own aircraft. Falck and Tomlinson met again fifty-four years later in Cape Town, South Africa. (Falck)

generous nature. Wolf recalls one such event that occurred on 22 September 1941. His actions towards the RAF officer, Squadron Leader Peter Tomlinson, would result in another meeting with the airman fifty-four years later, and the formation of a new friendship:

> I am flying back in my Me110 from a conference in Hamburg to our operational airfield at Deelen in Holland. On the way I get a report: 'Enemy aircraft leaving Hamburg heading 270 ° – shoot him down!' So – full throttle, eyes open! But there is nothing to be seen. Finally I arrive at Deelen, and below me I see a Spitfire that had tried to land.
>
> What had happened? I learnt that it was an unarmed reconnaissance Spitfire that had experienced technical problems on its way back home and had therefore been forced to land immediately ahead of me. I greeted the pilot, a Squadron Leader, a nice, young, smart man. As it was midday I took him into the officer's mess, introduced him to the officers and invited him to lunch. The conversation was lively and comradely. After lunch we went for a stroll together and chatted about our individual experiences, and in doing so we discovered that we had flown operationally over the Channel at the same time. I spoke of the Spitfire with great respect, while he said that the Me110, with its considerable fire power, was a very unpleasant opponent when it managed to get in behind a Spitfire which, fortunately, was only rarely the case.
>
> As the nightly RAF bombing attacks on the Rhine and Ruhr area were already on the increase, I wanted to spare him being taken by rail through these very areas in RAF uniform. He had spoken very knowledgeably about the Me110, so I instructed my Technical Officer, Oberleutnant Rademacher, to fly him to Frankfurt in my Me110. I gave him a good supply of chocolate and cigarettes to take with him, assuming that he could make good use of them in the immediate future. The flight was, quite naturally, an impressive experience for him. That same evening the Kommandeur of Oberursel rang me up and passed the handset over to the prisoner, who thanked me effusively.

On 17 January 1995, almost fifty-four years later, the two former airman met again at Peter Tomlinson's home in Cape Town, South Africa. As a result of the meeting the men struck up a close friendship which was to last until Peter Tomlinson's death in 1998. This is just one of a number of examples, which reveal the true character of this man and explain how, after the war, he was easily able to make friends with people who had once been regarded as his enemies.

During the post-war years he continued his love of flying by joining a number of flying clubs. He also served, for a short time, as the President of the German Fighter Pilot's Association (*Gemeinschaft der Jagdflieger*), of which he is still a member. He now lives quietly, perched high in the Austrian Tyrol, with his enchanting partner, Gisela, and a whole host of family pets. Much of his time is spent at his picturesque home entertaining guests from all over the world. Wolf Falck is a remarkable man who, even on the eve of his ninetieth birthday, has the ability to recall events from over sixty years ago, as if they had occurred yesterday. His unique story guarantees his place in aviation history, but I am sure that all who have had the privilege of meeting him will remember Wolf as being an outstanding officer, a perfect host and indeed, a perfect gentleman.

2

Hauptmann Georg Hermann Greiner

The glow of the fires that emanated from the north German town of Bremen penetrated the dark, cloudy night sky, as wave after wave of RAF bombers continued to drop their deadly loads into the inferno below. This raid, one of Bomber Command's first thousand bomber raids, caused many fires. This was particularly true in the southern and eastern sectors of the town where strengthening winds helped fan the flames, increasing the destruction.

In response to the raid on Bremen, elements of the *Nachtjagd* had been scrambled to counter the incoming bomber force, and these night fighters were very effective in harrying the bombers to and from the target. As was usual practice in the German night fighter force, the most experienced and successful crews were scrambled first. This gave them the best opportunities to shoot down bombers and thus improve on their individual scores, while the lesser-known and established pilots were normally demoted to the last

Hauptmann Georg Hermann Greiner,
Gruppenkommandeur of IV./NJG 1. (Greiner)

Oberstleutnant a.D. Georg Hermann Greiner,
now in his eightieth year. (Greiner)

waves of aircraft to be scrambled. It was to one of these last waves that Georg Hermann Greiner found himself allocated to in the early hours of 26 June 1942. Unfavourable weather conditions, in the form of heavy cloud, combined with his late entry into the fray meant that *Leutnant* Greiner was not optimistic about his chances of contact with the enemy. However, he goes on to explain:

> My first downing involved many problems as will become apparent from the following description – nothing went right. It was the 26 June 1942, and as often happened I had been assigned to the 'last wave'. This patrol normally lasted until dawn and did not usually lead to any combat activity. This early morning patrol was quiet except for one late arrival who must have thought that he was almost home. This led to my first enemy contact.
>
> It was already getting light when we set off. We were directed by the Jägerleitoffizier on to the enemy's course through massive stratocumuli clouds. [My aircraft] was shaken constantly by turbulence, and thus it was a liberating feeling to be able to return to visual flight and relatively calm conditions having cleared the clouds. By now, it was bright daylight over the clouds and I was just wondering what had kept this late arrival over enemy territory for such a long time, when I saw him, a Wellington, approaching from out of one of those high-reaching cumulus clouds.
>
> This cloud formation offered ideal possibilities for him to quickly escape into and re-emerge again when necessary. But, at this time he was visible to the vigilant eyes of the fighter, standing out sharply against the clouds through which the rising sun was emerging. Nevertheless, his 'cards' were still better than mine because he would see me before I could get close. I fired at the Wellington from a great distance. I very carefully aimed and tried to correct any deviations to my 'Cone of Fire.'
>
> As expected, the Wellington disappeared into the clouds. I was sure that I had hit him but I had been unable to see whether it went down or was only damaged. This uncertainty as to whether this was a downing or only an enemy contact was somewhat depressing. However, shortly afterwards it was confirmed that the Wellington had in fact crashed into the ground.

With his first victory safely under his belt, Georg Hermann Greiner's star began its ascent. After just a few short, tumultuous years, filled with constant fighting and the very real threat of death, he would survive to become one of the *Nachtjagd*'s most respected and highly decorated night fighter pilots. To have survived these bitter years of aerial combat with the RAF, a battle unprecedented in its magnitude and ferocity before this clash-of-arms, was itself no mean feat. As well as this, he was one of only a handful of night fighter pilots to have achieved more than fifty confirmed victories by war's end. This may well have had something to do with the fact that Georg Greiner fought with the most successful night fighter unit in the *Nachtjagd – Nachtjagdgeschwader 1*. Not only did he serve under some of the finest *Geschwaderkommodore*, such as Wolf Falck, Werner Streib and Hans-Joachim Jabs, but he also fought alongside some of the best night fighter pilots the *Geschwader* had to offer, chiefly Heinz Schnaufer, Martin Drewes and Hans-Heinz Augenstein.

In order to examine the life and career of Georg Hermann Greiner one must travel to a time twenty-five years prior to the cessation of hostilities, to the small Bavarian town of Heidenheim located in the administrative district of Middle Franconia.

It was here on 2 January 1920 that Georg, the only child of Albrecht and Sophie Greiner, was born. Due to the poor nutritional conditions that were prevalent in post-war Germany at the time, Albrecht moved his wife, prior to their son's birth, to this rurally located town so that she could raise the child in an area where food was more readily available.

Having made suitable provisions for his family, he returned to Bochum, a small town in the Ruhr, where he was employed as a trainee banker with the *Reichsbank*. This area of the Ruhr, which under the provisions of the Treaty of Versaille was controlled by the French authorities, sorely lacked adequate housing. This inevitably resulted in Albrecht being unable to bring his family to Bochum with him and, as a consequence of this, Georg rarely saw his father in the early years of his childhood. It was left to Sophie to raise her son. Under his mother's influence and guidance, these early, formative years were to mould Georg Greiner into the sensitive and thoughtful man he was to become and remain.

As the years passed, his father was finally given an opportunity to rent a small flat in Bochum. On securing the property Albrecht immediately sent a message for his family to join him there. Although they were now finally together life did not become any easier, in fact the opposite was to be true.

Albrecht Greiner was very intolerant of his son and punished him severely whenever he strayed from the straight and narrow. This caused a great deal of friction and disharmony within the family, which usually resulted in Sophie Greiner arbitrating between father and son in order to maintain a fragile peace. As a direct result of this almost tyrannical treatment, Georg developed a strong desire to succeed in everything he participated in, in an attempt to prove himself worthy in the eyes of his father.

At the age of seven he joined the German Gymnasts Association (*Deutscher Turner Bund*) and three years later he became an active and enthusiastic member of the German Scout Movement (*Deutscher Pfadfinder Bund*). Membership of both organisations was to prove rather fortuitous, as they provided him with opportunities he would have otherwise missed. Recounting the events sixty-five years later, two episodes in particular stand out in his memory from these rather happier times.

The first of these occurred in 1933 when, as a member of the Scout movement, he participated in an educational tour of Switzerland and Italy. Compared by today's standards this is nothing remarkable. But, sixty-five years ago, for a young boy of thirteen who had never travelled beyond his own country's borders, it was quite an event. This tour, and in particular the journey through Italy, left a deep and lasting impression on Georg:

> In 1933, after we had moved to Offenbach/Main due to my father being transferred again, we Scouts went on an organized trip to Switzerland and Italy. From Offenbach we went to Airolo-Bellinzona by train and from there by foot along the shores of Lake Maggiore. Then on again by train to Milan where we had been invited to stay for a few days with local German families there. After that, Rome, with all of its historic and architectural masterpieces, including the Sistine Chapel with frescoes by Michelangelo and famous marble statuettes of Moses and David by the same exceptional artist. This was the ultimate experience for us, a unique experience of truly overwhelming perfection without which no-one could possibly define 'beauty' if they had not seen and studied it themselves.

The second of these memorable episodes occurred three years later, in 1936, when he was selected by the National Olympic Committee to participate in the International Youth Camp of the XI Olympic Games held in Berlin. This was chiefly as a result of the German Gymnasts Association's support, which nurtured and developed Georg's natural athletic ability. The Games were a memorable event that he fondly, but philosophically remembers:

> Those were unforgettable days. Above all because one got to hear about subjects and information which we had hardly known about until then as one was able to move rather freely in those circles. We were able to speak about and discuss questions and problems more openly.
>
> The sporting ability of the top sportsmen, especially that of the German team was astonishing. However, nothing could hide the fact that this demonstration was serving a political end. I was less interested in what the organizers of the Games obviously wanted to show and communicate to the world. I therefore mainly concentrated on contact with the young foreign guests and the possibility of making friends with them to further mutual understanding.
>
> I received invitations to Hungary for 1937, to Bulgaria for 1938, to Canada for 1939 and I was determined to follow them up. The trip to Hungary took place according to plan. The impression that this city, the elegant metropolis of the Magyars, with its castles, bridges and magnificent buildings had on me sixty-one years ago is still unforgettable, clear and vivid.

Not only did Georg enjoy broadening his own horizons by visiting other European countries and meeting foreign visitors to Germany, but he was also able to indulge in another favourite pastime – flying.

As a consequence of the Nazis coming to power in 1933, the Scout movement was disbanded and its members integrated in to the Hitler Youth (*Hitlerjugend*). For young men of this period, who were vehemently against joining this organization, the realisation that there was little they could do was accepted with an air of resignation.

After four monotonous years of being in the Hitler Youth, Georg Greiner decided to join the Flying Hitler Youth (*Flieger Hitlerjugend*)[1] having already completed the aptitude test to become an officer in the Luftwaffe. As well as the aptitude test, any young German volunteering to join the Air Force with a view to becoming an officer was required to pass the *Abitur*.

In February 1938, due mainly to political reasons, students were made to take this exam a year earlier than normally would have been expected. These unusual circumstances presented Georg with an ideal opportunity to finally leave the Hitler Youth and he quickly applied for a leave of absence in order to study. The request was granted and much relieved at this stroke of luck, and free of this organization's influence, he would never again have any contact with them.

On 5 April 1938, having obtained the all-important *Abitur*, he underwent six months of Reich Labour Service or *Reichsarbeitdienst*, which was compulsory in Germany at that time.

---

[1] The Flying Hitler Youth was established in 1933, and was a specialist unit within the Hitler Youth. In 1937 it was absorbed in to the *Luftsportscharen* or Air Sports Association.

A copy of Fahnenjunker-Unteroffizier Greiner's pilot's licence. (Peter Heinrich)

This involved young men aged between eighteen and twenty-five participating in such work as farming, construction and land reclamation. In Georg's case he took part in a road building scheme in the rugged and wild Rhön Mountains.

The Nazi regime had many motives, militaristic as well as nationalistic, for introducing this type of labour service. Not only did it improve Germany's road network and dramatically reduce the nation's unemployment figures, but it was also hoped that regular exercise, combined with regimented discipline, would prepare these youths for war. For many of those involved the end of their six months could not come quickly enough. The work camps were hastily erected and this was more often than not reflected in the poor living and sanitary conditions endured by those involved. Few of those who attended these camps would remember them with any fondness.

Within fourteen days of completing his compulsory period with the Reich Labour Service, Georg found himself undergoing basic recruit's training with the Second Pilot Replacement Unit at Detmold in Westphalia. Four intense and gruelling months were to follow, commencing on 8 November 1938 and finishing on 20 March 1939. The training was particularly hard and regularly pushed the recruits to their physical and mental limits.

At the conclusion of this basic military training *Fahnenjunker* Greiner was posted to the Air Warfare School at Berlin-Gatow where his flying training with the Luftwaffe began. During the next ten months he underwent intensive schooling on such aircraft as the Focke-Wulf 44 'Stieglitz', the Bücker 131 biplane and the single-engined Arado 96. After months of mastering the fundamentals of flying he successfully qualified for his pilot's badge and A/B flying certificate, which was given in recognition of being qualified on elementary and advanced single-engined aircraft.

The Zerstörer School at Memmingen in the winter of 1940. On this particular day, during a break in the training, Greiner met one of the foremost German pilots involved in the Battle of Britain, Josef 'Pips' Priller (second from the left). (Günther Lauser)

Being attached to NJG 1, Georg Greiner had the privilege of flying with some of the Nachtjagd's best pilots and crews. From left to right: Hans-Heinz Augenstein (46 victories – killed in action on 6/7 December 1944); Wilhelm Gänsler (Schnaufer's Bordmechaniker); Heinz Schnaufer (the highest scoring night fighter of all time with 121 victories); Greiner; and Fritz Rumpelhardt (Schnaufer's Bordfunker). (Greiner)

From here, in order to qualify for the C-Certificate, which would allow a pilot to fly multi-engined machines, he attended the C-*Schule* at Alt-Lönnewitz in Saxony. There he was able to fly and master twin-engined aircraft such as the Heinkel 111 and Junkers 86 but, most importantly, he would master the one aircraft in which he would later excel as a night fighter – the Messerschmitt 110:

> I preferred the Me110 which had been designed, named and used as a 'Destroyer' or 'Heavy Fighter' because I was convinced that it had more advantages than disadvantages for me as a night fighter. In terms of construction, weaponry and type, it was a 'Fighter' with features that I wanted to have. The Me110 had greater mobility and was easier to manoeuvre. The pilot only just fitted into the cockpit which gave him the feeling of being an integral part of the machine.

After obtaining the 'C' grading to his pilot's licence, Georg Greiner completed a succession of courses all aimed at moulding him into a proficient pilot. He attended a multitude of flying schools, detailed below, giving some insight into how comprehensive the training was.

The first of these was the Long-Range Reconnaissance School at Großenheim followed by the Blind-Flying School at Neuburg/Donau. From there he was posted to the 'Destroyer' School at Memmingen, the Fighter School at Schleißheim near Munich and then finally on to the Night Fighter School at Stuttgart/Echterdingen. The training programme was a long and arduous one, at times frustratingly so.

From the time that his flying career began in March 1939, to the time he completed the final part of his training in September 1941, over two years had elapsed.[2] Georg feared that the war would be over before he'd had a chance to prove himself. However, the war was still raging when he was transferred to II./NJG 1 in October 1941. He recalls his first few months of being with a front line unit:

> I reported, as ordered, for duty with II./NJG 1 at Stade near Hamburg on 1 October 1941. Hauptmann Walter Ehle was the Kommandeur and my Staffelkapitän was Oberleutnant Gresens. A few months later I became the Gruppe's Adjutant.
>
> I had been transferred to this Geschwader, which had been formed when night fighting was in its infancy. I was allowed to be a member of this unit right up to the end of the war and I was loyal throughout. I could not imagine a better military order and hierarchy because we hardly had any disciplinary problems at all. The atmosphere was good, humour and tolerance were part of everyday life. The majority of us were well brought up and formed young men who were able to weigh feelings and intellect appropriately. According to a maxim of that time, 'A soldier was to be self-confident but modest, upright and loyal, as well as a valuable member of society.' These words are timeless, even if they were formulated in the Third Reich.

---

[2] Usually the training programme lasted approximately two years. As a result of a flying accident during his time at the Long-Range Reconnaissance School at Großenheim, Georg Greiner was unfit to fly for a period of several months. This resulted in a slightly longer training period (approximately two-and-a-half years) than was normal.

On 1 October 1941 Greiner joined II./NJG 1 based at Stade, near Hamburg. To his left is the Staffelkapitän of 11./NJG 1, Oberleutnant Gresens. (Lauser)

Pre-mission briefing of II./NJG 2 at Leeuwarden in Holland. From left to right: Heinz Vinke (killed on 26 February 1944 – 54 kills); Walter Kubisch; Leopold Fellerer (41 kills); unknown; Greiner. (Lauser)

In the middle of January 1942, and much to his dismay, *Leutnant* Greiner was transferred to II./NJG 2. This *Gruppe*, comprising of the 4th *Staffel* of NJG 2 and the 6th *Staffel* of NJG 1, had been formed in November 1941 and was based at Leeuwarden on the north-west coast of Holland.

Within a matter of a few weeks Georg found himself participating in a special operation that would involve him, along with other night fighter pilots, operating during the day. The mission, code named *Donnerkeil* or Thunderbolt, was the escort of the battleships *Scharnhorst* and *Gneisenau* and the heavy cruiser *Prinz Eugen* through the English Channel and on to the relative safety of the Norwegian Fjords. The mission turned out to be a great success for the Germans, who were able to get all three ships through the Channel without serious interference from the RAF, and safely into German ports, namely Wilhelmshaven and Kiel.

On 20 April 1942, Georg was promoted to the rank of *Oberleutnant* and two months later, having achieved his first confirmed aerial victory over north-west Holland, he was awarded the Iron Cross Second Class. A second victory followed on 6 October 1942 when he shot down a Halifax over Leeuwarden. But, shortly after this, he received the dismal news that he had been selected to go to the night fighter school at Echterdingen as an instructor.

As a pilot with less than ten victories Georg had very little choice in the matter, although he was able to secure a promise from his Commanding Officer, *Hauptmann* Helmut Lent, that he would be returned to the *Gruppe* after six months.

Leutnant Greiner with his Bordfunker, Rolf Kissing. This successful crew achieved its first kill on 26 June 1942, following an attack by Bomber Command on Bremen. (Greiner)

At the wheel of the Kommodore's Dodge motorcar, which had been converted to run on gas. Leutnant Heinrich sits next to Greiner. (Lauser)

Posing in front of a parked Bf110 with a captured American flying jacket. (Greiner)

The attachment to the night fighter school commenced on 23 November 1942 and *Oberleutnant* Greiner found himself responsible for turning newly qualified airmen into competent night fighter pilots. At Echterdingen, no missions could be flown against the RAF as the school did not have the required technical equipment. This, however, did not deter Georg, who on one dark March evening took-off and successfully infiltrated the incoming bomber stream. The ensuing combat proved successful for this young German night fighter who was able to chalk up a further victory by shooting down a Short Stirling near Rastatt.

After completing almost exactly six months as an instructor at the training school, Georg was, as promised, transferred back to his former *Gruppe* which had from 1 October 1942, been re-designated IV./NJG 1.

Exactly a week after returning to the *Gruppe*, on the night of 25/26 May 1943, *Oberleutnant* Greiner increased his tally to five, accounting for two Lancaster bombers that had participated in an attack on Düsseldorf. This raid by Bomber Command is generally regarded as having been a failure because the city was covered in several layers of cloud. As a consequence, the Pathfinders experienced great difficulty marking the target, resulting in widespread bombing that caused few casualties and very little structural damage. A total of twenty-seven bombers were lost during the mission and Georg Greiner briefly recounts the events of that night which saw him shoot down two of them:

> In the mission plan I was to be a reserve, but this changed when the Kommandeur's (Helmut Lent) Bf110 broke down and the head of operations appointed me as his replacement. It goes without saying that the Raum 'Tiger' in which I now flew for the first time was a Kommandeur's Raum - a good potential transit area for the RAF.
>
> The Raum and Himmelbett night fighting system that we had been using for almost a year, was carried out now with almost no noise apart from the odd burst of gunfire. I was led in perfectly by the Jägerleitoffizier and shot down two Lancasters without much of a fight and after a relatively short period of time. Both of these bombers crashed into the Züider Zee in North-West Holland.

According to Bill Chorley's *Bomber Command Losses*, one of these aircraft was Lancaster ED695 PO-J of 467 Squadron, based at Bottesford in Leicestershire. It crashed in flames at 03.21 hours, and all but two of the crew survived to become prisoners of war.

The Iron Cross First Class was bestowed upon *Oberleutnant* Greiner on 1 June 1943, as visible recognition of his achievements. Over the following three months the young night fighter was able to account for a further five bombers, taking his tally to ten. Three of these bombers, a Halifax, a Lancaster and a Wellington were all shot down during the devastating raids on Hamburg in July and August.

As a consequence of the continued night offensive directed against Germany, many thousands of young men from both sides lost, and were to lose their lives, during this titanic struggle. Although it is known that this was a brutal battle of attrition there are documented incidents of acts of chivalry and humanity. One such act occurred on the night of 27 September 1943 and is worthy of mention here. It is a fine example of human decency during trying times and helps reveal the true character of Georg Greiner. The following account took place over the North Sea, and occurred after he had already shot down one Halifax (his thirteenth victory):

> Having located the [second] Halifax, my radio operator continuously updated me with the range to the bomber until we were very close. At first we were unable to see him even though we knew he was there. Still, he remained invisible. It seemed as if we had flown over him as I had not been able to react in time to my radio operator's directions. As a consequence I had not been able to adjust our flight speed to that of that Halifax and we had to fly a full circle in order to get back behind it. In order not to overshoot the target again I lowered our speed substantially. But again we gained so much speed that we missed the Halifax for a second time. I finally estimated the speed of the bomber correctly and we were then able to fly relatively close to its port side. What we were about to see would have amazed the most experienced flying personnel and sent ice-cold shivers down their spines!
>
> The bomber was only flying with two engines! It was only just managing to stay up in the air and above the waters of the North Sea. The starboard engines had failed and made no sound or movement. The blades of its propellers rose motionless and ghostly into the dark evening sky. At the end of the starboard wing almost 2m were missing, probably due to heavy anti-aircraft fire over the target. What had been its target? What encounters had it been involved in? How serious was its overall damage? And, how long had it already been flying in that condition? When one takes all of this into consideration it had been a great achievement by the crew, and especially that of the pilot, who one could only show the utmost respect.
>
> After flying alongside the badly damaged Halifax it was clear to me that the crew of the bomber had performed a unique achievement which had to be rewarded. Without a moments hesitation I rocked my wings a few times in time-honoured tradition, a conciliatory and peaceful gesture even among enemies. We then turned for home in a steep left curve.

Although this had been a gallant gesture on behalf of the young German night fighter, the decision to let the crippled bomber carry on unmolested hadn't been an easy one for him to make. He was constantly troubled by an inner conflict. He saw Germany being systematically and relentlessly attacked and, as a consequence, his friends, neighbours and colleagues were being killed in the bombings. On one period of home leave a neighbours house was badly damaged and set on fire during a raid. The exits from the building were blocked and all efforts to rescue them were to prove fruitless. All perished in the fire. Incidents like this increased his insensitivity, however, it did not change his attitude towards humanity. One way in which he found to compromise between his duties and his conscience was to shoot the bombers between the engines. In this way its crew was afforded a better chance of parachuting out and, at the same time, guaranteed its almost certain destruction. A small but decent act from a young German soldier trying hard to do the right thing in the middle of a bloody and murderous conflict.

On 4 October 1943 *Oberleutnant* Greiner was made *Staffelführer* of the 10th *Staffel*, this was a rank for an officer who temporarily led a *Staffel,* usually with a view of promoting him after a probationary period to *Staffelkapitän*.

It was at about this time that his aircraft was fitted with a revolutionary type of armament known as *Schräge Musik*. This weapon is usually believed to have had its origins in the

Schräge Musik gave the German night-fighters a distinct advantage in its battle with Bomber Command. In the first photograph a pair of 30mm MK 108 cannon have been installed in the rear of the cockpit. In the second, the twin cannon can be clearly seen on top of the fuselage just behind the cockpit. (author's collection)

Second World War, this is, however, not the case. As *Schräge Musik* is repeatedly mentioned throughout the book this would seem to be an ideal opportunity to describe in some detail how it both originated and worked.

In the closing stages of the First World War, a German airman called Gerhard Fieseler had a novel idea about fitting a pair of machine guns to his aircraft. This was nothing unusual except that these were aligned so that they fired upwards, allowing the pilot to shoot vertically while flying underneath a target. This weapons system was not universally known about, or used at the time, but its principles were to be successfully adopted and improved twenty-five years later to devastating effect.

In early 1942 *Oberleutnant* Rudolf Schoenert, *Staffelkapitän* of 4./NJG 2, began experimenting with upward-firing machine-guns in a Dornier 17Z *Kauz* II. When he was transferred as *Gruppenkommandeur* of II./NJG 5 he took with him a Do217 that had already been equipped with the same weapons system. It soon caught the eye of an armaments technician, *Oberfeldwebel* Mahler, who designed and built a prototype using two 20mm Oerlikon MG FF machine-guns. These were then built into the cabin roof of an Me110 in which Schoenert was to score the first recorded *Schräge Musik* victory in about May 1943. This first kill was soon followed by others.

Later, twin cannon, either 20 or 30mm, were fitted into the top of the night fighter's fuselage and positioned at an angle of 70 or 80° to it. The pilot was then able to aim the weapon by means of a reflector-sight in the cabin roof. *Schräge Musik* enabled the night fighters to get in underneath a bomber with only a small risk of being seen by its gunners. Once under the enemy machine, and hidden by the dark backdrop of the ground, the German pilot could take his time and aim with care. This usually resulted in more accurate fire and a better chance of success, but with considerably less risk of being shot down. Like many of his colleagues Georg adopted this style of attack and, with only a few exceptions, his future victories were all achieved using *Schräge Musik*:

> The enormous advantage for the night fighter attacking with Schräge Musik was that he was flying to the side of and slightly lower than the bomber. He was then able to move below it without being noticed, thereby getting safely into firing position. With Schräge Musik, when the bomber performed evasive manoeuvres, I was able to follow each of his flight movements exactly.
>
> Before changing over to this weapons system the guns of the Me110 were directed horizontally towards the front. The starting point of the attack for the night fighter was therefore from a position behind and below the bomber. The fighter would commence his attack by climbing and using the horizontal guns as soon as the bomber appeared in the cross-hairs of his sights. During this manoeuvre he had to pass the tail of the bomber which was armed with an immense four-barrelled machine-gun. This was by far the most dangerous area of the bomber and with Schräge Musik the main danger from this weapon was thus avoided.

However, it was to be a further three, long and frustrating months before he could claim his next victory. On the night of the 14/15 January 1944 Bomber Command made its first raid on Brunswick. As a result of the German early-warning system detecting the bomber stream at a very early stage, the *Nachtjagd* was able to infiltrate it as soon as it crossed the German frontier in the area of Bremen. Consequently, eleven Pathfinder machines were

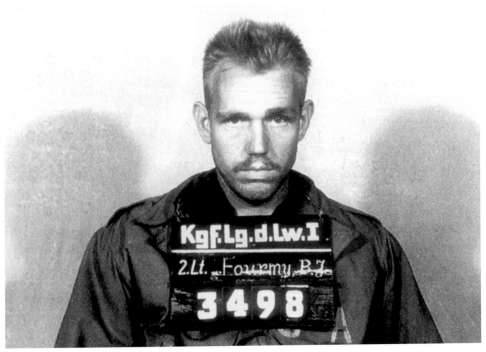

A very dejected looking Lieutenant Ben Fourmy has his photograph taken before internment in a prisoner of war camp. Oberleutnant Greiner shot down the B-17 that he piloted on 6 March 1944 over Quakenbrück airfield. (Fourmy)

shot down. With the loss of so many of these aircraft, responsible for accurately marking the target with flares, the bombing that followed was widespread and inaccurate. Very little damage was caused to the Brunswick, and the majority of the bombs fell in countryside to the south of the city. A total of thirty-eight Lancasters were lost from the raiding force, one of which Georg claimed as his fourteenth confirmed kill of the war.

The early months of 1944 saw a marked increase in daylight raids by the USAAF after its heavy losses over Schweinfurt on 14 October 1943. Now, with the emergence of the P-51B as a long-range escort fighter, the bombers could once again venture deep into Germany – but this time with suitable protection. On 31 January and 10 February respectively, the 8th Air Force carried out daylight raids attacks on Brunswick. Consequently, on each raid, Georg Greiner accounted for a B-17 over the Westphalian town of Osnabrück. This was by no means a small feat for a pilot only accustomed to attacking large bombers under the veil of darkness. The Me110 was best suited as a night fighter, because when it was opposed by fast single-engined day fighters, such as the P-51 and P-38, it was totally outclassed, just as it had been during the Battle of Britain.

The most significant raid by the USAAF in early 1944 was the first large-scale daylight raid on Berlin on 6 March. One of the B-17s that took part that day was aircraft 42-38118 from the 91st Bomb Group stationed at Bassingbourn in Cambridgeshire. During the course of the mission this aircraft was damaged by a combination of German fighters and flak. The pilot, 2nd Lieutenant Ben Fourmy, recalls the raid that saw two of his crew killed:

A short time after we crossed the English Channel we were attacked by German fighter planes, both Me109s and Fw190s. Our plane was badly damaged. The top turret was blown off and a piece of the nose cone was destroyed, the right outboard engine was knocked out and we could not feather the propeller. The top turret gunner, Fred Walker, was badly injured so we had to have the radio operator come forward and take him to the radio room to try and stop the bleeding. At this point we were having trouble keeping up with the Group and eventually we had to fall back behind the 91st. We were then hit by flak (west of Hanover causing damage to an engine on each side of the aircraft) and a little later by more Me109s and Fw190s. To make matters worse the co-pilot did not have heat any longer and was being to freeze. We could not find the problem, but at this point it did not matter, as we could no longer keep up with the Groups and had to leave the formation. It was sixty below zero and we had a draft through the plane from the hole in the nose and the missing top turret. This left us with a choice of either bailing out or trying to get home. We tried to make it back to England as there were clouds below us and we knew that they would protect us from the German fighter planes. [When] the clouds disappeared we went down to treetop level as that was the only chance we had of getting back to England. We were doing great until we passed over a German fighter field and were [subsequently] picked up by a German night fighter, an Me110, that was taking off from the airbase. He followed us and stayed out of range of our fifty calibre machine-guns and set us on fire with his 20mm cannons. Our plane at this point was out of control and crashed. The pilot of that German plane was Oberleutnant Georg Greiner.

Oberleutnant Greiner was indeed the pilot of the aforementioned German fighter. He had seen the American bombers pass over the airfield at Quakenbrück, north of Osnabrück and, fearing an attack on the base, he took off. Here he vividly recounts his version of the aerial encounter that took place on that particular March afternoon:

By the beginning of 1944 the Americans had considerably strengthened their fleets of bombers, which were responsible for the daylight attacks on Germany. Additionally, within the framework of the measures taken in this development, the fighter escorts had been reinforced accordingly. The attacks subsequently became heavier and heavier, and their targets were now no longer restricted to the west of Germany. The central point, the focal point of the attacks, was Berlin, which was bombed several times in succession within a short period of time.

For some short time the Nachtjagd had also been in action as reinforcements against the day attacks, a miscalculation with severe consequences to send highly qualified flying personnel to their doom in this way. They could only be replaced over a long period of time, and their Messerschmitts and Junkers could not match the speed of the US escort fighters, the Lightning and Mustang, nor could they achieve a great deal against the concentrated, blazing power of the B-17s that operated in close formation. In those days I was one of the privileged circle excused from flying daylight missions.

On the 6 March 1944 my Me110, which hadn't been cleared for operations after my last mission, had been certified airworthy by the ground crew. An operational air-test was urgently due in order to make sure that the machine was fit for action for possible use that evening. A short time afterwards I took off on the air-test and, as usual, I pulled my aircraft up into the air in a steep climb with full flaps in order to gain height as quickly as possible. I was probably at about 100m altitude, intending to begin to test the aircraft to its stress limits – requirements that were specified for combat – when I made a discovery. It was a discovery that baffled me and which was so unusual and peculiar that at first I simply couldn't believe it. I had to look several times in order to rid myself of my astonishment. Flying always has a few surprises in store, but I had never before seen a B-17 flying so low, without observing any obvious signs of damage, on a parallel heading to mine in the direction of Den Helder and on the periphery of my own airfield. Indeed, I had to think what to do. Because of my own aircraft's instability I could scarcely open fire without endangering myself. It was also inadvisable to pull up the flaps at a relatively low altitude in order to gain stability, because in such a manoeuvre the 110 lost height and might have dropped lower than I would have liked. While I was thinking along these lines the B-17 was drawing further and further away so that I feared that it would escape from me, which I could not allow to happen. After this review of the situation my mind was made up. I would have to stay in a state of instability because I was unable to alter it quickly, and I had to open fire immediately, even if there was a risk of doing so at a greater range from the target than was usual. I acted on this decision immediately. In discussions I have repeatedly emphasised that this kill seemed to me to be unpleasant and unfair, even though all thirteen guns on the B-17 were intact and no engine fault was impeding its thrust and speed, but I couldn't just let him get away.

In order to compensate a little for the comparatively long distance when I attacked I tried to aim with as much concentration as possible, and to correct my bursts of fire by means of my

Oberleutnant Greiner with Feldwebel Kissing (left) and Feldwebel Vinkler (right), all wearing recently procured American leather flying jackets. (Greiner)

tracer, in order to direct my aim with precision. In addition I fired in a flat profile, that is to say, on the watering can principle, which admittedly resulted in a worse shots-to-hits ratio but nevertheless ensured a greater overall number of hits on the target. The pilot did not change his pattern of flight and the B-17 soon showed the effect. A number of lesser and bigger fires could be seen rapidly growing bigger, in the fuselage of the Flying Fortress. As there was an ever-increasing danger of explosion and total destruction the pilot, Second Lieutenant Fourmy, put down in a potato field near to Quakenbrück. Because of the danger his crew took to their heels in a great hurry and I heard subsequently that with the exception of two crew-members, who had died in the fuselage in the course of the crash-landing, the remaining eight crewmen were taken prisoner. Finally a huge explosion sealed the fate of the B-17.

A little over three hours later that same day, at 15.53 hours, *Oberleutnant* Greiner added a B-24 Consolidated Liberator to his days cache. After positioning himself underneath the unsuspecting bomber, he opened fire. This burst of gunfire tore off the tail section, which caused the bomber to dive steeply and spin out of control. Before it crashed, alongside a munitions factory at Münsterlager, eight of the ten-man crew were able to take to their parachutes. As a result of having shot down a total of four American four-engined bombers in a little over five weeks, a credible figure for a trained night fighter, his tally of victories now stood at nineteen. This figure was raised to twenty-one when he accounted for a Halifax and Lancaster on raids to Düsseldorf (22/23 April) and Karlsruhe (24/25 April) respectively.

By this time *Oberleutnant* Greiner had been decorated with the German Cross in Gold and promoted to *Staffelkapitän* of the 11th *Staffel*. This unit was part of IV./NJG 1 and was

Oberleutnant Heinz Schnaufer, Kommandeur of IV./NJG 1 and close friend of Georg Greiner. (author's collection)

Hauptmann Adolf Breves (Staffelkapitän of 12./NJG 1 – eighteen kills) and Leutnant Kurt Matzak (fifteen kills). (Lauser)

commanded by *Oberleutnant* Heinz Schnaufer. This young, successful pilot was already the holder of the prestigious Knight's Cross and had fifty-three victories to his credit. Georg Greiner had met Schnaufer briefly when they had both been members of the night fighter school at Echterdingen. They met again when they both joined II./NJG 1, but before a friendship could develop, Greiner was transferred to Leeuwarden with II./NJG 2. These two pilots were fated to meet again in August 1943, when Schnaufer joined IV./NJG 1 as the *Staffelkapitän* of the 12th *Staffel*. Heinz Schnaufer was destined to become the top night fighter pilot in the Second World War, and these two pilots were to become close friends during the conflict. Georg Greiner describes in detail the character of this outstanding man:

> Leutnant Schnaufer and I met each other shortly before we finished our training as night fighter pilots at Echterdingen (Night fighter School No. 1), and subsequently when we were on operational duty with II./NJG 1. Then, however, as we went our separate ways after the almost legendary Operation Donnerkeil, in which the whole of the Nachtjagd flew escort, we did not get to know each other more closely.
>
> At that time he was nineteen years old, but he was already of striking appearance – tall, athletically motivated and healthily ambitious, but quite naturally he lacked the character and aura which, it was reasonable to expect, his future experience of life would bring to him. His features were still to some extent those of a growing boy of his age, but the physical and mental stresses and burdens of the difficult night operations to come would soon change them. It was a phenomenon of war that battle could change boyish faces in a relatively

short time into the features of prematurely aged men. The severity of the operations, which spurred on the young man in his rapid advance in his career, which he too was aiming towards, were destined in a remarkably short time to form him into a grown man.

In this short but succinct development one could clearly perceive the astounding physical and intellectual potential of an extremely talented, but still young man, who, by the tokens of his time, of his job, of his day-to-day responsibilities, had grown manly and mature. The rigours of the nightly operational flights, the difficulties of the ever-increasing responsibility for men and material that ran parallel to his rising career, were destined in an unexpectedly short time to compensate in Schnaufer for the negative factors mentioned above that are part and parcel of youth.

Within three short years the young man from Calw, a small town in the Black Forest, had changed into a mature man with self-esteem coupled with a pleasant modesty in his awareness of his qualities and capabilities, into the most successful night fighter of the Second World War as well as being a charismatic leader of men, and into the sort of multitalented individual that only emerges once in decades.

After all this I must add that I met up with Heinz Schnaufer again in August 1943 in IV./NJG 1, and that we soon became friends, getting on with each other really well until our second separation on 1 November 1944. On this date Heinz took over as Kommodore of NJG 4 while I became Kommandeur and so became his successor on IV./NJG 1. It is worth adding that after the war, despite the fact that we lived a long way apart, we remained loyal to each other. Our relatively close contact would certainly have lasted a long time had his tragic death not occurred. The event deeply affected us, simply extinguishing as it did a bright shining star. In conclusion I should like to say that from the time of a separation up to the capitulation we remained in solidarity with each other until the bitter end, signs of the coming of which we had long been aware of, endeavouring in the face of ever-increasing attacks from the air to help in the alleviation of the wounds and hardships of a hard-pressed civilian population.

In April 1944, IV./NJG 1 was transferred to Saint Trond (St Truiden) in Belgium, a Flemish provincial town between Liege and Brussels. As a consequence of the tense war situation, opportunities for night fighter crews to have home leave were extremely limited. Consequently, the *Gruppenkommandeur* of IV./NJG 1, *Hauptmann* Schnaufer, rented a four-bedroomed house on the outskirts of the town. Crews that needed rest after long periods of strenuous operational flying were temporarily housed here as home leave was only being granted in exceptional circumstances. As the month of April wore on, it became the turn of *Oberleutnant* Greiner's crew to take up residency in the house. Reluctant to miss an operation, Georg asked a junior NCO from the operations room to call him the moment approaching enemy aircraft were reported. On 27 April, Bomber Command attacked the railway yards at Montzen in France. Georg Greiner takes up the story:

We were sleeping the deep sleep of the just and over-stressed when the telephone rang. Almost immediately we could hear the first of the bombers above us. They were not coming, as they usually did, in a stream, but were flying separately – spread out over a large area. The battle controllers forecast an attack on regional targets, which in the event

In April 1944 IV./NJG 1 was transferred to Saint-Trond in Belgium. The officers were accommodated here, in the chateau at Nonnen-Mielen. (Lauser)

turned out to be correct. Speed was the order of the day, as was the necessity to dispense with putting on my full operational flying clothing. I pulled my flying overalls on over my night-shirt with the confident feeling that even though I was not dressed according to regulations, I was not scruffy or untidy. Dressed in this outfit I took off, as I always did, cautiously but without undue concern. After climbing to an altitude of about 4,000m, because the enemy aircraft were much lower than they usually were for a major attack, I took note of the fact that the night was extremely dark, no doubt because the night sky was cloudless. I did not let the firmament above my position out of my sight, and I caught a short glimpse of the shadows of four-engined bombers above me. It was quite obviously far more dangerous for the enemy to approach in a widespread formation, as he was flying today, than to fly in a bomber stream, which was concentrated in height and proximity.

I saw two four-engined aircraft far above me, the size of small model aircraft. Despite their camouflage they stood out quite clearly from the black night sky. And, laden as they were with deadly material, they were not flying very fast. I was able to follow them quite comfortably, and at once I began to climb steeply so that I could begin my attack. Every attack was naturally a risk, particularly when you came in to attack behind the four machine-guns. Sometimes I was surprised by the degree of inattention on the part of the enemy, but there were certainly a number of reasons for such seeming carelessness of which I was unaware, and perhaps I often had good fortune on my side and profited from the luck of the hour.

The standard method of attack that I had worked out – and which had often been put to the test – took these whims of fortune into account, and I made use of it once more. First of all I manoeuvred to the port side of the Lancaster, a little below it and on a parallel heading,

On the front terrace of the chateau, spring 1944. From left to right: Koltermann, Weissflog, -?- (journalist), Breves, Greiner, Rumpelhardt. (Lauser)

A visit to Saint-Trond by the Geschwaderkommodore of NJG 3, Helmut Lent. (Lauser)

Members of the Geschwader share a joke proving, even in difficult times, their ability to retain a sense of humour. Left to right: Weissflog, Schnaufer, Drewes, Sutor, Jabs, Dormann, Förster, von Bonin, Knickmeyer. At their feet is Georg Greiner. (Lauser)

Breakfast in the officer's mess. Greiner is flanked by Hauptmann Dormann (left) and Major Sutor (right). At the far end of the table is Oberleutnant Weissflog, the Bordfunker of Major Jabs. (Lauser)

As was typical of most fighter pilots, Georg Greiner graphically describes an aerial victory by using his hands, much to the amusement of his colleagues. From the left: Matzak, Rolland, Schnaufer, Potthast and Fengler. (Lauser)

and then moved from this position until I was almost beneath him – 'almost' because when I pulled up and shot between the two engines I had to fly past the fuselage of the bomber. I used this variant of following the bomber up to the point when I opened fire to avoid, on the one hand, being picked up by his radar and, on the other, to avoid the dangerous quadruple guns in his tail. Then I pulled my Messerschmitt up a short way, quite gradually, and opened fire at the tanks between the engines, which caught fire immediately. I always, without exception, aimed at the fuel tanks, because I simply could not bring myself to fire directly into the fuselage and the human beings in it. For that reason I am, to this very day, grateful that I can sleep in peace. In this way I wanted to give the members of the crew the chance that fate had granted them. In a short time the flames of the Lancaster's port wing had spread through out the whole aircraft and shortly afterwards it went into a dive.[3] I was only marginally aware of it hitting the ground because I was looking out for the second bomber, which had in the meantime disappeared.

Half an hour later a Halifax bomber crossed in front of the prowling German night fighter which, after a short exchange of gunfire, was dispatched in the same manner as its unfortunate predecessor.

[3] The only Lancaster lost that night was one piloted by Squadron Leader Blenkinsopp DFC, Croix de Guerre. The Lancaster was JA 976 (LQS) from No. 405 (PFF) Squadron stationed at Gransden Lodge, crashing near Diest not far from the night fighter airfield at St Trond.

25 March 1944. Officers of IV./NJG 1 line up outside their mess to celebrate the Gruppe's 500th victory (author's collection)

On 27 July 1944, Georg Greiner received the Knight's Cross from Generalleutnant 'Beppo' Schmid. Next to Greiner is Hauptmann Schmidt-Dietrich, and next to him is Oberfeldwebel Wilhelm Gänsler (Schnaufer's Bordfunker). (Lauser)

From this point on, until the end of the war, there would be a marked acceleration in Georg Greiner's successes. In almost two years, from the time of his first confirmed victory, to the end of April 1944, his tally of kills had risen to twenty-three. From May, which saw him score eight kills, the highest number of victories he ever achieved in a single month, to his final victory of the war in March 1945, he would more than double this figure of twenty-three in just ten months.

May 1944 started well for the young night fighter, accounting for two of the three Halifaxes lost by Bomber Command when its bombers raided the railway yards at St Ghislain and Malines in Belgium. Similar targets of military importance were attacked during the run-up to the invasion of the European mainland, which saw Harris' bombers fly a total of 11,353 sorties in an attempt to paralyse the German military machine. In the hectic weeks that were to follow he scored a string of single victories between 9 and 25 May, taking his total of kills to twenty-nine.

On the night of 27/28 May, he recorded victories thirty and thirty-one when Bomber Command targeted the Belgian town of Bourg-Leopold. Its main objective was a large military camp situated there and, as a result of accurate marking by Pathfinder aircraft, was severely damaged. Two of the nine Halifaxes lost during the raid were claimed by Georg Greiner, the first of which fell victim to him at 02.28 hours over Antwerp and was probably a Halifax from 640 Squadron. It came down close to the port of Antwerp, and is recorded in Chorley's *Bomber Command Losses* as having crashed at exactly the same time as recorded by Georg Greiner.

The pilot of this machine was Flying Officer F. Williams DFM who, along with two other members of his crew, was killed during the attack. Just eleven minutes after this encounter, a second Halifax fell in the same area as the first and so became Greiner's thirty-first victim. On 1 June 1944, *Oberleutnant* Greiner was promoted to *Hauptmann*, a rank equivalent to that of Flight Lieutenant in the RAF.

In contrast to May, the months of June and July were relatively quiet for this particular pilot. Between the D-Day landings in Normandy on 6 June and 21 July, a period of six weeks, he destroyed only five further bombers. However, the most significant event to occur during these weeks was the much overdue award of the Knight's Cross. Usually this highly sought after medal was bestowed after an average of twenty-five kills, but at this stage of the war, it was being awarded only after its recipients had achieved a higher and higher number of victories. On the day the Knight's Cross was conferred upon Georg Greiner, 27 July 1944, his total number of victories stood at thirty-six. Standing alongside him when he received the medal from the hands of *Generalleutnant* Joseph 'Beppo' Schmid was Wilhelm Gänsler, the *Funker* of Heinz Schnaufer, and *Hauptmann* Schmidt-Dietrich, whose own tally of kills stood at thirty-two.

As a *Ritterkreuzträger* or holder of the Knight's Cross, and recognised not only by his peers but also by the German public, he had finally made his mark as a night fighter pilot. It is easy to forget though that behind every successful pilot there is inevitably a competent *Funker*. This was certainly the case for Heinz Schnaufer, Helmut Lent and the other top *Nachtjagd* pilots, and Georg Greiner was no exception to this rule. Since September 1941 his long-time and experienced *Funker* had been *Feldwebel* Rolf Kissing. Up to August 1944, this crew had never been shot down or injured in any way but their run of luck was about to change – with tragic consequences. Here Georg describes his first encounter with a roaming RAF night fighter and its calamitous outcome:

Hauptmann Georg Greiner wearing his recently awarded Knight's Cross. (Greiner)

The young lady on the left is a member of the Luftwaffen-Helferin (equivalent of a WAAF), to her left is Oberleutnant Koltermann, summer 1944. (Lauser)

During a mission in August 1944, the inconceivable happened. Nothing special had been announced or noted and we were thus flying in a straight line, unlike normally, when we curved around in order not to present an easy target. As a result of all this I did not see the danger or our attacker coming. We were suddenly attacked from behind, and a fierce, precise burst of fire set our starboard engine on fire and struck Rolf Kissing in the head. He must have been unconscious immediately as his head had sunk forward to his chest.

My first reaction was to switch off the burning engine so as to stop the flow of fuel to it. It was clear that a burning engine at night and the reduced speed that inevitably went with it would immediately show the attacker the way to a decisive second attack. Therefore I carried out defensive manoeuvres that were dangerous for us, and indeed contrary to the principles of flight, given that we had one intact and one unserviceable engine. I took no heed of the excessive demands I was making on the machine and the considerable danger of going into a stall, which would probably spell the end for us. There was still the question of whether or not to bale out or, with the condition of our Funker in mind, should we stay with the aircraft and await our fate. From my pilot's seat I had no access to Kissing, who was in the fuselage seat, and our gunner who was scarcely eighteen years old, was only on his second operational flight, was in a state of shock and unable to speak. I made a quick but positive decision to try and make a landing – there was no way we could leave Kissing in the lurch.

We were quite unable to believe our eyes when the fire in the engine, blown hither and thither by the slipstream of our dive, went out. We were still not out of danger, although most unusually, and quite contrary to the rules, tactics and common sense, the second attack did not materialise. The area below us was dark and I could see no possibility of performing an emergency landing, we were running out of fuel and it was impossible to keep the machine in straight and level flight. There was no chance of reaching our own airfield, so I needed to find an emergency field, but it was dark all around me – no light to guide a late homecomer. In order to make our identity clear to our colleagues I fired off Very cartridges with the colours of the day. Seconds later, and directly beneath us, the airfield lights of Düsseldorf shone out in their full glory. In consideration for Kissing – and for my Messerschmitt – I decided not to try a belly-landing. I lowered the undercarriage by means of compressed air. As a result of the enemy fire I could not place any reliance on my automatic pilot. I saw the ambulance, which we had requested by radio, from some distance away and we landed safely despite the defective landing gear. Feldwebel Kissing died that same night. With a large number of shell splinters in his head, the extremely difficult operation had to be abandoned. By then Rolf's suffering was over and an outstanding radio operator and radar specialist had gone to his eternal rest. I thought very highly of him and missed him a lot. After our lengthy and eventful association I found it very hard to hold his funeral oration.

Losing Rolf Kissing, an experienced radio operator and trusted friend, after three long years of war was inevitably a devastating blow. There was, however, no let up in the hostilities and *Feldwebel* Kissing was soon replaced by another experienced *Funker*, *Feldwebel* Hammerdörfer.

An early photograph of the Greiner/
Kissing crew. This successful partne
-ship came to a tragic end in August
1944 when Kissing was killed
during an attack on their aircraft by
an RAF intruder. (Greiner)

Several weeks after shooting down a single Lancaster on 12 August 1944, Georg
Greiner, along with the entire *Geschwader*, found themselves uprooted from the unit's
long-standing airfield at St Trond. On 2 September 1944 IV./NJG 1 was transferred back
to Dortmund-Brakel situated on the eastern side of the Ruhr. This upheaval was due
exclusively to the inexorable advance of the Allies through France and into Belgium, which
threatened the *Nachtjagd's* ability to operate efficiently. With much of Belgium occupied,
the night fighters were unable to use this advanced area to climb to operational height,
and this was an essential prerequisite if they were to get airborne in time to intercept the
incoming bomber stream.

In the confusing weeks that followed *Hauptmann* Greiner shot down three further
bombers, a double on 22nd and a single on 24 September, to take his tally of kills to
forty. In recognition of his growing stature within the *Geschwader*, having trebled his
number of kills in less than a year, Georg was made *Gruppenkommandeur* of IV./NJG 1
on 1 November 1944, replacing Heinz Schnaufer who became *Geschwaderkommodore* of
NJG 4. Two former prestigious night fighter pilots, Helmut Lent and Hans-Joachim
Jabs had previously held the position of *Gruppenkommandeur* of IV *Gruppe*. The latter,
after a distinguished career as a *Zerstörer* and night fighter pilot, went on to become the
Kommodore of *Nachtjagdgeschwader* 1 on 1 March 1944. Georg recalls his first impressions of
this outstanding pilot and commanding officer:

To mark the occasion of the awarding of the Swords, Heinz Schnaufer was presented with a 'lucky pig'. From the left: Gänsler, Schnaufer's driver, Drewes, Schnaufer and Greiner. (Lauser and Greiner)

Georg Greiner made the mistake of agreeing to babysit the pig, which immediately, as is plain by the expression on his face, soiled his uniform. (Lauser and Greiner)

On 16 October 1944 Heinz Schnaufer was awarded the Diamonds to his Knight's Cross. Here he returns the salute from the officers and men of IV./NJG 1. Hauptmann Greiner accompanies him on the inspection. (Greiner)

In October 1944 Georg Greiner married his fiancée, Charlotte. The couple leave the county court after the wedding ceremony and are saluted by officers from the Gruppe. (author's collection)

Outside Park Hotel where the wedding reception took place. From the left: Frau Greiner, Jabs, Greiner, Sutor and Schnaufer. (author's collection)

The bridegroom and his best man, Georg Greiner with Heinz Schnaufer. (Werner Kock)

Georg Greiner with officers attached to the Gruppe. To his right is Major Kreisig, the Kommandant of the airfield at Saint-Trond. (Kock)

In August 1943, when Major Lent took over NJG 3, I met his successor as Kommandeur of IV./NJG 1, Hauptmann Jabs, for the first time. At that time I was a member of the 10th Staffel of the Gruppe. As a Staffelkapitän of the legendary Haifischgeschwader (Shark Geschwader) our new Kommandeur had already brought the so-called Zerstörergeschwader, which was equipped with the Me110, to astounding successes. As we all agreed, his introductory visit was very impressive. In his outward appearance, tall, very slim and athletically trained, well proportioned and erect, he looked dazzling and cultivated. He was generally thought to be approachable and sociable, but at first he was somewhat reserved, weighing up those whom he was meeting. His intellectual characteristics matched perfectly with those already mentioned. He was extremely intelligent, able to sum up a situation rapidly, and he reached clear decisions. His self-esteem was pronounced, but he did not behave self-importantly towards others.

He was an excellent pilot and airborne formation leader. His meeting with British fighters over the airfield at Saint Trond, which at first took him by surprise, proves that courage and willingness to take a risk were not alien to him. There was no alternative, no thinking about tactical options, only the necessity to take action, preferably immediately. He too used the element of surprise as well as his flying ability. He outwitted the Spitfires with his flying experience and brought them down with his tactical superiority. From his subordinates he expected good results and correspondingly set them high standards, but he demanded even more of himself, becoming an example to them. As a superior officer he was universally loved, appreciated and admired by his subordinates from the most lowly to the most highly placed.

Hans-Joachim Jabs became the Geschwader-kommodore of NJG 1 on 1st March 1944. He was considered to be an excellent pilot and very much respected by those whom he led. By end of the war he had risen to the rank Oberstleutnant and had added the Oak Leaves to his Knight's Cross. (Lauser)

Schnaufer, Jabs and Weissflog stand in front of a downed P-47, which fell victim to the airfield's flak defences. (author's collection)

Georg Greiner's final two victories of the year, both Halifaxes, came on the night of 4 November when Bomber Command attacked Bochum. A total of 749 aircraft were dispatched to this German town, which was targeted because of its important industrial centres. The raid was successful in that it severely damaged many of the town's industrial areas, and in particular the steelworks. Twenty-eight aircraft from the bomber force were lost during the operation which, of all the attacks on this target, was probably the most successful.

As the war approached its conclusion, Germany was being slowly and systematically destroyed from the air in a well-directed and determined offensive. The pilots of the *Nachtjagd* fought on bravely. Many had already resigned themselves to the fact that the air war by this stage was irrevocably lost. Their despondency was borne out by the fact that during the last nine months of the war, almost half the total tonnage of bombs dropped by the RAF in the entire air offensive was dropped during this period. It was also a sign of Bomber Command's growing confidence in the campaign that over a third of their operations were now flown during daylight hours.

To compound the German's problems, not only did it seem that the British were always one step ahead of them in the field of electronic warfare, but now the bombers were being escorted by increasing numbers of Mosquitos. These wooden aircraft, whose superior speed and manoeuvrability made them almost unassailable by night fighters, instilled fear into the hearts of many of the German pilots.

The New Year started well for *Hauptmann* Greiner who, on 5 January 1945, was to have the most successful night of his career, shooting down four bombers in ten minutes. The target for Harris' bombers this time was Hanover, the first time it had been raided since October 1943.

The young night fighter penetrated the bomber stream and sent three Lancasters down in flames at 19.12, 19.15 and 19.18 hours respectively. Minutes later, a fourth bomber appeared out of the darkness. This machine, Halifax LV952 MH-F from 51 Squadron based at Snaith, had been briefed to attack the rail network and shunting yards located within the city. As it flew over the target area Georg positioned himself underneath the four-engined bomber and fired a quick burst of 20mm cannon shells into its port side. A large explosion tore through the doomed machine, which immediately plummeted earthwards. One of the crew on board this Halifax was Don Thomsett, the rear gunner. He describes the operation and the events that led up to the destruction of his aircraft:

> After an hour's delay, we finally took off at 16.20 hours. During the delay, the ground crew were working against time to correct a 'Magneto Drop' on the Halifax, which they were able to correct just in time to make take off.
>
> We flew to the south coast to join the bomber stream and quickly reached 16,000ft, which previously had been a drag, but on this day she simply made the climb easily. We had an uneventful trip to the target. The stream appeared very tight, there was a Lancaster sitting right on our tail at our height and another close to the port side. [Suddenly] our mid-upper gunner was on the intercom saying 'Fighter to port!' He could not engage as his tail fin inhibitors had put his guns to 'Non Fire' I saw the Me110 so close that I could see the dark outline of the pilot. My sight with the Me110 illuminated in it, also gave me a Lancaster at 100 yards – sight in line with the Me110. I gave the order to 'Cork screw to port', in order to get another firing angle, and our plane dropped out of the sky violently.

There was a terrific explosion! I thought we had hit another plane in the stream, the skipper gave the jump call. I tried to line up my turret with the fuselage but the power had gone. I had to mechanically turn the turret. Opening the doors I saw fire rushing through the fuselage. On finding my parachute I banged it on in the dark, tipped myself backwards and out of the turret. One thing I forgot to do was to unplug my intercom, the wire from each side could have broken my neck! Fortunately I was upside down and they just pulled my helmet straight off. Next, I was on my way down and heading straight into the target area. There were planes above, bombs coming down and flak going up. The smell of cordite was overpowering! I could hear the silk of the parachute making a crackling noise, and I spent most of my time on the journey down trying to lay back to see if the chute was on fire. Next, I was close to houses and fires. Then, the roofs came up so quickly that my boots caught the apex of a house. The chute slackened and I fell, landing in front of an apartment block in Hanover-Herreshausen. I was in Germany!

Unfortunately, the remaining members of the crew were killed as a result of the attack, and the bomber crashed in the Lienhausen district of Hanover. Don Thomsett was soon picked up by members of the Volkssturm and taken to the local police station. On being beaten by some of the inhabitants after a second air raid on the city, Don was later taken by train to the interrogation centre at Dulag Luft, and from there on to a prisoner of war camp to see out the remainder of the war.

These, Greiner's forty-third to forty-sixth victories, were his only successes during January. In February he took his score to forty-eight by shooting down two Halifaxes that he intercepted in the area of Neuss, near Düsseldorf. They had been part of a force of 349 aircraft that had attacked Worms, resulting in substantial damage being caused to its residential and industrial areas.

In March 1945, he scored his final victories of the war. On 3 March Bomber Command attacked the Dortmund-Ems Canal, losing a total of seven Lancasters during the course of the mission. In a hectic period of fifteen minutes, three of these fell to *Hauptmann* Greiner while he patrolled in the area around Dortmund. These last three victories took his final tally for the war to fifty-one.

Although the conflict would drag on for a further eight weeks, his war was destined to end a lot sooner. Just days after scoring his last three kills, Georg Greiner and his crew took off to intercept RAF bombers that were on their way to bomb the East German town of Dessau. He describes this as having been the second most dangerous of his 204 missions. What happened on that night is best told in his own words:

When we set off on our last combat flight we, of course, could not know what was going to happen to us. However, a forerunner of what providence had in store for us (something that had never happened before) was an organizationally failed approach on predicting the target to be attacked by the bombers. We had to turn around shortly before the target without seeing any action although we would have been too late anyway!

The radio operator was, as usual, busy trying to fix our location as, after the relatively long flight, we had to know whether the fuel reserves would last until we were back home

Sergeant Don Thomsett was the rear gunner and only survivor in Halifax LV952 MH-F, which was shot down by Georg Greiner over Hannover on 5 January 1945. Greiner claimed a total of four bombers that night. (Thomsett)

Georg Greiner and Don Thomsett met for the first time in May 1998, and since then have become good friends. They are pictured at Don Thomsett's home in July 1999. (Richard Brandon)

or whether we would have to change our flight schedule accordingly. We were therefore not prepared for the next disaster that abruptly tore us out of our musing and calculations when we heard that we had completely lost radio contact and would remain without any further information. Everyone's adrenalin levels rose as we became more alert, this would definitely mean parachuting out into the freezing cold and into the unknown. In addition, I had to fly in a westerly direction for as long as possible in order to avoid bailing out over Russian territory. The Russians had already reached East Prussia and they may have even progressed further in the meantime!

There was almost no fuel left when my two crew members got ready to jump out. They climbed on to the wings, lay on their bellies and let the slipstream take them away before pulling their parachutes. Suddenly, it was my turn. First of all I had to throw off the cabin roof using the slipstream to break it at the so-called 'breakpoint'. My cabin roof was of a different opinion and it preferred to remain intact. The open cabin is always the best solution for an exit, so I tried to roll the aircraft sideways, however without any luck. Although I had sufficiently trimmed the aircraft beforehand, it continued to dive as soon as I took my hand off the control column. After several attempts I finally managed to achieve success by using a different method. I fully reclined my seat and then went into vertical flight at maximum speed. Having starved the machine of fuel I then used one foot to push the control column with all of my power, in order to achieve the highest possible lift effect on my body. I had freed myself, or so I thought, and in some respects this was true as I was lying out on one wing. I had pulled my parachute too early and was thrown against the rudder badly injuring my left knee. I was plunging down with the machine unable to understand why I could not free myself of it. I waited apathetically for death. In the meantime I had reached 1,000m having started from 6,000m and was still entangled with my machine, which I had previously loved and now hated. Suddenly I felt a strong shock as if a cable had been torn. When I realised that I was no longer tied down and that I had escaped I felt for the first time in my life that I had been born again. When I took off my parachute I could see what had happened. A long wire had wound itself around the straps of the shroud line and had cut the 6cm wide straps down to about 1cm. This long wire had been the trailing aerial of my machine and my parachute had become entangled in it, as it had not been retracted!

After a few painful minutes I knew I had to somehow inform my two companions of my whereabouts. For this purpose I fired the distress flare of the day and was most surprised when I received machine-gun fire in response. This could have come from either advancing American troops or a German rear-guard, however, I could not tell and fired off two further signals. From some distance I had seen blurred images and, as they came closer, I saw that they were carrying scythes and spades and that they had a uniformed man as their leader who carried a machine-gun. They were extremely suspicious despite me speaking German and it was difficult to convince them of my identity. One has to add that on combat missions we only wore overalls without badges of rank, and which only displayed a yellow armlet with the national emblem and the words 'Deutsche Luftwaffe'.

When I had finally convinced them of my identity I discovered they were farmers from the next Eifel village. They put me up in the village so that my knee could be treated and, in addition, they guided my crew to my accommodation. As there was neither an aircraft nor fuel available in order to pick us up, we had to return by train the following day.

So ended Georg Greiner's active participation in the war. By the time the armistice was signed he had already released himself from hospital and returned to his former *Gruppe*, who had quartered themselves in a disused camp at Ostenfeld, situated between Schleswig and Husum in North Friesland, Germany. After several weeks of further rest and rehabilitation the injury to his left knee had healed sufficiently for him to walk properly again. It was during these weeks of captivity that he received notification that as of 17 April 1945 he had become the 840th member of the German Armed Forces to be decorated with the Oak Leaves to the Knight's Cross. Georg had also been awarded the pendant to the Night Fighter Clasp for having flown over 200 missions. Sadly, both awards came too late on in the war and any pride he might have felt was lost in the depths of defeat and despair.

The area of Schleswig-Holstein became, in the turbulent weeks that followed the capitulation, one large camp for refugees and prisoners of war. In his correspondence he describes the time in the camp as being relaxed, with the internees responsible for their own discipline and the camp's normal day-to-day running. There seems to have been no breakdown in discipline or any reported problems, even though the British oversaw their imprisonment with the minimum amount of supervision. This was quite an achievement considering that in this particular area of Northern Germany there were some 1,500,000 prisoners of war and 4,500,000 refugees.

In recognition of his 51 victories Greiner became the 840th recipient of the Oak Leaves to the Knight's Cross on 17 April 1945. This is a post-war replacement set issued by the German government. (author's collection)

As the summer passed into autumn, the prisoners received the welcome news that they were to be transferred to an American camp where they were to receive their official discharge papers. Just fourteen days after arriving at the discharge centre, which was located at Frankfurt/Main, Georg Greiner received the relevant papers and set out for his mother's home near Stuttgart. Now, after almost seven years of being a soldier, of having everything in his life regulated by the military, he was a civilian once more.

However, the inactivity of the following months soon had Georg yearning to fly again. But, opportunities to find work as a flier in either Europe or the United States were few and far between. After the cessation of hostilities there were just simply too many qualified airmen looking for too few jobs. With this in mind he set off to seek the advice of his former wartime friend and colleague – Heinz Schnaufer. It was decided during their first meeting that the best chance of flying again, and indeed to earn a living from it, lay in South America, chiefly Argentina, Brazil and Chile. As a result of this meeting they decided that it would be prudent to seek further advice from the appropriate consulates, the closest of which was located in the Swiss capital of Bern.

In the meantime, and with this plan in mind, Georg left his mother's home in Stuttgart and moved to Basle-Offenbach situated on the German-Swiss border. Arrangements were made with the relevant Embassies in Bern, and on the day in question, the 23 September 1946, both former pilots met in Weil-am-Rhein. On his arrival, Heinz Schnaufer stated he could not be away from his family business for more than two days and so advocated crossing the Swiss border illegally. He was able to persuade his rather reluctant companion that this was the best course of action open to them and, with their decision made, the illegal border crossing took place soon after without incident. The meetings, however, with South American diplomats were bitterly frustrating. They were told, in no uncertain terms, that without having a substantial surety behind them their business venture would never get off the ground. Resignedly, both men left Bern and set out to cross the border once again. As they crossed into the French-controlled zone of Germany they were confronted and then arrested by a Swiss border guard. Georg Greiner describes their arrest and subsequent imprisonment:

> We were very surprised when somebody shouted from behind us, 'Halt, hands up and turn around, if you try and escape I will be forced to shoot!' A Swiss Gendarme had challenged us, but one could hear in his shaky voice that he was more scared of us than we of him. I advised Heinz that there was little point in trying to escape, as this guardian of the law would probably shoot out of fear. As he approached with his drawn pistol we were able to reduce his nervousness with a few reassuring words.
>
> He handed us over to a French Captain, a border official from Baden-Württemburg (later we discovered that our appointment in Bern had been betrayed). Out of pure boredom the official seemed to have consumed too much alcohol as he was completely drunk. He opened a door to an adjoining room and slurred to us elegantly, 'Now gentlemen, please make yourselves comfortable here'. We were soon able to recognise the alcoholic irony of his feigned courtesy. The said room was completely flooded under 20cm of water from which the sunken remains of lumpy blankets stared disgustingly out at us.

The next morning we were taken to Lörrach, a border town, for questioning at the prison where we were immediately detained. Here it was somewhat more comfortable, even if we did have to share our 10m^2 cell with a Spaniard. We were provided with a toilet, however, as the cell consisted of only one room, one could not freely utilise this facility. In spite of this, our German guard was a good man and was to play an important role at the end of our stay. Through him, I was promoted to cleaner of our corridor and was allowed to leave our cell for this purpose.

As we had already had to wait quite a while for a court hearing and, as Heinz Schnaufer was getting nervous about his absence from his business, we forged a plan to escape. We desperately needed our German guard and thus we involved him in our plan. He was immediately willing to help as Heinz had offered him a job. It was planned that he would open the prison doors for us at dawn and that we would flee in an appropriate number of vehicles with our relatives. However, thank heaven we did not have to face this great risk. Just a few days later we were surprised with the wonderful news that we were free and that the French Commandant and his wife were expecting us for dinner. We were able to collect the vehicle with which we had journeyed to Weil-am-Rhein, and which had been confiscated after our arrest. We were welcomed very politely that evening, shown wonderful hospitality and even given good provisions for the onward journey. After saying our goodbyes we drove off the following morning in the direction of home. Our South American enterprise was finished.

A trip that had been planned to last just two days had in fact lasted six months, and during the entire period of imprisonment no charges were ever brought against either

A copy of the summons served on Georg Greiner by the French authorities, after he and Schnaufer were caught illegally re-entering the French-controlled zone of Germany from Switzerland. Both men spent six months in a French prison. (author's collection)

Oberstleutnant Greiner (front row, fifth from the right) with other officers at the NATO School of Operation in Baden. (Peter Heinrich)

man. After his Swiss escapade, Georg Greiner moved to Bonn where he spent four terms studying law. After marrying in 1949, and for purely financial reasons, he gave up his studies and became a sales representative for one of his relatives who owned a textile factory.

Slowly, life in Germany began to improve. A currency reform took place with the introduction of the *Deutsche Mark* in 1948 and, less than a year later, the Federal Republic of Germany was formed. The most significant event for Georg and many other former soldiers occurred in 1956, with the rebuilding of the German Armed Forces. Even though his job as a sales representative was lucrative, with regular foreign holidays and a car, the thought of being able to fly again excited him greatly. Without any hesitation, he applied to join the new *Bundes*Luftwaffe. His application was successful and he joined the Air Force as a *Hauptmann* in August 1957.

Over the next seventeen years, starting as a staff officer at the Pilot's School at Landsberg, Georg held various posts, rising to the rank of *Oberstleutnant*. By the time of his retirement in 1972 he was a staff officer for the German Federal Armed Forces in Bonn. Since 1980 he has lived in Wangen, a small town situated on the shores of Lake Constance, and lying in the beautiful Allgäu region of Southern Germany. This quiet, sensitive and very talented man spends most of his time with his wife, Rosemarie, listening to and playing music. He is a very gifted pianist and an enthusiastic correspondent. Now, as Georg enjoys the tranquil years of retirement he can reflect on a life and career which, like those of many of his wartime colleagues, has been accomplished with a sense of duty, fairness and honour.

3

Major Werner Hoffmann

On the western shores of the River Dabie, not far from the Baltic Sea, in an area that prior to the Second World War lay in the German state of Pomerania, but is now very much part of modern day Poland, lies the city of Szczecin, formerly known as Stettin. The history of this former German municipality has been as stormy and chequered as that of the country it now forms part of.

Stettin dates back to the eighth century when the Slavs built a stronghold there. It was annexed in 967 and became part of the newly formed Polish state. As a result of subsequent wars the city changed sovereignty on several occasions over the following 700 years. After the conclusion of the Northern War in 1720, the Swedes sold Stettin to Prussia, which held the region until 1945. Under their rule it grew and prospered as the main port for Berlin, connected as it was to the German capital by a canal. It was in this prosperous city that Werner Hoffmann was born on 13 January 1918, the son, and only child, of Walter and Gertrud Hoffmann.

Major Werner Hoffmann, Gruppenkommandeur of I./ NJG 5. (Hoffmann)

Werner Hoffmann, now aged eighty-two and living in retirement in Bremen. (Hoffmann)

In early 1918 proud parents, Walter and Gertrud Hoffmann, show off their newborn son. (Hoffmann)

Werner Hoffmann, *c*.1928. This was about the time he started Grammar School in Berlin. (Hoffmann)

It was on 13 January 1918, on the top floor of this apartment block in Stettin, that the future night fighter and Knight's Cross holder was born. (Hoffmann)

As was customary he began his schooling at the age of six, entering the local *Volksschule* in 1924. In the same year ship construction in Stettin came to an end and his father, a ship construction engineer, was forced to move to Berlin in order to continue working. Within a year, after finding work and a suitable apartment in the Wilmersdorf district of Berlin, Walter was able to send for his wife and son who quickly joined him in the capital.

In 1928, having meanwhile progressed on to one of the district *Gymnasiums*, the German equivalent to England's grammar schools, Werner's interest in military matters was first fired. In order to fulfil his growing fascination with this subject he began to read as many books, particularly those concerning the careers of former First World War German aviators, as he could find. Over the next four years he would progress from reading about flying to actively participating:

> In the following years I read a lot of adventure books about the First World War, particularly about fliers such as Immelmann, Boelcke and Richtofen. In this way my interest in the military things, particularly flying, was stimulated. I began gliding in 1932 and made my first three or four flights with the Deutscher Luftsport-Verband (DLV)[4]. In the summer of 1933 the DLV Youth Group was absorbed into the Flieger-Hitlerjugend (Flying Section of the Hitler Youth), which I didn't join. At the same time as this I was a member of the Scout movement (Pfadfinder), which was also transferred into the Hitler Youth.
>
> I found service in the Hitler Youth to be far more exciting than carrying out my school studies, so my parents decided to have me sent to a boarding school in 1934. At this school, in the mornings, we took part in various types of sport, such as rowing, fencing and motorcycling.
>
> During the summer holidays of 1935 my classmates and I had the opportunity to take part in a gliding course at Hirschberg in the Riesengebirge (a high mountain range in the vicinity of the border between Germany and the former Czechoslovakia, today in the Czech Republic). On conclusion of the course I passed my A and B gliding examinations flying a Grunau SG 35 glider. In the Easter holidays of 1936 I then passed my C examination in a Falte glider. For this I had to fly for five minutes at a height of 2-300m along a valley. In doing so I had the happy feeling of really flying and could have indeed stayed up much longer if I hadn't been ordered to come down and land.

Following Hitler's rise to power in 1933, his policies and military ambitions led to an accelerated build up in the size and strength of the German *Wehrmacht*. This was especially true with regards to the Luftwaffe, which emerged out of clandestinity from the ashes of the defeated Imperial German Air Service in March 1935. As a direct result of this build up, Werner Hoffmann, excited at the prospect of joining this rapidly expanding force, left school early in the autumn of 1936 with a view to applying for the new air force. Having completed two months of his *Reichsarbeitdienst* (Reich Labour Service) in the

---

[4] The DLV (German Air Sport Association) was established in March 1933, and was made up of all civilian flying clubs throughout Germany. Its task was to promote interest among the civilian population in balloon, glider, model and powered aircraft flight.

Above left: As a member of the Pfadfinder or Scout movement. After the National Socialists came to power in 1933 the organization was amalgamated into the Hitler Youth. (Hoffmann)

Above right: In October and November 1936 Werner completed two months of his compulsory Reich Labour Service in the Riesengebirge Mountains in Silesia. He is seen here wearing the uniform of the Reichsarbeitdienst. (Hoffmann)

Left: An identity card issued by the Reichsarbeitdienst. (Kock)

Riesengebirge during October and November, he entered the *Luftkriegschule* (Air Warfare School) at Wildpark-Werder, in the vicinity of Potsdam, as a *Fahnenjunker* (officer-cadet) on 4 December 1936.

Between then and March of the following year, and before being able to commence any flying instruction, he had to undergo a period of intensive basic military training. This usually lasted anywhere between two and four months and had to be endured by all recruits, regardless of which branch of the armed forces they joined.

From April 1937 Werner began his training to become a pilot, a process that usually lasted two years and began with initial flying training. During this time, and depending on how well the candidate performed, not only would a decision be made as to whether or not to let the recruit continue further training but also, if he was successful, whether he would be best suited flying single or multi-engined aircraft. After successfully completing this stage of the training, the nineteen-year-old *Fahnenjunker* Hoffmann commenced his elementary and advanced flying training, designated in the Luftwaffe as 'A' and 'B' respectively. Instruction for his 'A' certificate followed on the Heinkel 72 'Kadett' and the Focke-Wulf 44 'Stieglitz', that were both fabric-covered, metal construction biplanes with a top speed of 115mph. These aircraft were used extensively at many of the Luftwaffe's training schools and were ideally suited as trainers, built as they were with tandem seats (usually with the instructor sat directly behind the student) and an open cockpit. To give an insight into what the young recruits like Werner Hoffmann had to achieve in order to qualify for their pilot's licence, there follows a description of the difficult and extensive training they received.

In order to qualify for this first category of the licence, which was divided into two parts, A1 and A2, the student was required to complete a number of wide ranging and demanding tasks. These included completing a 300km triangular course, and altitude flight to 2,000m, as well as executing a loop and carrying out three precision landings. Once this had been achieved successful trainees received further intensive instruction for the B category of the pilot's licence that also came in two parts. By this stage of the training, and to qualify for the B1 certificate, the student had to have flown at least 3,000km, performed an altitude flight to a height of 4,500m and, within nine hours, completed a 600km triangular course. A minimum of fifty flights had to be made in B1 category aircraft, these being classed as single-engined aircraft, weighing up to 2,500kg, with between one and three seats. Further precision landings, including two night landings, and a night flight, lasting at least thirty minutes, were required. The B2 certificate demanded an increase in flight experience and additional night flights.

Werner Hoffmann received B1 instruction piloting the *Gotha* 145, a two-seat biplane constructed of wood and fabric. His long months of flying training finally concluded at Wildpark-Werder with the B2 examination on the Junkers W-34. By this time, as can be seen by the following dates, he had risen rapidly through the cadet ranks having initially entered the Luftwaffe as a humble *Fahnenjunker* (1.6.37 *Fahnenjunker-Gefreiter*, 1.8.37 *Fahnenjunker-Unteroffizier* and 1.12.37 *Fähnrich*).

In the spring of 1938 he attended the Officer's Academy at Wildpark where the cadets were encouraged to develop their leadership potential and increase their knowledge of tactical and strategic matters. On 2 June 1938 he was awarded his Pilot's Badge and the

Werner Hoffmann's Pilot's Badge
awarded on 2 June 1938. (Kock)

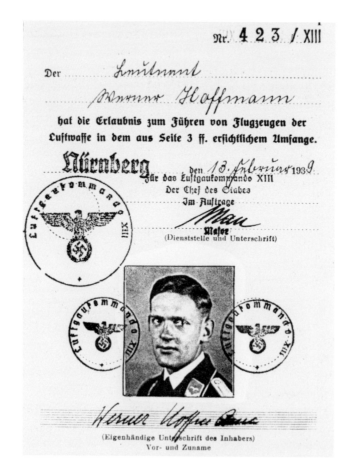

Photograph of Leutnant
Hoffmann taken from his pilot's
licence. (Kock)

A/B certificate, which meant that he was now qualified on both elementary and advanced single-engined aircraft.

The officer's course concluded prematurely because of the imminent occupation of the Sudetenland and he was immediately transferred to the newly formed III./JG 234 'Schlageter'. This *Gruppe* was activated on 1 July 1938, and was initially based at Düsseldorf under the command of *Hauptmann* Karl-Heinz Lessmann. On his arrival at the *Gruppe* Werner immediately found himself being sent for fighter pilot training at Fighter Pilot School No. 1 at Werneuchen, located to the east of Berlin. There he flew both the Heinkel 51 and the Arado 68. The latter entered service with the Luftwaffe as its last fighter biplane, and was introduced to replace the ageing and somewhat out-dated Heinkel. With the advent of the first monoplane, the revolutionary Bf109 with its superior speed and handling characteristics, it was clear that these two aircraft had had their day and were consigned to the training schools. At the conclusion of the training, on 15 August, he returned to recommence active service with 7./JG234, which had in the meantime been transferred to an auxiliary airfield at Schweidnitz in Silesia. Two weeks later he was promoted to *Leutnant*.

Meanwhile, political tensions in Europe over Hitler's demands for the annexation of the Sudetenland were mounting. Initial talks held at Berchtesgaden and Bad Godesberg, on 15 and 22 September 1938 respectively, failed to diffuse the worsening crisis. Werner Hoffmann suddenly found himself, as did thousands of other young German combatants, on standby

Award certificate for the Commemorative Medal of 1 October 1938, which was issued to celebrate the bloodless takeover of Czechoslovakia. (Kock)

for a possible military confrontation. If further diplomatic attempts failed to resolve the situation before 1 October, Hitler's planned date for the invasion of Czechoslovakia, (code named *Case Green*) these young men would soon find themselves at war – many for the first time. War was successfully avoided, but the cost for the Czechs was high. On 30 September the now infamous Munich agreement was signed and Europe was rescued from the brink of war. The price for that peace was the sacrificial annexation of the Sudetenland and almost three million of its inhabitants were absorbed into the *Reich*.

In November, following the conclusion of the Czechoslovakian Crisis, III./JG 234 was transferred to Crailsheim and re-equipped with the Arado 68. By the spring of 1939 the *Gruppe* found itself on the move once again, this time being relocated to Illesheim in Bavaria. In May 1939, III./JG 234 was re-designated I./ZG 52, thus becoming one of the Luftwaffe's first *Zerstörer*, or 'Destroyer' units. Frustratingly though, due to early production problems, there was an initial shortage of Bf110s, which resulted in many of the newly formed *Zerstörer* units being equipped with the C and D variants of the single-engined Bf109 instead.

In preparation for flying multi-engined aircraft it was necessary for pilots to attain their *C-Schein* (C Certificate) or Advanced Pilot's Certificate. Therefore, as a precursor to flying the Bf110, Werner attended the Pilot's School at Erding in Bavaria, where he duly obtained this qualification.

Just prior to the outbreak of the war, towards the end of August, I./ZG 52 was moved west to a temporary airfield at Biblis near Worms. From then, until the beginning of the French Campaign in May 1940, the *Gruppe* operated from a number of different airfields, flying countless numbers of sorties in defence of Germany's western borders. During February 1940 Werner Hoffmann, along with other pilots from the unit, was sent to Garz, on the Baltic Island of Usedom, where they received the necessary conversion training to fly the Bf110. Once this had been completed the entire *Gruppe* was re-equipped with the new aircraft.

Two days after the commencement of *Fall Gelb* or Case Yellow, the invasion of France and the Low Countries on 10 May 1940, *Leutnant* Hoffmann experienced his first operational flight and, two weeks later, his first aerial victory:

> It was our job to attack a French airfield in the vicinity of Strasbourg and, in order to avoid the flak, we flew at a height of about 3,000m in a loose formation while another Staffel attacked the aircraft on the ground with their cannon. The small black flak bursts were more amusing than disturbing.
>
> The French Air Force was overcome after a few days, but we continued to fly escort duties for the bomber formations attacking tactical targets on the ground (railway installations, crossroads and bridges). After our armoured formations had reached the coast and the French troops had split from the British, the British Expeditionary Force fell back to the Channel. Spitfires and Hurricanes protected the embarkation.
>
> As the front moved forward, we moved from our base at Mannheim-Sandhofen to a grass airfield at Charleville-Mèzieres. On 24 May I took off for the Channel Coast where the British Expeditionary Force was preparing to retreat. Between Dunkirk and Calais I saw a Spitfire. We had been told that the Bf110 was superior as a fighter to the Spitfire, so

Im Namen des Führers
und Obersten Befehlshabers
der Wehrmacht

verleihe ich
dem

Leutnant Werner H o f f m a n n

das
Eiferne Kreuz 2.Klaffe.

Gefechtsstand.., den ..15...Juni.....1940
Der Kommandierende General
des V. Fliegerkorps

Generalleutnant
(Dienstgrad und Dienststellung)

On 15 June 1940, in recognition of his first aerial victory and participation in numerous ground attack missions during the French campaign, Hoffmann was awarded the Iron Cross Second Class. (Kock)

> I tried to get on its tail. We turned around each other and I quickly realised that it could turn more tightly than I could. I therefore relied on the superior armament of the Bf110 and flew head on at the Spitfire, firing my guns from a range of 200-100m, at which point it began to disintegrate. I had difficulty in diving away under the Spitfire so as to avoid ramming him. When I had recovered from my fright there was a Hurricane in front of me and I opened fire immediately. After one burst of fire it went down in a steep glide, but I didn't see the impact on the ground because of the amount of smoke that was coming from Dunkirk.

Immediately following on from this somewhat exhilarating encounter, his first against the RAF, Werner Hoffmann submitted a detailed account of his experience, claiming both British fighters as destroyed. But, due to the strict regulations imposed by the Luftwaffe's High Command concerning the verification of aerial victories, the uncertainty over the Hurricane's demise meant that he was only credited with one of them.

The weeks following this aerial kill, his first and only daytime victory of the war, I./ZG 52 was employed in operations against French troops in the Paris area. On 15 June 1940, having flown a total of fifty-three combat missions, Werner was awarded his first medal of the campaign, the Iron Cross Second Class.

On 19 June, just days before France capitulated, and while attacking enemy troops that had dug themselves in around Badonviller (a region of Alsace), Werner was shot and wounded in the left arm. A hail of small arms fire met the sudden and unexpected appearance of his Bf110 as it skimmed low over the French positions. Miraculously though, of the hundreds of rounds fired at the German fighter, only one found its mark. The round, which was fired from a rifle, tore its way through the aircraft's thin metal exterior before entering the aircraft's cockpit from the port side. It then struck the young German pilot in the left elbow, penetrated the joint and exited from the other side of the arm, before finally lodging itself inside the chest area of his flight overalls. With a great deal of effort and determination he was able to fight off the veil of unconsciousness that threatened to overcome him, and flew the twin-engined fighter back to Karlsruhe where his badly injured arm was immediately operated upon.

After several weeks of convalescence Hoffmann was transferred from front-line duties and sent to the *Ergänzungs-Zerstörer Gruppe* at Vaerlöse in Denmark. Initially posted there as a flying instructor, his previous combat experience was to prove an invaluable asset to the young pilots who had arrived direct from training school, having just completed their basic flying training. Shortly after the transfer he was promoted to *Oberleutnant* and awarded the Iron Cross First Class. In the summer of 1941 he took over the command of a *Staffel* in this *Gruppe* and became its *Staffelkapitän* on 1 July. The primary role of the unit, which usually comprised nine aircraft, was to escort shipping convoys to Norway. These convoys principally supplied the German garrisons stationed there and were protected with a defensive aerial umbrella as they sailed through the Skagerak and Oslo Fjords.

In the meantime, the *Wehrmacht* had launched its all out attack against the Soviet Union in June 1941, and this new theatre of war was to see a resurgence of the Bf110 as a *Zerstörer*. In the Battle of Britain its inferiority against British fighter aircraft had become apparent at an early stage of the battle, and this had been reflected in its mounting losses as the campaign progressed. However, not only did this twin-engined fighter receive a new lease of life in Russia, but it also proved itself a capable night fighter in the night skies over Germany, as the fledgling *Nachtjagd* attempted to counter the growing threat posed by Bomber Command. As a result of the Bf110's changing fortunes, the *Ergänzungs-Zerstörer Gruppe* was disbanded on 3 August. Part of the *Gruppe* went to Russia as a *Zerstörer* unit and the remainder, to which Werner Hoffmann belonged, were destined to become night fighter pilots.

Previously, during May and June 1941, he had been posted to Blind-Flying School No. 4 at Copenhagen-Kastrup. This was a course that normally lasted for a period of about eight weeks and required about fifty or sixty hours of blind-flying practice. Having already attained this qualification, *Oberleutnant* Hoffmann was sent directly to Night Fighter School No. 2 at Manching near Ingolstadt. It was here, between 1 September and 15 November, that he received all the training necessary to become a night fighter pilot. This usually began with performing and mastering rudimentary night flying, such as carrying out numerous take-offs, landings and cross-country flights. Once pilots had become proficient at flying by night they went on to learn how to co-operate, and integrate with, the other elements involved in defending Germany's homes and industries. These were principally the searchlight batteries and radio beacons, both of which performed significant roles in the operation of the 'Kammhuber Line'. The latter were used by the night fighters to identify a holding area in which they would circle continuously while waiting for the approaching bomber stream. Some theoretical and practical implementation of night fighting techniques,

Adolf Hitler instituted The Iron Cross First Class on 1 September 1939 and approximately 300,000 were awarded. Werner Hoffmann received his on 10 July 1940. (Kock)

such as airborne interception, was taught at the training schools, but this was only at a very basic level and further intensive practice of these methods would then take place once they were with their operational unit.

With his training complete, Werner Hoffmann was transferred to 5./NJG 3, one of three *Staffeln* that made up II./NJG3, which was under the command of *Hauptmann* Günther Radusch and based at Schleswig in Northern Germany. From here, during the winter months of 1941/42 and spring of 1942, Werner flew his first missions in *Helle Nachtjagd*, but failed to make contact with the RAF. It did not help that this was a period when Bomber Command, restricted by frequent periods of inclement weather, were only able to carry out limited operations. This resulted in few opportunities for the men of the *Nachtjagd* to increase their personal scores or, indeed, for the young, inexperienced pilots to achieve their first kills.

On 13 February 1942, along with other night fighter units, he actively took part in the break out of the *Scharnhorst*, *Gneisenau* and *Prinz Eugen*, from their berths in Brest, through the English Channel and into German waters. Operation *Donnerkeil* as it was called, was masterminded by the newly appointed *General der Jagdflieger* – Adolf Galland. In order to make up the short fall of aircraft required to carry out the operation effectively, Galland re-employed approximately thirty Bf110s to provide further fighter protection along the intended route of the three ships. During the course of *Donnerkeil*, Scharnhorst struck two mines and was forced to dock at Wilhelmshaven to effect immediate repairs. Hoffmann and his *Funker*, Rudolph Köhler, subsequently found themselves forming part of a protective umbrella flying escort missions in the area of Wangerooge, a small North Sea Island situated some twenty-five miles north-west of the port.

Following the successful conclusion of this operation Werner returned to frontline duties with 5./NJG 3 still desperately seeking an opportunity to score his first night time victory. Overall, this was a frustrating time for everyone involved in the *Nachtjagd*, which claimed only five kills in the entire month of February. A further four long months were to pass before he was able to claim his opening success of the night campaign, by which time the tactics employed by Bomber Command had changed considerably.

These changes were implemented by the new Commander-in Chief of Bomber Command, Air Chief Marshal Sir Arthur Harris, soon after his appointment on 22 February 1942. Within months of him taking over, Bomber Command had carried out a number of raids, most notably Lübeck (28/29 March) and Rostock (22-27 April), which demonstrated how effective concentrated, well-planned attacks, using target-marking aircraft could be. The following month saw these tactics being used on a much grander scale with the first of Harris' 1,000 bomber raids directed against Cologne on 30/31 May. These concentrated attacks highlighted the weaknesses of the German defences because the bombers, which now flew in bomber streams, penetrated fewer of the areas patrolled by the night fighters and they did so quickly and on a much narrower front. One of the main problems with the Kammhuber Line was that only one night fighter patrolled each area. Once this one fighter had become embroiled in intercepting a bomber, any other bombers flying through the same area were able to pass through unmolested. In order to counter this problem the Germans were forced to change their own tactics. They did so by abandoning the existing system of *Helle Nachtjagd*, the use of searchlights to illuminate the bombers, in favour of *Dunkel Nachtjagd*, which led the night fighter to the bomber by means of close-controlled interception from the ground. It was by using this method that *Oberleutnant* Hoffmann scored his first two night time victories on 25/26 June 1942, during a 1,000 bomber raid on Bremen:

> During the night of 25/26 June 1942 I was scrambled against returning bombers on the western coast of Schleswig-Holstein after an attack on Bremen. Using Dunkelnachtjagd we were able to approach the enemy without being seen by him, we positioned ourselves underneath, adjusted our speed to match his, and finally pulled up and fired from beneath.
>
> The ground control unit vectored me onto the enemy, a Lockheed Hudson, until I was so close I could easily see him. My Funker, Oberfeldwebel Köhler, said to me, 'Herr Oberleutnant it must be a four-engined aircraft, but it doesn't look that big – get in close!' After I had attacked from astern and shot the starboard wing into flames I had difficulty in diving away without ramming it.
>
> Following this I was vectored on to a second aircraft, a Whitley V, which I also attacked from astern, but it did not catch fire and evaded pursuit by going into a dive. I had, however, damaged the Whitley so severely that the crew did not dare to make the return flight over the North Sea, but made a forced landing on a beach to the north of Büsum and were taken prisoner.

On looking through the losses sustained by Bomber Command during the Bremen raid, it is quite likely that Werner Hoffmann's second victim was Whitley V Z6730 UO-Z piloted by Sgt J.J. Makarewicz, one of twenty-three aircraft lost by the Operational Training Units. This very high and demoralising loss rate, which equated to over eleven and-a-half percent of the OTUs involved, was probably due to the fact that these units were usually equipped with old aircraft that had been withdrawn from front-line service. Overall, the raid itself achieved only limited success, but the most alarming aspect of the raid as far as

Abschrift

Der Reichsminister der Luftfahrt   Berlin, den lo.8.43
und Oberbefehlshaber der Luftwaffe
Az.29 Nr. lo357o /43 (L P 5 VII)

Bezug: Abschussmeldung vom 26.6.42.

        An
        5./N.J.G. 3

        Der 5./N.J.G. 3
        wird der Abschuß eines Lockheed-Hudson

        durch Olt. H o f f m a n n in Zusammenarbeit mit 6./Ln.Rgt.2o

        als zweiter (2) Abschuss der Staffel anerkannt.

                                I.A.
        F.d.d.d.A.
                                gez. Unterschrift

        auptmann

Official confirmation from the Luftwaffe's High Command of his two first night time kills, a Whitley V and Lockheed Hudson, shot down on the night of 26 June 1942. (Kock)

A b s c h r i f t

Der Reichsminister der Luftfahrt   Berlin, den 2. Sept. 1943
und Oberbefehlshaber der Luftwaffe
Az.29 Nr. 103937/43 (LP5 VII)

Bezug: Abschußmeldung vom 27.6.42
        An 5./N.J.G.3

    Der   5./N.J.G. 3
    wird der Abschuß eines   Whitley

                            am 26.6.42, 03.24 Uhr
    durch Oblt. H o f f m a n n in Zusammenarbeit mit 6./Ln.Rgt. 2o2

    als d r i t t e r (3)   Abschuß der Staffel anerkannt,
                                I. A.

        F.d.R.d.A.
                                W o l f f.

    berleutnant

These two silver victory cups were given to Oberleutnant Hoffmann in recognition of his first two victories at night. (Hoffmann)

Bomber Command was concerned, were the total number of aircraft lost to the German defences. A total of fifty-five aircraft were lost, five of which were from Coastal Command,[5] representing a new record loss of five percent.

As the months rolled by and the year came to an end he had failed to add to his tally of two kills. During these long and disappointing months Werner Hoffmann operated against Bomber Command intrusions over Schleswig-Holstein and the Baltic, but he only actually made contact with the bombers on two or three occasions. None of these resulted in any kills and this lack of success understandably increased his already growing frustrations. Perhaps sensing this, his *Gruppenkommandeur, Major* Radusch, arranged for him to be posted to the newly formed II./NJG 5 that was stationed at Greifswald on the Baltic coast.

Arriving at the airfield on 11 February 1943, barely a week after being promoted to *Hauptmann*, he took over command of the 4th *Staffel* and then spent the next two months fine tuning his tactics and expertise in a determined attempt to improve his chances of future success. He recounts the two major changes that effectively changed his fortunes:

> In the following months I used to rehearse interception flights with the ground radar stations in order to intensively practice attacks. In addition I met a physicist from an optical factory who was attached to a test unit and who was probably of great significance not only for me but for the whole night fighter force.

[5] Coastal Command provided 102 aircraft for the Bremen operation. It was made up of Wellingtons and Hudsons, one of which was claimed by Werner Hoffmann 6km south-east of Heide at 02.26 hours.

From the start of the Nachtjagd the reflector sights had been equipped with a blue filter to reduce the brightness and not cause dazzle. Nevertheless dazzle caused by the cross-hairs in the target circle was so great, even at the lowest brightness setting, that one had to guess where the target was, rather than being able to see it clearly. I told the physicist about this difficulty and he replied that in the industry they had been surprised for a long time that we had used a blue filter rather than a red one, which was much kinder to the eyes. He promised to get me two red filters for the reflector sight, one of which I had put in my aircraft, and I put the other one at the disposal of my Gruppenkommandeur (Rudolf Schönert). Afterwards I wrote a report on my favourable experiences and sent it to the leadership of the Luftwaffe. As a result all the reflector sights in the Night Fighters were fitted with red filters, and subsequently in 1944 even the fluorescent indicator screens were covered with red foil. Perhaps this was an explanation for my earlier lack of success.

This lack of success, however, was soon forgotten once his hard work began to pay dividends. On the night of 20/21 April the Baltic port of Stettin was targeted by a force of 339 bombers which, as a result of good target marking by the Pathfinders, caused considerable damage to the centre of the city. The raiders were not without their own losses, and twenty-one of their number failed to return from the raid. Of the seven Halifaxes lost from the bombing force, two were shot down by Werner Hoffmann.

After having been scrambled from Greifswald at 00.10 hours, he took off in Bf110 G9+AM with his *Funker*, *Unteroffizier* Tschmiedler, and plotted a south-easterly course towards Stettin. A little over half-an-hour later, while under the direction of a ground controller, the prowling German night fighter was vectored on to its first unsuspecting target. The bomber fell from the dark night sky at 00.45 hours after receiving a devastating burst of fire from the Messerschmitt's lethal frontal guns. It subsequently crashed approximately 45km to the north-west of Stettin, near the town of Eggesin. Werner's second victim that night fell five minutes later, close to the small village of Borken, some 35km from the target area. Using W.R. Chorley's book (*Bomber Command Losses 1943*) to check the aircraft lost by Bomber Command during this raid, it is possible to identify Werner Hoffmann's likely victims that night.

The first was a 419 Squadron Halifax, serial number JB912 and coded VR-B, that took off from Middleton St George and was shot down by a night fighter while flying at 16,000ft. It crashed an estimated 47km north-west of Stettin, within a mile of the point where Werner claims to have shot down his first bomber. The entire crew was able to bail out of the stricken aircraft except for F/S D.A. Watkins DFM, who was killed during the encounter.

The second bomber was more than likely to have been a 77 Squadron Halifax, serial number JB804 and coded KN-Q that was piloted by F/L T.S. Lea DFC. It took off from Elvington and later crashed at Pasewalk, approximately 38km west-north-west of Stettin. All on board were killed.

Following this multiple kill, which doubled the number of his victories to four, over a month was to pass by before he was able to achieve his fifth kill. This was a significant figure because it would entitle him to be officially classed as an 'Ace', an important milestone in the career of an up-and-coming night fighter pilot desperately seeking to make his mark amongst the other young pilots of the *Nachtjagd*.

Oerleihungsurkunde

Im Namen des
Oberbefehlshabers der Luftwaffe

verleihe ich dem
Flugzeugführer
Hauptmann Werner H o f f m a n n

Staffelkapitän der 4./N.J.G.5

die

Frontflug-Spange für Nacht-Jäger
in Gold

O.U. , den 8.Juli 1943.

Major u. stellv. Geschwaderkommodore

The certificate to accompany the Night Fighter Clasp in Gold. This was awarded to Hauptmann Hoffmann on 8 July 1943 after having achieved 110 operational missions. (Kock)

Midway through 'The Battle of the Ruhr', which began on 5/6 March 1943 and concluded on 24 July 1943, Werner Hoffmann and Rudolph Köhler, along with other successful operational crews, found themselves posted to Holland and Belgium to help counter the intensive and sustained air offensive against the heart of industrial Germany. From 26 May he was subordinated to II./NJG 1 at St Trond in Belgium where he was able to shoot down a further four bombers. The first of these fell during the early hours of 30 May when Wuppertal was attacked by a force of 719 bombers. This raid was seen as the most successful of the entire Ruhr campaign, causing uncontrollable fires that destroyed a large area of the Barmen region of the town and killed over 3,000 inhabitants. Hoffmann's victim that night, a Halifax, fell at 01.45 hours. This was one of thirty-three bombers that failed to return from this particular trip, and one of eleven accounted for by crews from II./NJG 1.

Wuppertal was again the subject of a raid almost a month later, on the 24/25 June, and on this occasion a slightly smaller force of 630 aircraft were sent back to destroy the remaining Elberfeld region of this already devastated town. At 00.36 hours Bf110 G9+1M took off from St Trond, and just forty-five minutes later its crew, *Hauptmann* Hoffmann and *Oberfeldwebel* Köhler, encountered a Lancaster near Erkelenz (60km west of Wuppertal) and shot it down. Exactly half-an-hour later they were vectored onto a second bomber, which was quickly identified as a twin-engined Wellington. This aircraft was later discovered to have been a 166 Squadron machine from Kirmington in Lincolnshire, piloted by P/O R.E. Currie RCAF. All five members of the crew perished when it crashed at 01.51 hours near the small town of Dessel, near Antwerp in Belgium.

His fourth and final victory while attached to II./NJG 1 came four days later when he shot down a homeward bound Short Stirling that was returning to England having just bombed Cologne. According to W.R. Chorley's *Bomber Command Losses* this aircraft was from 15 Squadron, based at Mildenhall in Suffolk, and was one of 608 aircraft tasked for the operation. It crashed at Lommel in Belgium at 02.20 hours, and all but one of the crew (F/S J.D. Duckett RNZAF) was killed.[6]

Following the death of *Hauptmann* Siegfied Wandam, the *Gruppenkommandeur* of I./NJG 5, on 4 July 1943, Werner Hoffmann was recalled from Belgium to become the acting *Gruppenkommandeur* of the *Gruppe*.

Within weeks of him taking over command of I./NJG 5, the very nature and tempo of the battle was to change dramatically. Before the Battle of the Ruhr came to an end, Harris had already planned the next phase of operations and he decided to turn the focus of Bomber Command's might towards Germany's second city – Hamburg. From the time of the first raid, which took place on 24/25 July, to the last on 2/3 August, Hamburg was bombed on four occasions by the RAF and twice in daylight by the Americans.

The devastation caused to the city, as well as the great loss of life, has already been well documented, but the raids are also significant because they marked the end for *General-Major* Kammhuber's inflexible *Himmelbett* system, which had been rendered useless by the introduction of 'Window'. This was the code name used by the RAF for what were basically strips of aluminium foil cut to half the length of the German radar frequency. Dropped in sufficiently large numbers 'Window' would effectively jam the German defences resulting in numerous returns appearing on their radar screens, which would in turn cause widespread confusion amongst the ground controllers and night fighters.[7] The effectiveness of this simple device was reflected in the very low losses suffered by Bomber Command on the night of the first Hamburg raid, a total of twelve aircraft were lost, equivalent to just one-and-a-half per cent of the force. Several new methods of night fighting were introduced immediately after Hamburg to counter this new threat as Werner Hoffmann explains:

> During the night of 24/25 July 1943 Bomber Command first used 'Window' on an attack on Hamburg and thereby jammed out both the ground and airborne (Lichtenstein B/C) radars. In this way close control of the Night Fighters was no longer possible. Oberst Herrmann, a former bomber pilot, developed the so-called Wilde Sau system. With this system the Night Fighters were directed to a position above the target area and if there was a layer of cloud the bombers were illuminated from below, thus making them highly visible. The attack on the bombers then followed like a daylight attack from above.
>
> At the same time the close-controlled, so-called Himmelbett system, in which the fighter orbited a light beacon until he was directed by the ground-controller on to an enemy target, came to an end. Some of the Bf110 Night Fighters were already equipped with Lichtenstein airborne radar, and in this way we could, after we had been infiltrated into the bomber stream, look for our own targets independently – so-called Zahme Sau.

6 This was Short Stirling serial number BK694, coded LS-C, and was piloted by Sgt J.B. Keen. All of those who died now lie in the Heverlee War Cemetery.

7 The Germans had also been experimenting with the same idea but had been apprehensive about introducing it, fearing the British would retaliate and use it against them. The Germans referred to it as *Düppel*.

Here a female factory worker gathers together the aluminium foil before it is cut into strips. These strips were then bundled together and dropped by the bombers prior to reaching their targets. (author's collection)

On the night of 24/25 July 1943 Bomber Command effectively rendered the German night defences blind by dropping millions of aluminium strips, known as 'Window', prior to its raid on Hamburg. (author's collection)

Confirmation for one of two kills claimed by Werner Hoffmann on 7 September 1943. As the war progressed it took longer and longer for confirmations to be processed and this one is dated seven months after the claim was first made. (Kock)

Although he did not actually operate himself during the Hamburg raids, Werner did play an active role in countering Harris' next phase of operations directed against the German capital, which took place between August 1943 and March 1944. Over the course of the next eight months Bomber Command mounted a total of nineteen raids against Berlin losing over 600 aircraft in the process. By actively implementing the *Zahme Sau* method of night-fighting Hoffmann was able to account for the demise of twenty bombers, the first of which, a Lancaster, he shot down to the north of Berlin in the early hours of 4 September, raising his number of kills to nine.

Three nights later during a rather unsuccessful attack by the RAF on Munich, and this time operating from an airfield at Ingolstadt, his tally of victories reached double figures when he claimed two Halifaxes as his tenth and eleventh victories. The first of these fell at 00.24 hours and crashed to the east of the city from an altitude of 5,800m. The second followed suit twenty minutes later and exploded on impact in an area to the north of the target. These were just two out of a total of sixteen bombers that failed to return, the majority of which fell victim to either the predatory night fighter or flak.

Later on that month Hanover became the target for a series of four heavy raids that were to be the first major attacks on the city in over two years. Although he was not actually involved in this particular operation on the 22nd, Werner Hoffmann did operate on the night of the second and fourth attack, which took place on 27/28 September and 18/19 October. On each of the nights in question he accounted for a single bomber, claimed as

107

Hauptmann Hoffmann poses proudly for the camera as he displays his newly awarded German Cross in Gold. (Hoffmann)

a Lancaster and Halifax respectively. It is interesting to note, however, that no Halifax bombers were dispatched on 18 October, as it was an all Lancaster affair. This is just one example that highlights very well how difficult aircraft recognition must have been, with genuine mistakes often being made under the most difficult and trying of conditions.

Before the month was out he added a 'double' to his growing list of successes by shooting down a pair of Lancasters on 22nd, taking his tally to fifteen. Three weeks later, on 15 November 1943, this achievement was officially recognised with the awarding of the German Cross in Gold. This was the next grade of decoration usually awarded to recognise a degree of bravery or achievement of an individual above that of the Iron Cross First Class, but was not quite enough to justify the award of the Knight's Cross.

There now followed what was to prove the most outstanding period of *Hauptmann* Hoffmann's career, during which time he would actively participate in the defence of Berlin and, in a little over three months, he would almost double his number of confirmed kills. A number of technological advances, combined with a growing confidence in his own abilities, undoubtedly contributed towards this rapid increase in personal success as he now recalls:

> While my first kills were obtained entirely with the frontal weaponry, with effect from December 1943 I shot the majority of my bombers down with Schräge Musik. I preferred Schräge Musik because at first, when I attacked with my frontal guns, I was not always

The German Cross in Gold and its accompanying
certificate. (Kock)

successful. In addition there was practically no danger of being detected by the enemy rear-gunner and running into defensive fire. The approach to the enemy bomber, whether one was being controlled from the ground or by one's own radar, was made from one side and below so that one could pick him out better against the lighter sky. Then I would position myself beneath the bomber and match my speed to his and then direct fire from below. In addition to Schräge Musik the existing radar equipment, Lichtenstein B/C, which was susceptible to jamming by 'Window', was replaced by Lichtenstein SN-2.

This new type of air-interception radar was impervious to the effects of 'Window' as it operated on a lower frequency than its predecessor. The first sets were fitted in September 1943, and by the early part of 1944 the vast majority of night fighters had had the new radar installed. The effects of *SN-2* and the upward-firing guns of *Schräge Musik* soon became apparent as Bomber Command's losses began to mount. However, although the chances of shooting down a bomber had been improved, the risks to the night fighter had also increased:

> I remember an attack on a Lancaster with Schräge Musik I fired at him from a distance of about 25 to 30m into his fuselage and caused his bombs to explode. I was so completely dazzled by the flames that I was unable to see my instruments for between thirty and sixty seconds so that for some time I had to fly by the sense of sound only until I could see again. From another operational flight I came back to base with four or five incendiary bombs that had struck my aircraft but had not ignited.

Winter 1943/44. Left to right: Werner Hoffmann, Willi Elstermann (nine victories – killed 2.2.45), Gustav Thamm (fourteen victories), Paul Szameitat (Knight's Cross holder with twenty-nine victories – killed 2.1.44). (Kock)

Martin 'Tino' Becker in front of his SN-2 equipped Bf110. This new airborne radar was able to counter the effects of 'Window' and by early 1944 most night fighter aircraft were fitted with it. (Hinchliffe)

On the night of 18/19 November 1943 Harris mounted the first of sixteen raids against Berlin, a concentrated, destructive offensive that would cost him in excess of 600 bombers destroyed and the lives of over 6,500 of Berlin's inhabitants. Werner Hoffmann's first involvement in the battle took place on 23 November when he shot down a Halifax directly over the capital. Two further bombers, both Lancasters, fell to his upward-firing cannon on 2 December to take his total at the years end to eighteen.

The new year started well for the young night fighter with his next kill coming in the early hours of 2 January 1944, a fiery banner of flame marked the final journey of the unfortunate Lancaster as it plunged earthwards from an altitude of 6,500m. The Hoffmann crew did not operate again until 20 January when they were scrambled at 18.30 hours to intercept an incoming bomber stream that had been detected while still some 100 miles off the Dutch coast. Although this proved to be a successful mission with the interception and shooting down of a Lancaster on its way to Berlin, it almost proved to be their last:

> I had already shot down a Lancaster above the city when I attacked another at 5,500m. I immediately came under fire from his rear gunner and my starboard engine caught fire. As I couldn't extinguish it the only thing my crew and I could do was to jump out using our parachutes. We got out of the aircraft without any trouble. I counted twenty-one, twenty-two, twenty-three and then deployed my parachute as I had been taught. After the shock from the jerk of the parachute opening I was suspended at about 5,000m with the British aircraft and the German Night Fighters flying around me. From above the bombs were falling and from below the flak was firing – it was not a pleasant situation to be in. Finally I floated into a more peaceful area at about 2,500m. Then came the next shock. On

A Dornier 217 fitted with Lichtenstein B/C antennae. (author's collection)

the ground there was a huge building on fire and I feared that I would fall into it. During the first minutes the ground had scarcely seemed to get any nearer to me, while at the end it all happened so quickly and I landed in a field on the edge of a village. After I had gathered together my parachute I took refuge in a cellar of a deserted farm as the bombs were still falling and the flak was still firing. In the darkness I caught sight of two green eyes that belonged to an Alsatian dog. I was afraid that he would attack me so I took out my pistol to shoot him in case he went to bite me. However, the poor animal was in such a state of fear himself that he ran straight past me and out into the open air.

This had been the first occasion on which he'd had to resort to a parachute and, while on the ground among the falling bombs and showers of flak splinters, he gained a real insight into the utter misery suffered by the residents of Berlin during such a raid. Driving through the city on his way to Döberitz airfield, seeing the capital's buildings and streets burning, as well as peoples belongings piled high in the street, left him thoroughly depressed but determined to carry on nevertheless.

The whole experience seemed to spur him on to achieve greater success against the bombers. This was all too evident when he proceeded to shoot down five of them during the next two attacks on Berlin. Three Halifaxes, the most he had shot down in any one night up to that time, fell between 03.12 hours and 03.55 hours on 29 January. In the course of the next raid on Berlin he sent two of the thirty-two Lancasters lost from the bomber force crashing into the burning suburbs of the *Reich's* capital for his twenty-fourth and twenty-fifth victories.

During the night of 15/16 February, the penultimate attack in the Battle of Berlin, he took off from Greifswald at 19.20 hours flying Bf110 G9+AB and set out on a westerly course towards Rostock. Two hours earlier a Halifax V from 76 Squadron, serial number LL140 and coded MP-A had taken off from its airfield at Holme upon Spalding Moor in Yorkshire. This was the bomber crew's fifth mission and their third to the 'Big City'. Several hours later, at approximately 20.48 hours, shortly after the pilot of the Halifax, F/S D.A. Eaton, had turned south over the Baltic Coast, these two aircraft met between Rostock and Schwerin. What happened next is recounted by the Halifax's navigator, F/S Geoffrey Wilson, who describes the final minutes of what was to be the crew's last mission:

> Apart from the lively reception from the flak ships off the Schleswig Coast and some desultory firing from shore-based batteries, our flight was uneventful. On turning south over the enemy coast we observed two aircraft, both some five or six miles away, going down on fire. The target indicator markers were about three miles away on our port beam.
>
> Only a few minutes later there came the dreaded sound of cannon fire; and almost simultaneously the rear gunner called for a corkscrew. Before the pilot could properly initiate this manoeuvre, there came another burst of cannon fire. Through my flimsy curtain I could see a bright glow rapidly becoming a lurid glare. On pulling aside the curtain, I saw that the port inner engine was on fire.
>
> As we came to pull out of the corkscrew there was another brief burst of fire along the fuselage and I was somewhat alarmed to see my Gee box explode just above my head. The skipper (who I subsequently learned no longer had rudder control and whose attempts to put out the engine fire had failed) at once ordered us to bail out.
>
> When it came to my turn to sit on the edge of the forward escape hatch and launch myself into the cold German night I found that somehow my parachute had tried to open itself prematurely, so I dropped out holding it as a bundle in my arms. However, on letting it go I had not far to fall before there was a savage jerk – my boots fell off – and there was this great canopy far above my head. It seemed to take a long time to reach the ground. I emerged from the snow-bearing cloud at about 150ft and made a soft landing in the middle of a parade ground of an army barracks, where I was soon surrounded by a group of soldiers who, to my relief, were more interested than hostile. Sad to say the mid-upper gunner drowned in one of the lakes near the crash site. The rest of us suffered only slight injuries that quickly healed.

Another member of the crew, the flight engineer, Sgt Robert 'Bob' Becker had a grandstand view of Werner Hoffmann's attack, here he describes the events as they unfolded:

> We started getting Monica[8] beeping and then we heard reports from the gunners that there was a night fighter behind us. Then the chaos started. The rear guns all seized up and 'Ginger' Watson tried to clear them. The mid-upper turret manned by Basil Upton, who was our 'Spare Bod' that night, received quite a lot of bullets into the turret because I remember looking back down the fuselage and seeing the remains of his turret on the

---

[8] A device that transmitted radio pulses, which reflected off other aircraft in the vicinity and produced a clicking noise in the headset of the pilot. In this way an early warning could be given to the crew as to the approach of another aircraft.

On the night of 15/16 February 1944 F/Sgt Dennis Eaton was the pilot of Halifax LL140 when it was shot down by Werner Hoffmann to become his twenty-sixth victory. (Robert Becker)

F/Sgt Geoffrey Wilson, navigator on board Halifax LL140. (Geoffrey Wilson)

floor. He was sitting on the rest bay seat and the internal light had come on. I then looked out and their was our friend sitting almost above the tail fin, he was angled up quite nicely and pointing towards our port wing. You could see that his forward-facing cannon were firing. I've always thought that I was in a very detached state, not really believing that I was there and that I was just an observer.

He then came across the aircraft and completely devastated the astrodome where I had been looking out. He then hit all the oxygen bottles underneath that went off like flak themselves; one little bit went through my battle dress and tweaked my arm. It was then I realised that all of our controls had been shot away. We were at 21,000ft, the highest we had ever been, when there was a general call to say we should get out. This is where things went all wrong again.

I went down the little step next to the wireless operator who was on my left, and in front of the escape hatch were the bomb-aimer and the navigator who could not get the hatch up – it was sort of partially open as it had been damaged. The wireless operator gave me a direct order to 'something OFF!' Which I thought was reasonable under the circumstances. So, I sat forward with my legs dangling and edged my way out of the aircraft. I finally remember grabbing the floor on the way out, which wasn't a sensible thing to do because I was dragged along the bomb bay doors. As I was going along the underside of the aircraft the ripcord was pulled and the parachute opened in the slipstream. There was a tremendous movement of the harness up to my throat and I then had the most terrible pain in my matrimonial prospects.

I found myself at 21,000ft, it was very cold and I think I was suffering from lack of oxygen. I then woke up to the fact that I was coming down in a horizontal plane with

F/Sgt Robert 'Bob' Becker. He witnessed the German night fighter as it carried out its devastating attack on Halifax LL140 while en route to attack Berlin. This was the crew's fifth mission. (Becker)

the parachute coming out of the small of my back. There was an aircraft going down on fire, which I thought was Werner's aircraft, but it transpired later that it wasn't – it must have been ours still burning brightly and going around and around. Obeying the laws of jumping with a parachute I brought my knees up in a horizontal plane and landed straight on my kneecaps. So there I was on the ground feeling very, very lonely when I heard the sound of hunting horns and out came the Volkssturm with their dogs looking for us. I went through the procedure of burying my parachute and was shortly surrounded by gentlemen who sort of more or less implied in German 'For you the war is over!' I spent that night on the kitchen floor of the Burgermeister of Schwerin. From there I went to Schwerin itself and was later joined by the rest of the crew except for poor old Basil who was the next man out after me. That was the luck of the draw, I came down on the side of the lake and he went down into it and was never seen again. Then of course it was off to Dulag Luft, the Frankfurt interrogation centre, and then off to a transit camp.

Although the entire crew was able to escape from the stricken aircraft they were all later interned by the Germans except for Sgt Basil Upton, the mid-upper gunner. He had followed Bob Becker out of the burning bomber but had the misfortune to land on, and plunge through, the ice-covered surface of Lake Schwerin, he subsequently drowned and his body was never recovered from its watery depths.

Five nights after claiming this, his twenty-sixth victory, Werner found himself scrambling against a large force of bombers destined for the important industrial city of Leipzig. Its importance as a priority target was due to the aircraft assembly factories located there, and a force of some 832 Lancasters and Halifaxes was assembled with the aim of destroying it. At their briefings the bomber crews were told to expect a steady and prolonged head wind en route to Leipzig, however, the head wind encountered was not as strong as expected and many of the bombers arrived over the target area before the city had been marked by the Pathfinders. This resulted in hundreds of aircraft circling the target area and several collisions were reported. The other consequence of the lighter than expected head wind was that the bomber stream became strung out as many of the crews did not recognise the problem early enough. This produced ideal conditions for the German night fighters, which, after being fed into the distended bomber stream by their ground controllers, harried the bombers all the way to the target.

Flying this time from Döberitz Werner Hoffmann took off at 01.49 hours and was directed to a holding area near Brunswick. He was successfully infiltrated into the bomber force on its inward bound flight and made two kills in twenty-six minutes. The first of these, a Lancaster, crashed at 02.51 hours close to Brunswick and the second, a Halifax, crashed between Stendal and Genthin, north-east of Magdeburg. This was a calamitous night for Bomber Command, which lost a total of seventy-eight aircraft – its highest loss at that point in the war.

Over the next ten weeks Werner Hoffmann only flew operationally against the RAF on two or three occasions, none of which resulted in any kills. The most significant event to take place during this time occurred on 4 May 1944 when he was awarded the Knight's Cross. In 1943/1944 the usual prerequisite for the award was twenty-five kills, which he had achieved on 30 January 1944. It usually took from several weeks to several months

Hoffmann wearing the Knight's Cross. It was awarded to him on 4 May 1944, by which time he had achieved thirty confirmed kills. (Hoffmann)

Werner Hoffmann's actual award piece. (Kock)

FÜR TAPFERKEIT

NJG 3, 5

Major Werner Hoffmann

wurde am 13.8.1918 in Stettin geboren und wuchs in Berlin auf. Er erhielt am 4.5.1944 für seine Leistungen als Nachtjäger das Ritterkreuz des Eisernen Kreuzes. Bisher erzielte er 29 Nacht- und 2 Tagabschüsse. Zur Nachtjagd kam Major Hoffmann von den Zerstörern, bei denen er sich im Frankreichfeldzug durch schneidige Tiefangriffe auszeichnete.

Hauptmann Hugo Frey ✠

wurde am 14.4.1915 in Heilbronn geboren. Bei den Tagesangriffen gegen die anglo-amerikanischen Terrorbomber errang er 28 Abschüsse. Der Führer verlieh ihm nach seinem Heldentod das Ritterkreuz des Eisernen Kreuzes am 6.3.1944.

Above and right: The awarding of the Knight's Cross was a prestigious event and worthy of reporting, as is evident by various articles which appeared in Berlin newspapers on 14 May 1944. (Hoffmann)

Neue Ritterkreuzträger

Berlin, 14. Mai.

Der Führer verlieh auf Vorschlag des Oberbefehlshabers der Luftwaffe, Reichsmarschall Göring, das Ritterkreuz des Eisernen Kreuzes an Hauptmann Hoffmann, Gruppenkommandeur in einem Nachtjagdgeschwader, und an Hauptmann Frey, Staffelkapitän in einem Jagdgeschwader.

Hauptmann Werner Hoffmann, als Sohn eines Ingenieurs am 13. Januar 1918 in Stettin geboren, hat im Kampf gegen die englische Luftwaffe 28 Nachtjagdsiege errungen.

Hauptmann Hugo Frey, als Sohn eines Schneiders am 14. April 1915 in Heilbronn geboren, hat sich im Kampf zum Schutz der Heimat gegen die englisch-amerikanische Luftwaffe als einer der besten Staffelkapitäne seines Geschwaders besonders ausgezeichnet. Trotz ungünstiger Wetterbedingungen und starker Abwehr errang er 31 Luftsiege, wobei der Abschuß von 25 viermotorigen Bombern besondere Hervorhebung verdient. Der tapfere Offizier starb inzwischen den Heldentod.

Stettiner mit 28 Nachtjagdsiegen

Das Ritterkreuz für Hauptmann Hoffmann

Berlin, 14. Mai.

Der Führer verlieh auf Vorschlag des Oberbefehlshabers der Luftwaffe, Reichsmarschall Göring, das Ritterkreuz des Eisernen Kreuzes an Hauptmann Werner Hoffmann, Gruppenkommandeur in einem Nachtjagdgeschwader. Hauptmann Werner Hoffmann, als Sohn eines Ingenieurs am 13. 1. 1918 in Stettin geboren ist ein kampferprobter, hochverdienter Offizier, vorbildlich, tapfer, zäh und hart, der es versteht, auch seine Besatzungen mitzureißen. Er hat im Kampf gegen die englische Luftwaffe 28 Nachtjagdsiege errungen.

Left: On 1 June 1944 Werner Hoffmann received this document from the Führer's Headquarters informing him that he had been promoted to the rank of Major and made Gruppenkommandeur of I./NJG 5. (Kock)

until a decision on the recommendation was agreed by the OKW (*Oberkommando der Wehrmacht* – Armed Forces High Command). By the time the award had been agreed Werner Hoffmann, and eight to ten of his most experienced crews, had been transferred to St Dizier in France. Although he was now tactically attached to the 4th Fighter Division in Metz, he still remained, for administrative purposes, subordinate to the 1st Fighter Division in Berlin. As a consequence, and to prevent further delay of the award, the Knight's Cross – a highly prized and sought after medal – was unceremoniously hung around his neck by an *Oberstleutnant* from the Divisional Staff on 19 May 1944. There were no other witnesses present during the presentation, a total anti-climax to what should have been an occasion for much celebration.

However, this was soon forgotten as on 1 June he was appointed the full time *Gruppenkommandeur* of I./NJG 5 and simultaneously promoted to the rank of *Major*. By this time, having been stationed in France for almost a month, he had been able to shoot down a further two four-engined bombers taking his personal tally of kills to thirty. Both of these aircraft were shot down over Mailly-Le-Camp (west of St Dizier) on 4 May, during an attack on German Panzer armoured units stationed there.

As a prelude to the invasion of mainland Europe Bomber Command had switched its attention to strategic targets such as the French railway network, German troop positions and flying-bomb sites. During these operations, and those mounted after the Normandy invasion, Hoffmann accounted for three further four-engined bombers on 3, 28 and 29 June respectively. On the last of these, having already shot down one bomber, he came under accurate fire from the rear gunner of another. The Messerschmitt's starboard engine was hit and immediately began to leak coolant. Due to the sheer weight of the aircraft, combined with the weight of the *SN-2* aerials, the night fighter was unable to maintain altitude on just one engine and it began to steadily lose height. Following accurate US bombing attacks on the airfields at Laon/Athis and Reims, aircraft looking to make emergency landings could not use the runways there and this forced the crew of the night fighter to take to their parachutes for the second time in six months. Unfortunately, as he was caught by the slipstream and blown clear of the cockpit , Werner struck the tail unit with his right hip causing a large contusion that prevented him flying for over a week.

After recovering from this rather painful injury he was again in action in the early hours of 8 July when he scored his thirty-fourth, thirty-fifth and thirty-sixth kills by shooting down three Lancasters. This time the target for the 208 bombers was the flying-bomb storage dump at St Leu, situated just to the north of Paris. The dump, a former mushroom growing facility, was made up of a number of tunnels that contained a large number of the new German 'Wonder' weapons. The subsequent bombing was accurate although the attack cost Bomber Command twenty-nine of their number. Werner Hoffmann was again able to infiltrate the bomber stream without being detected and his three victims fell at 01.31, 01.40 and 01.50 hours. It is very difficult at this stage of his career to identify the location of his kills accurately because he begins to log them by means of a grid reference system (see Appendix VIII). This map was made up of rectangles that measured fifteen minutes of latitude by thirty minutes of longitude, which meant that each rectangle represented approximately 360 square miles, making identification of individual bombers almost impossible.

By the end of July, after having accounted for three more Lancasters, *Major* Hoffmann and his *Gruppe* returned to their airfield at Stendal where they were re-equipped with the G-6 variant of the Junkers 88. From here, the *Gruppe* was transferred to East Prussia where they operated against both British and, for the first time, Russian bombers. Werner comments on the differences he experienced flying against these two different adversaries:

> After the invasion had succeeded, my Gruppe was transferred to East Prussia for operations against both English and Russian attacks. In the course of an attack on Königsberg (29/30 August) I shot down a four-engined bomber (my fortieth). Compared with the RAF who were using Lancasters and Halifaxes, the Russian DB3-F and PS84 were considerably slower. Operating against the Russians required a great change in tactics, because they flew much more slowly than the British. On my first contact with a Russian, which we had picked up on our AI radar, I had so much surplus speed that I almost flew right into the enemy machine and I had to dive away beneath him in order to avoid ramming it. In doing so we lost both visual and radar contact. After that, when we picked something up on the radar, we always approached much more slowly.
>
> During this period the Gruppe was brought up to its full wartime strength of forty-four Ju88s. However, the American attacks on the German fuel-producing factories were having an effect and supplies of fuel were becoming less and less. So, as time went by, fewer and fewer aircraft were put into action until more supplies could arrive. While we were in East Prussia we felt ourselves to be markedly superior, particularly to the Russians; but when we were flying in the air defence of the Reich our inferiority to the British was more than apparent.

While operating from Jesau, situated due south of Königsberg, Werner Hoffmann claimed a total of four Russian bombers all of which fell victim to him in and around the Latvian city of Libau during December 1944. A final victory, while operating on the Eastern Front, came his way on the 6 January 1945 when he claims to have shot down a Halifax, for his

Hauptmann Ernst Georg Drünkler, Staffelkapitän of 1./NJG 5. He was awarded the Knight's Cross on 30 March 1945 after his fortieth victory. By the end of the war he had taken his total to forty-five. (Kock)

forty-fifth victory, into the Danzig Bay. In fact, this aircraft was most likely to have been one of the forty-nine Lancasters that set off tasked with laying mines off the Baltic ports – two of which did not return.

With the opening of the Russian offensive on 12 January 1945 *Major* Hoffmann's *Gruppe* was forced to give up its night fighting and went over to a ground attack role against the Red Army. On 25 January, while still carrying out their low-level attacks on advancing Russian troops, I./NJG 5 was moved back into Germany to operate from airfields at Parchim and Erfurt-Bindersleben.

It was now painfully obvious to all those concerned that the war was drawing inevitably towards its close. The German night fighters had long been evicted from their Belgian, Dutch and French airfields and the night skies over Germany were now filled with long-range intruders, such as the much feared Mosquito, which justly made the German crews fearful and nervous. On top of this they had to contend with the fact that their radios and radar, both on the ground and in the air, were being jammed to such an extent that it was not always possible to detect or even locate the bombers.

On 13/14 February 1945, the night of the infamous raid on Dresden, Werner Hoffmann took off from Parchim airfield and made his way to the beleaguered city. What he saw when he arrived there deeply shocked him. From the short flashes of the exploding bombs, combined with the fires that were raging far beneath him, the sky was lit up as bright as day. In among the flashes of light he could see the bombers passing over Dresden as they dropped their lethal cargo on to the city below. Frustratingly though, no matter how hard he persevered he just could not get any of the bombers in his sights. It seems as if he was not the only night fighter pilot to experience this frustration as only 6 Lancasters from a total of almost 800 were shot down that night.

The following day Werner made up for his lack of success by shooting down two bombers, one of them was a Lancaster participating in the attack on Chemnitz, and the other he has recorded as being a Boeing. As has already been explained, the confusion caused during the closing stages of the war made it very difficult for the German crews to accurately record the locations of their claims, this has resulted in no location being given in his *Leistungsbuch* (Achievements Book) as to where this encounter with the Boeing actually took place. As the only B-17s operating that night were tasked with dropping leaflets on Hanover, it is more than likely that this was another genuine misidentification of a four-engined aircraft.

His last successful night of the war came a little over a month later, on the night of 16 March when Bomber Command sent 277 Lancasters to Nuremburg, its last major raid on this city of the war. The raid was also significant for two other reasons. Firstly, not only did it mark the last major victory for the *Nachtjagd*, but, it was also the last occasion on which they would shoot down more than 10 bombers in any one night. By the conclusion of the attack the burnt and twisted remains of 24 Lancasters lay strewn over the German countryside, a result of early infiltration of the bomber stream while it was en route to the target. This is particularly true in the case of Werner Hoffmann who accounted for 3 of the mighty four-engined bombers in just twelve minutes, taking his tally of night-time kills to 50. This night, however, was not yet over for the young German pilot as he now explains:

Shortly before the RAF attack on Nuremburg one of my crews had been shot down during an attack on Halle and Leipzig at an altitude of between 4-500m. When coming back from Nuremburg to Erfurt, as I was concerned the same might happen to me I stayed at an altitude of 700m. In the vicinity of Bamberg (north of Nuremburg) a string of pearls of tracer hit my starboard wing and very suddenly the Ju88 started to go down. I ordered the crew to bail out through the belly hatch, which we had already jettisoned, and I myself bailed out last. As I didn't know how much time had elapsed between being hit and bailing out I didn't wait for three seconds of free fall, but opened my parachute after one and-a-half seconds instead. Consequently, when the parachute deployed about 3m^2 of silk were torn from it and my flying boots flew off. Therefore I hit the frozen ground much more heavily than on other parachute jumps. Apart from massive bruising to my chest caused by the parachute straps, I was uninjured.

The unknown assailant responsible for shooting down Hoffmann's Ju88 turned out to be a prowling Mosquito from 239 Squadron, crewed by S/Ldr Dennis Hughes and F/Lt Richard Perks. Hughes had taken off in his Mk XXX Mosquito from West Raynham at 19.07 hours, and was detailed to escort the bombers to Nuremburg. What follows is an extract from his combat report written by Hughes after arriving back safely from the raid:

Bomber route followed out, our height 17,000ft. Flashing beacon was seen in approximate position of beacon 'Otto', time 21.55 hours. Four white fighter flares were seen to appear. On turning towards this a contact was obtained at a range of five miles crossing port to starboard and slightly above. This was chased on a general heading of 030 degrees (m) and was taking fairly strong evasive action. Closed in and visual obtained

On the night of 16 March 1945, while escorting 277 Lancaster bombers to Nuremburg, Flight Lieutenant Richard Perks (left) and Squadron Leader Dennis Hughes DFC (right) intercepted and shot down Werner Hoffmann's Ju88 near Bamberg. (Hazel Hughes)

at 1,200ft. Ross night glasses were used and aircraft identified as a Ju88. Closing slowly, fire was opened at 200 yards and strikes were seen all over the enemy aircraft. A second burst set the root of the starboard wing and engine on fire. Enemy aircraft turned to port and slowly lost height in wide orbits. These developed into a vertical dive with explosion in mid-air shortly before hitting the ground in three pieces, which continued to burn for sometime – time 22.17 hours.

Two weeks after his close brush with death Werner was fit to fly again. In the course of attacks in the area of Halle and Leipzig on the 7/8 April (this was probably the attack on the Benzol plant at Molbis near Leipzig) he claimed a Lancaster as destroyed. There were, however, no aircraft lost during the course of the attack, which completely destroyed the plant and put an end to Benzol production at the facility. This victory was never officially recognised and does not appear in his list of kills.

Between 21-25 April he was actively involved in further night time operations against Russian troops that were approaching Berlin from the south-east. In the course of these operations he strafed enemy convoys and in the process destroyed a number of enemy vehicles. He was then withdrawn from these duties and posted as a desk officer to the fighter commander at Berlin-Gatow airfield. Within days of this, and with the Russians closing in from all sides, he was ordered to leave the devastated capital. This was most fortuitous for him as Berlin was totally surrounded and cut off from the west just hours after his hurried departure.

On 1 May 1945 *Major* Hoffmann, along with three of his best crews, was transferred to Husum in Schleswig Holstein, where they became part of 7./NJG 3. He did not fly any more operations from this time and was subsequently taken prisoner by the British on 5/6 May 1945 when they occupied the airfield. Over the following months the Allies processed the hundreds of thousands of German prisoners of war that had been herded into the Schleswig Holstein peninsula, which had been turned into a makeshift holding area for almost a million-and-a-half prisoners of war. The long summer months came and went and finally, on 15 October 1945, he received his discharge papers and was released.

As a former officer in the German *Wehrmacht* opportunities for employment were severely limited, and this was reflected in the fact that for the next two and-a-half years he could only find work as an agricultural labourer. Determined to improve his personal circumstances he began five years of pharmaceutical training, which culminated in him becoming a registered pharmacist in Goslar. From October 1957 to his retirement in February 1981 Werner was employed as a scientific worker for the Farbwerke Hoechst A.G. Company in Bremen. In the years that followed he worked part time in his wife's pharmacy until she too retired in December 1997. He and his charming wife, Sabine, were married in August 1977 and now live quietly in the picturesque suburbs of Bremen overlooking the Rivers Weser and Lesum.

Among all those pilots who flew with the *Nachtjagd*, Werner Hoffmann will be remembered as being one of a select band who achieved the distinction of having shot down 50 or more bombers at night. He flew almost 200 combat missions during this time and was rewarded with the Knight's Cross of the Iron Cross, as well as a recommendation for the addition of the Oak Leaves. A fine record that attests to the bravery and the fortitude of this former Luftwaffe officer.

On 1 May 1945 Werner Hoffmann and three of his best crews were transferred to Husum. Just days before the British overran the airfield they posed for one last photograph. (Kock)

From left: Karl Klucke, Werner Hoffmann, and Ernst Georg Drünkler. (Kock)

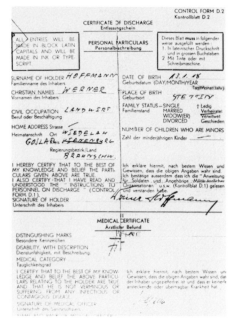

After more than five months in captivity Werner Hoffmann was released, receiving his discharge papers on 15 October 1945. (Kock)

124

4

Hauptmann Peter Spoden

The dark of night completely enveloped *Leutnant* Peter Spoden's Messerschmitt Bf110 night fighter. Its Daimler Benz engines droned rhythmically as the aircraft flew steadily on towards the outskirts of the German capital, which had been identified by the German ground controllers as the RAF's likely target that night.

The cockpit was filled with an eerie, dull glow which emanated from the multitude of dials on the aircraft's instrument panels. At an altitude of 4,000m the air was bitterly cold, so cold in fact that it even managed to penetrate the thick electrically heated flying suits worn by the three-man crew.

Strong winds and turbulence buffeted the lone German machine, causing it to pitch and lurch in a most unsettling manner. The monotonous hum of the engines was broken periodically by the radio as it crackled into life. A calm and steady voice could be clearly heard over the airways as the ground controller sought to guide the German night fighters

Hauptmann Peter Spoden, Gruppen-kommandeur of I./NJG 6. (Spoden)

In post-war years Peter Spoden had a successful career flying for Lufthansa, retiring in 1981 after twenty-six years service. He now lives with his wife in Frankfurt. (Spoden)

towards the incoming bomber stream. The controller's voice not only had a calming and reassuring effect on the night fighter crews, but he constantly gave up-to-date information as to the changing course and position of the RAF bombers.

A little after midnight on the 23 August 1943, having taken off from Parchim airfield, Peter Spoden set course, as ordered, towards Berlin and his allotted radio beacon. Accompanying him on the mission was his *Funker, Unteroffizier* Rüdke, and his *Bordmechaniker, Unteroffizier* Franz Ballweg.

For this particular operation Bomber Command dispatched a force of some 727 aircraft to the German capital city. By the conclusion of the mission, 56 of those four-engined machines would fail to make it back to their respective airfields. This represented an overall loss of 7.9% of the main force, and, up to that point of the war Bomber Command's greatest loss of aircraft in a single night.

An hour into the mission, *Leutnant* Spoden found himself flying over Berlin. The city was already ablaze. The scene that presented itself reminded the young German pilot of a scene from 'Dante's Hell'. A kaleidoscope of colours from detonating aerial mines, incendiaries and high explosives split the dark night sky. Slowly-descending marker flares, bursts of flak and powerful fingers of light emanating from hundreds of searchlight units added to the rich tapestry of colours below.

Looking out from the cockpit into the bubbling and seething inferno below, Peter could see the silhouettes of other aircraft against the lighter background of the burning city. The air space over the German capital was filled with hundreds of machines from the *Nachtjagd* and RAF, all vying for position over the maelstrom that was Berlin.

During this time Peter made several unsuccessful attacks on different bombers before finally locating a suitable quarry which, purely by chance, suddenly appeared in front of him.

Approaching the Lancaster from behind, Peter carefully opened fire at a distance of approximately 200m. He pressed the trigger firmly and the Bf110 shook with the recoil of four MG 17 machine-guns as they exploded into life. Hundreds of 7.92mm rounds tore through the thin exterior of the Lancaster, destroying everything they came into contact with. The bomber caught fire and plunged earthwards, on what would become its final journey. Minutes later it crashed in the centre of the city. The time was 01.10 hours.

Peter peered hard into the gloom, searching the dark sky for another target, and he soon spotted the tell-tale red and orange glow from a bomber's exhaust vents. The RAF machine, a Short Stirling, banked sharply without warning and flew head-on at the German night fighter, apparently oblivious to its presence. Firing some well-aimed bursts at the bomber, Peter Spoden saw it catch fire and plummet vertically.

Even though his own aircraft had been badly damaged, the rear gunner of the Short Stirling was able to control his fear, and the awful realisation of impending tragedy, by returning fire. The rounds from his four .303 Browning machine-guns ripped through the fuselage of the German aircraft.

The impact from these rounds was clearly heard by the German pilot as they passed through the thin skin of his machine. Seconds later, Peter was struck by a bullet which entered the top of his left leg, shattering the femur. Worse was to come.

As a result of the accurate and withering fire from the Stirling's rear gunner, the Bf110 began to burn. Peter Spoden immediately screamed at his crew to bail out. Shouting four or five times he received no reply from either crewmember, and with the heat from the burning aircraft beginning to reach unbearable temperatures, he decided it was time to get out.

Releasing both the seat harness and radio leads, he reached out and jettisoned the section of canopy above his head. The situation in which he now found himself was becoming ever more precarious. Flames, which fanned out behind the aircraft giving it the appearance of a comet, were quickly consuming the twin-engined night fighter as it fell to earth at a frightening speed. Spasms of pain racked *Leutnant* Spoden's body as he feverishly struggled with increasing desperation to exit the cockpit. After what seemed like an eternity, he finally succeeded in pulling himself up on to the edge of the cockpit. Completely exhausted and drained by the effort, he simply allowed himself to fall into the welcoming safety of the darkness. However, his nightmare was not destined to end just yet.

The airstream wrenched him clear of the cockpit but not from the entire aircraft, and he struck the tailplane with a sickening thud. With the stricken aircraft in a near-vertical dive, the speed of its descent pinned the petrified German pilot tight against the elevator. The cold and pain now forgotten, and barely able to move due to the gravitational forces involved, he clawed in sheer terror at the surface of the tailplane.

Such moments of mortal fear are said to give a man untold strength and determination. Shouting and crying out for his mother, with the roar of the rushing air filling his ears, Peter Spoden made one last attempt to free himself. Then, inexplicably and without warning, the doomed German machine turned over, throwing its captive clear.

Fumbling desperately for the parachute's ripcord he fell helplessly, tumbling and spinning out of control towards the ground. Although totally disorientated, and with all of

Aged eighteen months, 1923. (Spoden)

A four-year-old Peter Spoden poses with his great-great grandfather, who, it is interesting to note, is wearing his medals won during the Franco-Prussian war of 1870-71. (Spoden)

his senses screaming out with fear, he remembered to pull the ripcord before passing out. Unconsciousness completely covered him like a heavy but welcoming blanket, shutting out the horrors of the previous few minutes. Seconds, or maybe minutes later Peter regained consciousness and found himself lying in a garden somewhere on the outskirts of Berlin. A crowd of Berlin residents, incensed by the raid, and filled with a desire for vengeance, began to beat the prostrate pilot, thinking that they had found a downed British airman. Screaming at them in German, Peter was quickly able to pacify the mob, which in its anger at the devastation wrought on the city, had failed to recognise the injured airman's Luftwaffe uniform.

The mob's anger was quickly replaced with compassion as they realised their mistake. The seriously wounded German pilot was carried to a local hospital where he was immediately rushed to an operating theatre. As a result of the operation, which proved to be successful in saving his leg, Peter Spoden was left with a permanent limp and one leg shorter than the other.

His *Bordmechaniker, Unteroffizer* Franz Ballweg wasn't as fortunate. He had been killed during the air battle, and sometime later, was found dead still trapped within the wreckage of the Bf110. However, Peter's *Funker* had been somewhat luckier. When it had become obvious to *Rüdke* that their aircraft was doomed, following the encounter with the Stirling, he jumped clear without any complications and had parachuted safely back to the ground.

It would take almost three months of recovery before Peter could return to active combat duty, a remarkable achievement considering the doctors thought that he would never fly again.

His fortitude that night, and that of his crew, was recognised a short time later when he was awarded the Iron Cross First Class, and the Wound Badge in Black for his first combat injury. The double victory scored on the 23 August 1943 had taken his tally to three.

It was to be a hard road back to full fitness for this aspiring ace. However, it had been an even longer road which he'd had to negotiate in order to fulfil a lifetime's ambition to fly. He would succeed now as he had succeeded then.

Peter Spoden was born on 8 November 1921, in Borken, near Münster. His father, a railway inspector, raised all of his children with a strict Catholic upbringing. From a very young age Peter decided to be a pilot. One incident during his youth influenced this decision more than any other.

In 1927, he attended an air show at Bochum, near Essen where he witnessed the aerobatic skills of former First World War pilots. Among them was the highest-scoring living German ace from that conflict, Ernst Udet:

> It was in 1927 that I decided flying would be my dream career after seeing former First World War pilots like Udet doing a display at an air show in Bochum. The pilots spun almost to the ground and I saw Udet waving his handkerchief at the crowds as he did so.

On completing year six at the local *Volksschule,* he progressed on to the Elementary School in Langendreer, and then onto the Alfred Krupp Upper School in Essen. It was at this last school, at the age of eleven, that he joined the National Socialist League of Pupils, which was later amalgamated into the Hitler Youth. In the following years, Peter Spoden progressed within this organisation to become a junior leader in the Essen company.

During his time with the Hitler Youth he won several awards, including the Reich Sports Youth Badge and the Proficiency Certificate from the German Life Saving Association. With this organisation he was also able to increase his working knowledge of aircraft modelling and construction, while also having the opportunity to fly gliders:

> Flying has always been the only thing that has interested me. Politics were uninteresting. In the Hitler Youth I could learn to fly, we young school children never spoke about politics when we worked on our models and gliders.
>
> Recognising that a technical education would be necessary to me in my later occupation I joined the technical section of my group. There I had a certain amount of instruction in aeroplane modelling, aircraft construction and glider flying. We were also given basic instruction in aerodynamics.

Having passed his *Abitur,* the equivalent of A-levels, and a course in aerodynamics, Peter Spoden left the Krupp Upper School in 1940. It was his firm intention to study aviation at the university of Hanover, but his father had other ideas and landed him a job as a technician on the railways. This was an extremely frustrating time for the young would-be pilot who had a burning desire to fly and nothing else. As his career with the railways began, the 'Phoney War' in Europe came to an end as the Germans advanced into France, Belgium and the Low Countries; within a few short weeks the victorious *Wehrmacht* stood triumphantly on the Channel coast.

In the meantime however, his hometown of Essen in the Ruhr was already being bombed by the RAF. These attacks angered a frustrated Peter Spoden whose ambition to

In the spring of 1939, while a student at the Krupp Upper School, Peter Spoden and his classmates went on an educational tour of Germany. At his feet (far left) is Hans Adelhütte, who went on to become a night fighter and shot down between fifteen and twenty bombers. (Spoden)

become a pilot gained even greater impetus:

> I wanted to become a pilot – a night fighter pilot. It was only natural for me to want
> to defend my hometown of Essen where my mother, and my younger brothers and
> sisters lived, and where so many bombs were falling. My father prevented this with his
> connections, and I was not released from the railways to join the military.

It took many months of hard persuasion before Peter's father finally relented and allowed his son to join the German armed forces. Peter's dream of becoming a pilot drew one step closer when he joined the Luftwaffe in October 1940.

Initial basic training began at the Air Warfare School in Fürstenfeldbruck, which involved all aspects of basic flight instruction, including aerobatics. After successfully completing the course and obtaining his Pilot's Badge and A/B flying certificate, he was transferred to the flying school at Pütnitz. Here he qualified for the C grade of his Pilot's Licence, which then enabled him to fly all types of multi-engined aircraft, such as the Junkers 52 and 86, as well as the Heinkel 111 and Dornier 17. During this period Peter was commissioned, becoming *Leutnant* on 1 February 1942.

From the 1 September 1942, *Leutnant* Spoden went to the Blind Flying School at Copenhagen where he trained on the Junkers 52. After completing this difficult stage of the

At the family home in Essen
after his eighteenth birthday.
(Spoden)

As a member of the Hitler Youth, Peter
Spoden won his proficiency certificate
with the German Life Saving Association.
This qualification later enabled him to
become a lifeguard with the organisation.
(Spoden)

After joining the Luftwaffe in October 1940, Peter Spoden (right) underwent three months of basic infantry training, which placed a great deal of emphasis on physical training and drill. (Spoden)

training he was transferred to Stuttgart and then to the prestigious Night Fighter School at Kitzingen, where he undertook what was probably the most important part of his training.

For the first time in his career, during these two phases of the training programme, Peter was given the opportunity to fly the two aircraft that formed the backbone of the day and night fighter arms, the Messerschmitt 109 and the twin-engined 110. This comprehensive training programme gave him an excellent grounding in instrument flying and night fighter tactics. Skills that would be essential if he wanted to become a successful *Nachtjäger*, and, more importantly, to survive the war. The training had itself spanned almost three years, and Peter's opportunity to put this newly acquired knowledge to good use wasn't long in coming.

From training school he was transferred to 5./NJG5, joining the unit on 1 June 1943. Although somewhat anxious about going into combat for the first time, he was determined to fulfil his duty and bring honour to his *Gruppe*. He would find, however, that his first mission was to be both disappointing and frustrating.

The night of 27/28 July 1943 saw Bomber Command resuming their attack on the city of Hamburg. As a result of this mission (one of four such raids by the RAF on Hamburg during July and August 1943, code named, Operation *Gomorrah*), one word would be born that would become synonymous with the raid on this North German town; that word would be 'Firestorm'.

On being scrambled from Parchim in the late evening of the 27 July, *Leutnant* Spoden set a course for his allocated *Himmelbett* area to the east of Hamburg. Each of these areas (*Räume*) was given a designated code name. On this particular night he was directed to *Raum* 'Reiher' situated on the Baltic Coast near the island of Rügen.

Although 'Reiher' was some 40 to 50km away from Hamburg, Peter was still able to see the city burning brightly on the horizon. Bombers and night fighters alike

Peter Spoden in flying overalls during his training at the Air Warfare School. From March to December 1941, he attended the A/B Schule at Fürstenfeldbruck near Munich. (Spoden)

Flieger Spoden wearing formal tunic with flying helmet and goggles. (Spoden)

During the early stages of training the student pilots had to fly sixty satisfactory flights with an instructor before being allowed to fly solo. Peter Spoden is seen here in a Focke-Wulf 44 in which he carried out most of those flights.

A rather cold looking Peter Spoden peers out from the rear cockpit of a Klemm 35. It was in this aircraft that he carried out numerous cross-country flights, performed aerobatics and practised formation flying. (Spoden)

Preparing for take off in an Arado 96B. This advanced trainer had an all-metal construction and was fitted with a fully glazed cockpit. It was used extensively in Germany's A/B Schulen, as well as in the Ergänzungsgruppe and Luftkriegsschulen.

Wearing the insignia and rank of a Fähnrich, during the winter of 1941/42. (Spoden)

Peter Spoden shortly after his promotion to Leutnant. Note the cloth version of the Pilot's Badge on his left breast pocket. (Spoden)

were silhouetted against the burning skyline, circling the city like moths attracted to a bright light. Such a grim sight would have incensed any patriotic soldier defending his homeland and Peter Spoden was no exception. Calling up on the radio, he continually requested permission to fly closer to the stricken city, but to his disgust and frustration the order came back to remain where he was. Feeling utterly helpless at not being given an opportunity to help defend the residents of Hamburg, Peter continued circling until a shortage of fuel forced him to return to Parchim airfield. On landing, he immediately sought permission to operate in the airspace over the city, but the request was again turned down. During this operation, which was its second mission to Hamburg, Bomber Command lost seventeen of its aircraft, a relatively small number due mainly to the recent introduction of 'Window' which proved very effective in jamming German ground and air radar. The operation was also successful in inflicting a severe blow on the morale of the German civilian population, and the 'Firestorms' that night claimed an estimated 40,000 lives.

Three weeks later on the night of 17/18 August, *Leutnant* Spoden achieved his first aerial victory of the war when Bomber Command attacked the German research facilities at Peenemünde situated on the Baltic Coast. It was here that German scientists, utilising labour from hundreds of prisoners of war, were secretly carrying out construction and testing of the V1 and V2 retaliation weapons.

The shattered remains of an RAF Wellington shot down by flak in the area of Hamburg. During four raids on this North German city in late July and early August 1943, a total of some eighty-seven Bomber Command aircraft were lost. (author's collection)

Although not actively involved in the defence of Hamburg on the night of 27 July 1943, Peter Spoden did witness the destruction wrought by the RAF bombers. A member of a local defence unit took this photograph clearly showing how intense the flak could be for the bombers. (author's collection)

In order to have a better chance of destroying the facility it had been decided to carry out the raid during the period of a full moon. It would also be the first such mission where a 'Master Bomber' would oversee a full-scale bombing raid. Of the 596 aircraft dispatched, 324 were Lancasters, 218 were Halifaxes and 54 were Stirling bombers. About an hour before the raid on the installation, 8 Mosquitos took part in a diversionary raid on Berlin, a feint that was successful in drawing a large part of the German night fighter force away from Bomber Command's intended target.

Having taken off from Parchim airfield, Peter Spoden quickly gained altitude and headed north towards the Baltic coast. It was a very clear night, so much so that as he neared the target he could clearly see burning bombers falling from the night sky to the west of his position. This time, after his experience of the Hamburg raid, Peter was determined to play an active part in the defence of his homeland, and left his *Himmelbett* area without seeking the appropriate authority. A feeling of excitement mixed with a little apprehension ran through him, as he increased speed and set a course towards the burning horizon.

Arriving in the vicinity of the target area, Peter was soon able to identify a Lancaster bomber due to the good visibility and the fact that the target area was covered in only a small amount of cloud. Approaching the enemy aircraft from below and astern so as not to be seen by its rear gunner, Peter raised the nose of the Bf110, aimed carefully between the engines on the bomber's port wing, and opened fire using the Messerschmitt's forward guns. Keeping the trigger locked firmly down he fired a long burst until the Lancaster's wing started to burn. The stricken aircraft nosed over immediately and fell from the sky. In a state of euphoria at having achieved his first victory, Peter Spoden followed the course of the Lancaster's descent rather than searching the dark skies for another target. He saw the bomber explode as it struck the ground between Hanshagen and Greifswald some ten to twelve miles west of Peenemünde. The time recorded for his first victory was 01.55 hours.

Landing his aircraft at Greifswald airfield, close to the Baltic Coast, the excited young German pilot made his way to the crash site on a borrowed motorcycle. His feelings of elation, however, soon turned to horror when he saw the remains of the burning Lancaster and its dead crew. The bomber, piloted by Sgt W.J. Drew, had been a 44 Squadron machine, serial No. JA 897, which had taken off four hours earlier from Dunholme Lodge in Lincolnshire. Drew's aircraft had been part of the third and final wave of the attack on Peenemünde and the only survivor from the Lancaster had been the bomb-aimer, Sgt William 'Bill' Sparks. The German night fighters were able to reorganise themselves quickly after the diversionary attack by Mosquitos on Berlin, and they turned northwards and headed for the Baltic Coast. They arrived over Peenemünde at the same time as the RAF's third wave was making its attack, and it was from this wave that many of Bomber Command's losses came.

At the crash site Peter Spoden tried speaking to Sgt Sparks who was clearly shocked and dazed by his near death experience. Understandably he spoke very little, other than to give the German officer his name, rank and number. Almost forty years later Bill Sparks recounted the events of that night to author Martin Middlebrook, who later wrote a very well researched book entitled *The Peenemünde Raid*. The following exert is taken directly from the book:

A young German pilot came to see me. He looked a typical, clean-looking German, square cut, trim and blond. I remember that he had no hat on. He treated me with great respect. He spoke to me in English and told me that he had shot my plane down. I felt amazed that I was talking to someone who had shot me down. I don't remember my answer. I do know that I didn't tell him anything much but I did ask someone what had happened to my crew; it was probably that pilot I asked.

When the prisoners of war were collected at Greifswald, I kept trying to find more of my crew and, when none of them turned up, I began to wonder whether they had got away after all and returned to England. It never occurred to me that they were all dead.

With the horrors of war indelibly etched into his memory, Peter never again visited the scene created by one of his victories. Two days later he was awarded the Iron Cross Second Class in recognition of his first aerial victory, and several months later, on the 15 November 1943, he was further decorated with the Iron Cross First Class. This was awarded chiefly for his double victory (his second and third confirmed victories) achieved on 23 August during the RAF's attack on Berlin. The very same mission during which Peter sustained a terrible leg wound, inflicted as a result of accurate defensive fire from the rear gunner of a Stirling bomber. Months of convalescence followed but, by the beginning of November 1943, he was able to return to his *Gruppe* and active duty.

An aerial view of Peenemünde and the remains of its buildings as they look today. On the night of 17/18 August 1943 Peter Spoden achieved his first victory, a Lancaster, which was one of 596 aircraft tasked to destroy the secret V2 rocket research facility located there. (author's collection)

Sgt Bill Sparks, bomb aimer on board Lancaster JA897 of 44 Squadron, was shot down by Peter Spoden during the Peenemünde raid. The bomber crashed between Hanshagen and Greifswald and Sparks was the sole survivor. (Bill Sparks)

Sgt Johnnie Drew (left) was the pilot of JA897 and he perished with his aircraft, along with Sgt Jack Joplin, the wireless operator (right). (Sparks)

Sgt Bassett, rear gunner in Sgt Drew's Lancaster, killed on 18 August 1943. He and four other members of the crew are now commemorated on the Runnymede Memorial. (Sparks)

Shortly after his return, Bomber Command sent 383 aircraft to the German capital on the night of 23/24 November 1943. This fleet of aircraft consisted of 365 Lancasters, 8 Mosquitos and 10 Halifaxes. In response to this, though plagued with low-lying cloud over many of its airfields, the German *Nachtjagd* was still able to put up a large number of aircraft. At least half of Bomber Command's losses were inflicted on the inward bound journey to Berlin even though there had been effective radio interference from stations in England. These radio transmissions were often successful in causing confusion and providing false information to the crews of the *Nachtjagd*. In many cases incorrect bomber altitudes, locations and even orders to land their aircraft were transmitted from England with varying degrees of success.

Four further RAF aircraft were lost on the actual bomb run over the capital, with the remaining twenty lost on this operation being shot down on their homeward journey; it was one of these aircraft that was accounted for by Peter Spoden.

Approximately 40km west of Berlin, he was able to recognise the ghostly silhouette of a Lancaster. Manoeuvring into a favourable position Peter successfully attacked this aircraft inflicting grievous damage to its mainplane. This damage was sufficient to cause the bomber to plummet, trailing a banner of flames behind it. He noted the time of his fourth victory as 20.02 hours.

It was to be a further six weeks before he enjoyed another victory, but 14 January 1944 was to be a memorable day for this up-and-coming night fighter pilot. By the conclusion of this mission he would be officially recognised as an *Experte* within the *Nachtjagd*.

The target for the RAF on this occasion was to be Brunswick; situated in the centre of Germany it was to be the first major attack directed against this city. A decisive factor in choosing Brunswick as a strategic target was due to the fact that it had two Messerschmitt aircraft factories located there. A force of almost 500 bombers consisting mainly of Lancasters was dispatched.

The German early warning system picked up the incoming bomber stream at an early stage while on its way to the target. With the benefit of adequate warning, the German night fighters had time to take off and climb to the required altitude, and with the element of surprise on their side, the waiting units of the *Nachtjagd* discreetly infiltrated the bomber stream. Peter Spoden was flying one of those German aircraft waiting for the unsuspecting bombers and their crews.

Shrouded in darkness, he flew steadily on the expected course of the bombers while constantly being updated by the ground controllers as to their direction and height. He was one of the many night fighters who had been scrambled to intercept the raiders and now he waited poised to strike. After a short period of time he located a four-engined bomber, a Lancaster, and quickly shot it down; the time was 19.30 hours. Within five minutes of his first success he located a second Lancaster, which he again successfully attacked and destroyed. These two aircraft were both shot down very close to Brunswick and became his fifth and sixth victories. Peter was now officially recognised as an *Experte* having achieved a minimum of five confirmed victories. He received further recognition, being decorated with the Night Fighter Clasp in Bronze having flown twenty operational flights.

Peter Spoden scored another multiple victory on the night of Thursday 27 January 1944, when Berlin was again the target for Bomber Command. His seventh and eighth

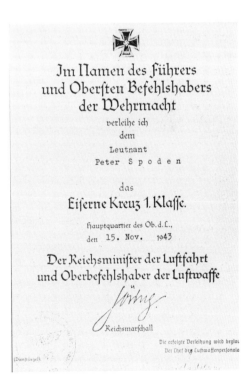

On 15 November 1943 Peter Spoden was presented with the Iron Cross First Class after shooting down three bombers. (Spoden)

Two of the elements that made up part of the German defences. Above: One of the massive concrete flak towers erected to protect Germany's major cities. This particular tower was erected in Hamburg and three of its double 12.8cm anti-aircraft gun emplacements can be seen mounted on the roof. Left: Seen in its protective trench, a 150cm Scheinwerfer 37 searchlight. (Spoden)

victories were achieved against two four-engined bombers but owing to the mêlée often associated with night-fighting, the type of bomber shot down was not known. Although Peter was unable to identify his victims, it is safe to assume that they were both Lancasters, as the bomber force dispatched that night consisted of 515 Lancasters and 15 Mosquitos.

This mission also gave Peter his first opportunity to use a new weapon that would revolutionise the art of night-fighting for its pilots, and had recently been introduced into the *Nachtjagd*. It was known simply as *Schräge Musik*:

> *Schräge Musik* was a good invention by my Gruppenkommandeur Rudi Schoenert in 1943, and Oberfeldwebel Gustav Mahle, who were both honoured for this. I preferred Schräge Musik instead of the forward facing cannons because it was much safer for the night fighter as you were not in the range of the rear gunner.

Prior to this attack against Berlin on the 27 January, a diversionary attack was made against the Baltic island of Heligoland, which was bombed by a small force of 'Pathfinder' Halifaxes, while a force of Wellingtons and Stirlings laid mines in the German Bight. These operations along with clever use of 'Window' drew part of the German *Nachtjagd* force away from the intended target and confused the German ground controllers. This resulted in the loss of very few bombers en route to Berlin.

Major Rudolph Schoenert, the man universally recognised as being responsible for the introduction of *Schräge Musik*. He achieved the first kill using the new weapon system over Berlin in May 1943. (author's collection)

During a break from operations, Peter Spoden takes time to relax with fellow pilots in the officer's mess. (Spoden)

Peter Spoden was scrambled after receiving the *Alarmstart* and took off in his Messerschmitt 110 now fitted with the upward-firing 20mm cannon of *Schräge Musik*. Long fingers of light emanating from the search light batteries and sporadic bursts of flak split the night sky; many districts of the capital were already well alight.

Lady Fortune was smiling on the RAF bomber crews that night as the defensive fire from the flak batteries was reported as being light and inaccurate. Through the eye-straining blackness of night, *Leutnant* Spoden, who was patiently circling the periphery of Berlin, was able to identify the dark silhouette of a four-engined bomber. He vividly recalls his tried and tested method of identifying and shooting down enemy aircraft:

> First you saw the eight exhaust flames of the four-engined bomber, then you flew under it, always staying in the dark so that you had the enemy plane above you. In most cases they had not seen you, but quite a number of RAF crews started shooting, or the bombers made abrupt manoeuvres so that you lost them. When under the bomber you didn't wait long, shooting with the upward guns between the two engines, port or starboard, whichever was suitable. Between the two engines each side were the fuel tanks. Even with one good shot they were burning fast.

His first victim, a Lancaster, was successfully intercepted and shot down at 20.27 hours. In a little less than ten minutes he had located and dispatched a second. Both bombers were shot down some 20 to 30km west of Berlin. Added to similar successes by other *Nachtjagd* pilots, and with several RAF aircraft forced to ditch into the English

Channel due to being seriously damaged, the bomber force lost a total of thirty-three Lancasters that night.

Further personal success was achieved three days later on the 30 January, when the RAF, as part of a continued and determined effort to reduce the German capital to rubble, targeted Berlin again. In the course of Bomber Command's assault on the battered city, another Lancaster fell to the upward-firing cannon of Peter Spoden's Messerschmitt 110.

Having been successfully directed to the bomber stream by his ground controller, Peter infiltrated it without incident. Visual contact was made with one of the mighty four-engined machines when its flaming exhaust vents were spotted through the gloom. The powerful slipstream created by the bomber buffeted the shadowing night fighter, which was simply dwarfed by the sheer size of the British aircraft. The Messerschmitt 110 by comparison was only half the size of its intended victim.

Reducing his aircraft's airspeed to match that of the bomber, Peter Spoden slowly and surreptitiously manoeuvred underneath it. This was the most critical time for any night fighter crew, and it caused unbearable tension within the claustrophobic confines of the German aircraft. The three-man crew of the night fighter could almost feel the straining eyes from the Lancaster's gunners peering out into the dark void for any sign of the enemy, fingers twitching on their triggers in nervous anticipation.

Looking up into the reflector sight, Peter kept his aircraft as steady as he could and aligned the upward-firing cannon against one of the Lancaster's wings. He squeezed the trigger. 20mm cannon shells tore through the thin metal veneer covering the Lancaster, and ignited the aviation fuel stored in the wing. Having badly damaged the British bomber and set it on fire, Peter Spoden instinctively banked his machine, slipping quickly and discreetly away in the darkness. From their position of relative safety, the German night fighter crew watched their unfortunate victim spiral downward towards the ground. It exploded several minutes later, a huge fireball marking its final resting-place. This encounter was recorded as having taken place at 20.29 hours, resulting in the Lancaster crashing to the south of Stettin, one of thirty-three lost that night.

During the early months of 1944, Peter Spoden also participated in several daylight missions against the US Air Force. Their growing numbers of men and machines were fast becoming a serious threat to the Luftwaffe, and to the population of the *Reich* itself. On one such mission he found himself being scrambled from Parchim airfield at approximately 10.00 hours to intercept a bomber formation from the US Eight Air Force. The date was 6 March 1944; significant because it was to be the first daylight raid on Berlin by the Americans.

A group of four Messerschmitt 110s from II./NJG5, led by Peter Spoden, were to intercept the US bombers on their return journey from the capital and break up their formation using a new 'Wonder Weapon'. Fixed to the wings of the German aircraft were rockets known as *Dödels,* which were to be used in conjunction with the *Lichtenstein* radar. The *Lichtenstein* would gauge the distance to the bomber formation and the rockets would then be fired at a distance no greater than 1.5km. It was hoped that the bombers would be shot down or at least isolated from their main formations so that the German day fighters could attack them more easily.

A group of fifteen to twenty B-17s were identified north of Rostock, but on seeing the formation of approaching Messerschmitt*s*, the vigilant, but somewhat nervous gunners

Messerschmitt 110s of 5./NJG 5 during daylight missions against the US Air Force in the early months of 1944. Peter Spoden's aircraft is in the centre. (Spoden)

of the American bombers opened fire at them from a distance of some 2km. Much to his surprise and disbelief, Peter found that his aircraft received numerous hits on the port side from this accurate fire, which thoroughly riddled both the wing and engine. He ordered his group to open fire with the rockets but on pressing his own trigger nothing happened. Either the firing mechanism had been damaged by gunfire or the rockets had been loaded incorrectly:

> Now I used my forward guns. I was shooting heavily into the enemy group but I could not see any success. At the same time my left engine showed a white flag and stopped running. I shut the engine down and turned away. Thank God there were no US day fighters nearby. Suddenly the B-17s were gone, I found myself alone with one engine and between the barrage balloons over the prohibited town of Kiel. The German flak did not shoot, thankfully they must have recognised me!

With the port engine out of operation, Peter was barely able to coax the damaged fighter back to Parchim airfield. This was quite a feat considering that a common complaint among those who flew this aircraft was that it was almost impossible to maintain altitude on one engine. With the added weight of the *Lichtenstein* antennae and the wing-mounted rockets, his already under-powered German fighter lost height rapidly.

While circling over the airfield, a further unexpected problem presented itself when Peter found it necessary to carry out a belly-landing due to a damaged undercarriage. Having successfully landed the crippled machine he later had time to consider that he had been more fortunate than several of his colleagues. Earlier in the mission he had witnessed two of his formation going down in flames having come under heavy defensive fire from the B-17s. These two aircraft crashed into North Sea between the Danish coast and Rügen, close to where the confrontation had taken place.

These daylight attacks by experienced *Nachtjagd* crews on American bomber formations were not destined to last long. This was almost totally due to the ever-increasing losses inflicted on them by the escorting Allied fighters, which came in growing numbers in the form of the P-47 Thunderbolt and P-51 Mustang.

By a strange quirk of fate eighteen years later in the spring of 1962, while training as a pilot for Lufthansa in Tucson Arizona, Peter Spoden was invited to the officers' mess for dinner at the nearby Monthan-Davis US Air force base. During the course of the evening the commanding officer, Brigadier-General William Garland spoke about his time as a B-17 pilot over Germany. Peter recalls:

> He mentioned that his group in early 1944 were attacked by four dark Night Fighters (we had dark paint at that time) and that the group shot down two Messerschmitt 110s. But he had been rather unlucky! Bullets from one of the Bf110s had damaged his fuel tanks, and he had had to ditch his B-17 close to the English shoreline. He was saved from his life-raft by the English coast guard. Well he asked, 'Is there a night fighter among you German gentleman?' Of course! – I stood up. I related my story and indeed comparing different details we knew that we had both been in the same battle.

Fortune again favoured the brave, for on the night of 26/27 March 1944 Peter found himself, for the second time during his career, on the wrong end of 'unfriendly fire'. While flying in the area of Stettin his aircraft was attacked by an unknown assailant and hit by gunfire that tore through the fuselage destroying much of the radio and navigational equipment on board. Determined not to have to ditch in the Baltic Sea, Peter set out in a southerly direction and ordered his crew to prepare to bail out.

Feldwebel Schmiedler, the *Funker* on board the aircraft, had already been forced to bail out on nine previous occasions, one of which had resulted in him breaking his legs. With this obviously at the forefront of his mind Schmiedler simply refused to jump again. Being unable to pinpoint their exact position over a darkened landscape, and with the radio unable to receive transmissions, Peter continued to fly on a southerly course.

At approximately 01.15 hours, having descended through the cloud layer, the anxious German crew spotted lights on the ground. Just as it seemed that their ordeal was finally over the engines spluttered and the propellers stopped turning. The fuel tanks were empty.

The Me110 lost height steadily as its pilot frantically wrestled with the aircraft's control column. Using all of his strength to pull the column back as far as he could into his stomach the fighter was barely being able to clear a row of houses that suddenly loomed up out of the darkness. When the aircraft finally plunged into the ground, it threw up a great plume of earth and turf as it careered across a number of tennis courts.

With the sheer impact of the landing all three members of the crew were knocked out. Through the clearing mist of unconsciousness, Peter could hear someone crying out in pain. It was his *Funker*, Schmiedler. On hitting the ground one of the aircraft's wings had been partially ripped off and was now lying across the fuselage, hot oil was running from it and dripping onto the unfortunate Schmiedler below. The aircraft crashed in Kornwestheim, a small town near Stuttgart; all three members of the crew were exceptionally lucky as local inhabitants arrived quickly at the crash site to pull them from the wreckage. It would take a stay of several weeks in hospital before they all returned to active duty.

Not long after returning to the front line Peter Spoden's *Gruppe,* now re-designated III./NJG 6, were transferred to Steinamanger (Szombathely as it is now called) in Hungary. He clearly remembers the reasons for the transfer and the conditions under which they had to live and fly:

> The reason our *Gruppe* moved to Hungary was that Harris had stopped the battle over Berlin because of the losses. We were needed more then to protect the southern borders from Allied bomber attacks on Italy and Sicily than to stay at Parchim to protect Berlin. The conditions in Steinamanger were very fair, the Hungarians were very friendly to us and our first missions were flown against the British night attacks in Austria, Hungary and Bohemia.

It was during this period that Peter had his only success with III./NJG 6. On the 21 July 1944, he shot down a Wellington bomber to the north-west of Neunkirchen at 23.22 hours. The targets that night were the oilfields at Pardubice, which were situated approximately 100km east of Prague. His victim was part of a mixed force comprising Liberators and Wellingtons, which reportedly took off from bases in Italy and were intercepted by elements of the *Nachtjagd* between Graz and Vienna.

This was Peter Spoden's tenth victory and was significant because it was his first flying the Junkers 88 as a night fighter. Having now converted to this aircraft he would never fly the Me110 again:

> The Ju88 was much better in blind flying, it had a wheel instead of the stick found in the Bf110. Besides the pilot there were two radio operators and one rear gunner. Two radio operators were needed in the last months of the war in the growing battle between the different radar used by each side.

III./NJG 6 were also utilised to attack and disrupt the nightly supply drops to the Tito partisans who controlled much of the Yugoslavian countryside. These supply flights were carried out by both the RAF and the Soviet Air Force under the cover of darkness. For the Germans however these missions often filled them with real fear. As a result of stories and rumours about the treatment received by German aircrew after being shot down and captured, few relished the thought of flying such missions. Peter Spoden recalls:

> Attacking low-flying Soviet and British planes from the east and south over mountainous Tito countryside was extremely difficult and full of danger. Our radar,

Lichtenstein, was useless. The partisans and Allied flyers had special radio contacts and light signals we did not know about. Normally they identified a German flyer right away and we received heavy fire from the ground. When shot down [German aircrews] were tortured and killed after questioning. I saw two German pilots murdered by the partisans. Our only chance was to fly without any German insignia and to speak English after parachuting, telling the partisans you were an English flyer, hoping then they would bring you to an English officer or agent, who would then treat you as a prisoner of war. We had lectures from our intelligence officers that this method was our only chance to survive. The war over Yugoslavia was very cruel and I was quite happy when I was sent back to the Western Front.

After being awarded the Night Fighter Clasp in Silver on completing his sixtieth combat flight, Peter was transferred back in order to defend the *Reich* against the Allies devastating round-the-clock bombing campaign. After his transfer to II./NJG 6, who at that time were based at Schwäbisch Hall, 60km north-east of Stuttgart, it didn't take too long before he again increased his tally of victories. The month of August saw him destroy two further four-engined bombers over Darmstadt and Rüsselsheim respectively, increasing his personal score to twelve.

On 11 September 1944, a clear autumn night, Bomber Command attacked the city of Darmstadt located to the south of Frankfurt. Darmstadt had been the target of an earlier

The award certificate for the Night Fighter Clasp in Silver for sixty operational flights. The Geschwaderkommodore, Major Heinrich Griese, made the presentation of the clasp on 8 July 1944. (Spoden)

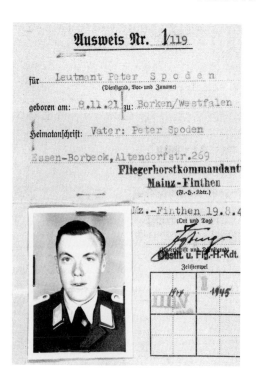

Peter Spoden's identity card. All combatants were required to carry one of these with them at all times. (Spoden)

raid in August but had sustained very little structural damage. The city was not the centre of any major industries or of any particular strategic value other than the railway system that ran through it.

With Darmstadt lying approximately ninety miles into Germany, this was far enough to give the night fighters ample time to scramble and intercept the incoming bomber stream. Peter Spoden and other elements of II./NJG 6 took off into the darkness and set a course towards the RAF's intended target. While circling the periphery of the city, the difficult task of locating one of the 226 bombers was made easier when one of the Lancasters was caught in the glare of a searchlight 20km north-west of Darmstadt's centre.

Flying at an altitude of 2,400m, the crew of the Lancaster was unaware that a German night fighter had latched on to them and was now discreetly shadowing their aircraft. This particular Lancaster was on its homeward journey having already dropped its deadly cargo on the city. The crew, much relieved at having completed the bomb run and now being on their way home, were oblivious to the dark form which was now directly behind them.

Positioning his aircraft beneath the Lancaster, an excited *Leutnant* Spoden of the much-feared German *Nachtjagd* carefully adjusted the airspeed of his machine to match that of the bomber and opened fire. The devastating and withering fire from the Junker's 20mm cannon ripped through the doomed Lancaster setting it on fire, and thus sealing its fate. Barely six minutes later, at 00.18 hours, Schmiedler, the *Funker*, picked up an echo on his radar screen of an aircraft flying at 3,000m. This machine, identified as another Lancaster, was stalked, and then dispatched in the same way as its unfortunate predecessor, crashing in flames 30km from Darmstadt.

Following on from this encounter, having meanwhile been promoted to *Oberleutnant* and awarded the Honour Goblet, Peter Spoden was to have his most successful mission on the night of 4 December 1944, when the RAF attacked Heilbronn north of Stuttgart. Peter was able to locate and shoot down his first victim of the night, a Lancaster bomber, at 19.33 hours. In less than ten minutes two further bombers were brought down 30km from the target, bringing his number of confirmed kills to seventeen.

One of the downed aircraft, flown by Flight Lieutenant Ian Herbert from the Royal New Zealand Air Force, was a MK1 Lancaster coded 9J-U, serial number LM259 from 227 Squadron, and had taken off from RAF Balderton in Nottinghamshire at 16.31 hours. Heilbronn was to be Ian Herbert's crew's twenty-eighth mission, two more and they would have completed their tour.

The purpose of 227 Squadron's mission that night was to bomb the railway marshalling yards, while the other squadrons involved were to bomb the town itself. For the purpose of bombing the marshalling yards the bomb load that night consisted of high explosives in the form of eleven 1,000lb and four 500lb bombs. As their squadron was to be the last to bomb the target it was already well alight when they arrived over the target area.

The bomb-aimer, Flight Officer Doug Cleary, found that cloud was covering the target to within a couple of miles of it. This meant that the bomb run would have to be a short one. Ian Herbert found that the marshalling yards themselves were covered in cloud so he decided to turn over the town and make a second pass. When they were approximately six or seven miles north of Heilbronn a warning was shouted over the intercom from the rear gunner, Sergeant Dick Whitbread, alerting the crew to the presence of German night fighters. Ian Herbert immediately carried out 'corkscrewing' manoeuvres in order to evade them but it was already too late. Cannon fire ripped through the starboard wing and engines, continuing on through the fuselage and narrowly missing Doug Cleary, but killing the mid-upper gunner, Sergeant Pete Webb. Ian Herbert recalls what happened after the attack:

> Firstly I decided to jettison our load when the starboard engine caught fire, the engine was feathered and the fire button operated, this did fix number four engine. However, our hydraulics were obviously damaged as we couldn't close the bomb doors and of course this was causing a lot of drag. This was further complicated because one of the 500lb bombs had become caught up in the bomb bay. But things were still thought reasonable and I set a rough course for the Rhine which I thought was approximately eighty miles away, and gave us a chance of getting over our own lines in France. But then the port outer engine caught fire, and I had a run-away propeller, constant speed control was out of action. Feathering and fire action failed to correct this and when the fire started to melt the fairings on the wing around the motor, I decided to instruct the crew to abandon the aircraft. When they had gone, that is the ones out front, I put the automatic pilot on and left myself.

The six remaining members of the crew successfully took to their parachutes and were taken prisoner. Sergeant Pete Webb, the only crew fatality was buried and now lies in the Dürnbach war cemetery.

Lancaster LM 259. Flight Lieutenant Ian Herbert piloted this aircraft on the night of 14 December 1944, one of three bombers shot down by Oberleutnant Spoden during the raid on Heilbronn. (Spoden)

Flight Lieutenant Ian Herbert. (Ian Herbert)

Sergeant Pete Webb, mid-upper gunner on Lancaster LM 259, was killed during the bombing run over Heilbronn. (Herbert)

Brussels, 12 May 1945. Two crew members from LM 259, who became prisoners of war, are pictured on liberation. Left: Jimmy Hudson (flight engineer) and Jodan Maxwell (navigator). (Herbert)

153

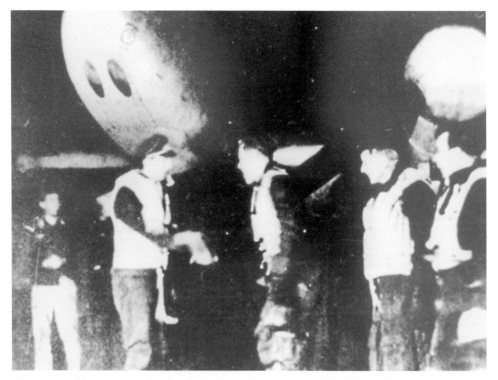

After a successful mission Peter Spoden is seen here shaking hands with Wim Johnen. Johnen later became the Gruppenkommandeur of III./NJG 6 and finished the war with thirty-four victories and the Knight's Cross. (Spoden)

Time to enjoy a quiet drink during a lull in the fighting. (Spoden)

On this one night alone Peter Spoden accounted for 25% of Bomber Command's overall losses, but it was not enough to prevent an estimated 7,000 civilians being killed in Heilbronn by the firestorm that ravaged the town.

Following on from this, further recognition was bestowed upon this rising star of the *Nachtjagd*, when he was given further responsibility and higher command by being made the *Staffelkapitän* of the 6th *Staffel* of II./NJG 6.

Having achieved his eighteenth victory over a four-engined bomber in the area of Trier the previous week, Peter and his three-man crew took off from Schwäbisch Hall just before midnight on 27 December 1944. At the briefing earlier that evening, it had been established that the encircled American troops at Bastogne were being supplied from the air with additional troops and ammunition flown in by gliders. The aim of the mission was to shoot down the gliders and thus deprive the hard-pressed defenders of essential supplies.

While flying over the front line scanning the night sky for the gliders, Oberleutnant Spoden's aircraft was suddenly and violently thrown about. Unknown to him at the time the Ju88 had been struck by 20mm flak fired from a flak battery manned by members of the Hitler Youth. The port engine immediately caught fire and Peter fought to keep the aircraft in the air. This was to no avail as it steadily lost height, due to the one remaining engine being unable to keep it aloft. With time quickly running out and the fire becoming progressively larger he frantically scanned the horizon for somewhere to land. As he skimmed low across the tops of trees and hedgerows, Peter quickly identified a snow-covered field near the town of Stadtkyll. The crew frantically tightened their seat harnesses, dropped their heads forward onto their chests and prepared to crash land.

On hitting the ground the aircraft careered out of control across the snow. The one good propeller threw up snow and earth before it buckled and stopped. The sheer impact of striking the frozen ground threw Peter forward in his seat causing the straps to cut painfully into his body. His head was thrown forward striking the Revi gun sight, knocking him unconscious. Amazingly the Ju88 did not explode, but the fire spread rapidly and it was only the quick actions of his crew pulling him from the wreckage that saved his life.

Although suffering from severe concussion Peter was able to commandeer a vehicle and drive to the flak emplacement where he found its Hitler Youth personnel painting another kill mark on the barrel of their gun. A very apologetic battery commander was able to placate the livid German pilot with an apology and 20l of fuel for the journey back to Schwäbisch Hall. The incident was soon forgotten. On 3 January 1945, having sustained his third combat injury, Peter was awarded the Wound Badge in Silver.

February 1945 saw him add three Lancasters and a Halifax to his victory tally while defending an ever-shrinking *Reich* from RAF raids on targets such as Mainz, Worms and Pforzheim respectively. These four victories took his personal score to twenty-two and he was awarded the German Cross in Gold as recognition of his continued achievements.

Peter Spoden's last two victories were achieved on the night of 7 March 1945 when the RAF attacked Dessau. The first bomber to succumb to his deadly marksmanship that night was a Lancaster, which was shot down and destroyed over the target at an altitude of approximately 3,000m. The second aircraft, also a Lancaster, was located 50-60km

The Wound Badge in Silver and the certificate that accompanied it, awarded for having been wounded three times in action. (Spoden)

south-west of Dessau while on its homeward journey. Peter Spoden vividly recalls this encounter which almost cost him and his crew their lives:

> When I arrived over Dessau the town was already burning like so many I had seen. Flying over burning towns was like daylight flying, everything was alight and everybody saw everybody. I spotted two four-engined planes and attacked with Schräge Musik and shot them down. I received accurate return fire [as a result of which] I had to feather one engine. We flew about two hours in the direction of Schwäbisch Hall, my airfield (Fliegerhorst), in the dark and did not encounter any Mosquitos – thank God. We were losing altitude constantly, the Ju88 with all the radar antennas was simply too heavy for single-engine flight. When I saw the trees near Crailsheim, at about 600ft, not far away from Schwäbisch Hall, I told the crew to jump out and I followed after switching on the automatic pilot. The plane crashed into the forest.

After parachuting safely the four crewmembers were almost immediately confronted by a group of excited and nervous old men armed with shotguns. These men turned out to be from the local *Volksturm*, who had been warned by the local authorities to be on the lookout for enemy paratroopers, which were likely to be in the area. Speaking very quickly in German, Peter was able to convince them that he and his crew were in fact German airmen. He hadn't endured eighteen months of continual combat, hardship and survived countless encounters with the RAF to be shot now by an old farmer with an itchy trigger finger. With these last two victories Peter Spoden's final tally stood at twenty-four.

With the war inevitably drawing to its close, many of Germany's towns and cities were now lying in ruins, however, the men of the *Nachtjagd* fought on bravely despite the overwhelming odds.

In recognition of his outstanding conduct and leadership, Peter Spoden was promoted to *Gruppenkommandeur* of 1./NJG6 on 19 March 1945. His command was to be short-lived however, as events outside of his control were bringing the war to its final conclusion. On 29 April the remnants of *Nachtjagdgeschwader* 6 surrendered to the Allies. The following day American troops occupied their airfield at Schleissheim in Munich where Peter Spoden's war finally came to an end. Unknown to him though, on 20 April 1945, during the last few confused weeks of the war, he had been promoted to the rank of *Hauptmann*. This fact remained undiscovered until many years later when he officially retired and applied for his war pension in 1981.

Barely a week later, the unconditional surrender of the German armed services was signed, and just like millions of other soldiers, Peter found himself herded into a prisoner-of-war camp. The first two weeks of captivity were the hardest as the prisoners received no food and water, but as the confusion cleared things did improve.

After being released in the autumn of 1945 he returned to Essen where he was reunited with his parents and two sisters. The devastation of the city horrified him, but this was soon forgotten as there were more pressing matters to concern him. Before the onslaught of winter the family home had to be repaired, and the garden needed to be prepared to grow vegetables, which would be vital to stave off hunger during the hard cold months ahead.

As Gruppenkommandeur of I./NJG 6, Oberleutnant Spoden shares a joke with the men of his Gruppe. (Spoden)

On 29 April 1945 I./NJG 6 surrendered to the Allies. Here Peter Spoden addresses his Gruppe for the last time. (Spoden)

As a former officer in the German Armed Forces things were made very difficult for him and his options for a post-war career were severely restricted. Peter's application to study at the University of Hanover was refused because of this fact. Undeterred Peter did eventually find a university at which he could study to become a mechanical engineer. As a result of hard work and determination Peter graduated, and was rewarded with a job as a technical advisor to the *Bundesbahn* in Essen.

In 1951 he joined the Essen Aviation Association and resumed glider flying as it was still prohibited in Germany to fly motor-powered aircraft. Two years later, having obtained his provisional pilot's licence, he flew regularly in Holland, Belgium and England. In the autumn of 1954 Peter was accepted for a *Lufthansa* training programme to become an airline pilot, which he successfully completed on 20 July 1955. Just a year later he was able to fly aircraft up to the size and specification of the DC-3, becoming an instructor shortly afterwards, with the qualifications to teach trainee pilots up to this level for the city of Hamburg. By April 1959 Peter had also qualified to fly the larger Constellation and was *Lufthansa's* Training Captain on this aircraft. In 1960 he had become *Lufthansa's* Fleet Commander 'North Atlantic' and received the award of the 'Blue Riband' for his Atlantic crossing between New York to Frankfurt. This journey was completed in an amazing five hours and fifty-three minutes with a little help from the jet stream. During the next ten years he completed maiden flights to Japan (via the North Pole), Central and South America, Africa, Bangkok and Hong Kong. In November 1970 he received his second 'Blue Riband' award for completing another Atlantic crossing, this time between New York and Cologne in only five hours and fifty minutes.

Testimony to the effectiveness of the Allied bombing campaign. (author's collection)

By the time of his retirement in 1981, Peter Spoden had completed 1,406 North Atlantic crossings and had flown an incredible 22,147 hours. This amazing man flies single-engined aircraft to this day and is a member of the Hanseatic Flying Association in Engelsbach, central Germany. He is also a member of the highly respected organisation, *Alte Adler,* (Old Eagles) for former German pilots who fought in either of the world wars, and the *Gemeinschaft der Jagdflieger,* the veteran's association for past and present fighter pilots of the Luftwaffe. Peter Spoden is a charming man who speaks fluent English and lives with his wife, who he has been married to for forty-eight years. He lives in a district of Frankfurt and has four sons. Although he admits flying against the RAF was the most frightening time of his life, this very modest man has nothing but the greatest of respect for the crews of Bomber Command, who like himself were fighting for their country. He pays a final fitting tribute to those men:

> I saw them making loops over Berlin in order to get rid of the searchlights, the RAF crews were very brave men, excellent navigators and perfect pilots.

5

Major Paul Zorner

On examining the history of the German night fighter force, the *Nachtjagd,* and the pilots who established its fearsome reputation, Paul Zorner can be instantly recognised as one of its most outstanding and successful *Nachtjäger* pilots. In only 110 missions he achieved 59 confirmed night victories, and ranks as the ninth highest scoring night fighter *Experte.* In recognition of this achievement he became one of only 882 members of the German Armed Forces to receive the Oak Leaves to his Knight's Cross, and rose to the rank of *Major.*

Paul Zorner was born on 31 March 1920, in Roben, a small village near Leobschütz in Upper Silesia, now in Poland. From a very early age, like thousands of other German children, Paul became very interested in flying. Unfortunately though, due to limited funds, young Paul was unable to take up glider flying as he longed to do. As one of eight children there was considerable financial strain on the Zorner family's resources. Although

Major Paul Zorner, Gruppen-kommandeur of II./ NJG 100. (Zorner)

Paul Zorner, now aged eighty years. After a successful career in the chemical industry he retired in 1981 and now lives in Homburg with his wife, Gerda. (Zorner)

his father was employed as a local primary school teacher, his wages were not sufficient to stretch to this indulgence. This however did not prevent his parents from ensuring that all of their children received a good education.

In the spring of 1938 Paul successfully passed his *Abitur*, equivalent to today's A-levels and then spent the next six months completing his national service, which was compulsory in Germany at that time.

His military training in the Luftwaffe began on 7 November 1938, when he underwent basic recruit training at Oschatz/Sachsen in Eastern Germany. On leaving here in March 1939, Paul went to the Air Warfare School in Berlin-Gatow. Here he received initial training as an officer cadet, and qualified for his A/B Pilot's Licence, permitting him to fly single-engined aircraft. The designations A and B were equivalent to basic and advanced flying training in the RAF.

From November 1939, with the war already underway, Paul underwent further flight training at the *C-Schule* at Alt-Lönnewitz/Sachsen where he qualified for his C class pilot's licence enabling him to fly multi-engined aircraft of all weight categories. With this part of the training completed by the end of February 1940, Paul stayed on at the school as an assistant flight instructor and was promoted to *Leutnant* on 1 April 1940.

From 5 July 1940 to the end of January 1941, having just successfully completed an instructor's course, he attended the *C-Schule* at Zeltweg/Steiermark, Austria, situated to the north of Graz. During these six months, as an instructor at the flying school, he was sent to the Blind Flying School at Neuburg-Donau in Southern Germany for three weeks. On returning from Neuburg-Donau, having obtained the appropriately named licence, Paul returned to Zeltweg where he completed the remainder of his six-month attachment.

At this time Rommel was advancing in North Africa, but he was experiencing problems with being adequately supplied and, in order to remedy this problem, a transport unit was formed and equipped with the Junkers 52 transport aircraft. Pilots, including Paul Zorner, were transferred from training schools all over Germany to this new unit, which was established at Wiener-Neustadt.

Paul was assigned as a transport pilot and flew supply flights in the Mediterranean between Sicily and North Africa. Just two months later he was again transferred, this time to Athens. With an Iraqi uprising against the British, Paul Zorner flew further transport flights between Athens and Aleppo, (now in Syria). These flights brought in supplies to support a Bf110-equipped *Zerstörerstaffel* from *Zerstörergeschwader* 76, which was being used to assist the Iraqis in their fight against the British.

With Germany now fighting a war on numerous fronts, many of its combatants found themselves constantly moved from one theatre to another. Paul was no exception. For the third time in as many months he was transferred, this time to the Ukraine in Southern Russia. The conditions on the Eastern Front were not to Paul's liking, but an opportunity to transfer away from there was not long in coming.

Back in Germany, during the latter part of 1940 and the beginning of 1941, the *Nachtjagd* was slowly being built up as a new wing of the Luftwaffe. With a wide range of flying experience and with a certificate for blind flying, Paul put in a transfer request to join this new operational unit. Paul Zorner's confidence in his own ability was obviously shared by

Between November 1938 and March 1939 Paul Zorner underwent basic military training at Oschatz/Sachsen, situated between Dresden and Leipzig. Here he wears the rank insignia of a Flieger. (Zorner)

Winter 1938/39. In the centre is Paul Zorner's father, a reserve officer in the Wehrmacht. On the left is his close friend, Erhart Kliene (killed flying a He111 in June 1944). (Zorner)

II Gruppe at Oschatz stands on ceremony for the camera. Zorner is second from the right. (Zorner)

Wearing his dress uniform, sometime during the four months of basic military training. (Zorner)

As an Unteroffizier. (Zorner)

The Air Warfare School at Berlin-Gatow where Paul Zorner qualified for his A/B pilot's licence. (Zorner)

With fellow students at the A/B Schule at Berlin-Gatow. From left to right, back row: Greiner, Fiedler, Müller, Felder, Schmied. Front row: Kruig, Schneider, Zorner.

The Arado Ar66. Used by the Luftwaffe as a primary trainer and assigned to most of its A/B Schulen. (Zorner)

One of the aircraft hangars at Berlin-Gatow. (Zorner)

The C-Schule at Alt Lönnewitz. Here, pilots who had already obtained their A/B licence were trained to fly multi-engined aircraft. Paul Zorner qualified for the C Certificate to his pilot's licence in February 1940. (Zorner)

his superiors as his application was quickly accepted. By October 1941 he was posted to the day fighter school at Schleissheim near Munich, where he was given the opportunity to fly the Heinkel 51 and Messerschmitt Bf110.

In January 1942, having completed the first part of the training programme, he and the other successful candidates were transferred to the night fighter school at Manching, near Ingolstadt, in southern Germany. With a desperate shortage of fuel caused by the Russian offensive, the whole training programme lasted nine months despite being scheduled for only four.

What Paul found most surprising was that much of the training took place in daylight with only a few hours dedicated to flying at night. Despite this and the fuel shortage, he enjoyed this period of the training which provided him with a generous amount of home leave. During this time he was promoted to *Oberleutnant,* which became effective as of 1 April 1942. Within a month of this promotion his training as a *Nachtjäger* was complete.

Paul Zorner was posted on 1 July 1942 to his first operational unit, II./NJG2 which was based at Gilze-Rijen in Holland:

> This was where I actually received the necessary training, especially theory for night fighter combat. Although I was regarded as one of the experienced pilots at that time with my 1,200 hours of flying, I still had to fly more than twelve hours in the Junkers 88 in the first six weeks. There was of course an extended tactical introduction held by the most successful pilots of the group. This included such well known men as Prinz zu Sayn Wittgenstein and Heinz Strüning, both holders of the Knight's Cross.

Above left: During a quieter moment in the training, Oberfähnrich Zorner enjoys a cigarette and a hand of cards. (Zorner)

Above: First formal portrait of Leutnant Zorner, commissioned on 1 April 1940. (Zorner)

Left: A steady arm and a keen eye – the hallmarks of an accomplished marksman. (Zorner)

Between March and October 1941 Paul Zorner flew as a transport pilot, operating in North Africa, the Mediterranean and Southern Russia. Stores and supplies are unloaded from a Ju52 transport aircraft in the Ukraine. (Zorner)

Studying hard during the winter of 1941/42, while attending the Day Fighter School at Schleissheim. (Zorner)

Leutnant Zorner proudly displays the ribbon to his recently awarded Iron Cross Second Class. (Zorner)

June 1942, while attached to the Ergänzungsgruppe at Stuttgart-Echterdingen. (Zorner)

Paul Zorner is pictured shortly after his promotion to Oberleutnant on 1 April 1942. (Zorner)

On 1 July 1942 Paul Zorner was posted to II./NJG 2, which was based at Gilze-Rijen in Holland. This train was used to transport the pilots from their accommodation to the airfield. (Zorner)

Paul's baptism of fire as a night fighter took place on 17 August 1942. While flying a Ju88 over Holland, he encountered an RAF Wellington bomber returning from a raid on Berlin. Eager to prove his worth, the whole incident proved a very disappointing start for this young pilot. Having closed the distance between himself and the bomber to about 200m he prematurely opened fire which did nothing more than warn the Wellington's crew of his presence. The bomber immediately carried out a 'split S' manoeuvre and quickly disappeared into the clouds, never to be seen again.

After flying a total of six missions Paul was retrained on the Dornier 217. With his *Gruppe* being split, he found himself transferred to Grove in Jutland. Once there he participated in a further six missions, all of which involved flying the Do217, an aircraft he greatly disliked:

> The Do217 was an aircraft that was very little suited to night fighting. Its maximum rate of climb was only 6m/second, and it was not very manoeuvrable, so that it could be scarcely be used for dogfighting. Its endurance was more than 5 and and a half hours but I didn't like this aircraft.

On 2 December 1942, Paul Zorner was transferred as a *Staffelführer* to the 2nd *Staffel* of NJG3, who were based at Wittmundhafen on the North Sea coast. The *Gruppenkommandeur* there was already an accomplished night fighter, and holder of the Knight's Cross, Egmont Prinz zur Lippe-Weißenfeld.

Paul didn't have long to wait for his first victory, which came on 17 January 1943, during his fourteenth mission. With a dislike of flying the Do217 he continually pressed *Prinz* zur Lippe-Weißenfeld to be able to fly the Bf110 instead. Weißenfeld finally gave into Zorner's request on the understanding that he flew both aircraft operationally in rotation. So, on the night of 17 January, Paul took off from Wittmundhafen in a Bf110, the only member of the *Staffel* to do so.

Flying out over the North Sea he scanned the dark night sky with the aim of intercepting the homeward-bound RAF bombers which had just attacked Berlin. At an altitude of 3,200m he located the silhouette of an aircraft that was identified as a Halifax. After two unsuccessful attacks on the bomber, Paul finally positioned the night fighter behind and slightly below the Halifax, closing to a distance of only 20m before opening fire. The effect of the attack wasn't immediately obvious as the bomber continued to fly a straight and level course. Then, suddenly without any warning the Halifax tipped over and went down vertically into the North Sea. It crashed some 45km north-west of Juist, a small island just off the north coast of Germany. The time was 21.55 hours.

His second aerial victory followed a month later on 11 February, again while flying a Bf110. On this occasion, the unsuspecting bomber was a Lancaster, which plunged into the cold waters of the North Sea approximately 40km north-west of Borkum, another island in the same chain as Juist.

With two confirmed victories to his credit, both achieved flying the Bf110, Paul received a further verbal warning from his *Kommandeur,* concerning his non-operational use of the Do217. Begrudgingly, and against his better judgement, Paul realised that he had no choice other than fly this aircraft on his next combat sortie. This decision would result in him experiencing his most difficult victory. Paul Zorner takes up the story:

On 19 February bombers were approaching Jutland for an attack on Berlin. There were no clouds, the moon was shining brightly and the air was very clear. The bombers followed the same route on their way home. It was late when I was suddenly ordered to scramble, and there were no further reports of enemy aircraft on their way back. Seven minutes after I had taken off I had just reached 1,000m altitude on a heading for the Fighter Control Station on the island of Juist, when the controller there ordered me on to an easterly heading. He directed me to a target that was coming from the east and heading west at an altitude of 2,800m north of the island of Nordeney. I climbed towards him at full power. When I had at last reached 2,700m I saw a small black point coming towards us ahead and to my left at a distance of about 1,500m. When I was at the same height, but on a reciprocal heading, and had in the meanwhile recognised him as a twin-engined aircraft, we began to curve around each other. Obviously the other aircraft had seen us as well. With his binoculars my Funker confirmed that the other machine did in fact have two engines but it wasn't a Wellington. I found myself in a slightly favourable position, but even with full engine power I couldn't get the heavy Do217 into a firing position behind him. We turned doggedly round each other, losing height all the time. After we had been turning around each other for about seventeen minutes and were 1,000m lower, I ordered the air gunner to open the fuel jettison valve of the tank in the fuselage and get rid of the remaining fuel, about 900l. In this way we were able to get behind the enemy machine, which I had in the meanwhile identified as a Boston. But I couldn't get into a firing position. Finally I decided to make one desperate attempt. I put my aircraft into a slight dive, told the flight mechanic to lower the flaps, and pulled the column right back into my stomach. The aircraft reared like a horse that had been spurred, and the Boston came into my sights. I only fired a very short burst from my 20mm cannon, but I didn't see any strikes on the enemy machine. Nevertheless it stood on its nose and went down vertically, disappearing into the sea mist.

It was finished and we breathed in with relief, but for a good fifteen minutes no one spoke a word. Then the flight mechanic pointed to the oil temperature gauge on the starboard engine; the needle was up against the maximum level! It was switched off and we flew back to base at a height of barely 1,000m. Just before we landed we switched it on again. It was a risky business landing the Do217 on one engine but the landing went smoothly. When we had a closer look at the aircraft there was a small round hole in the starboard wing and another underneath in the starboard engine casing. From the latter there was a widening oil smear up to the edge of the wing. During the combat we hadn't realised that we had been fired at, the Dornier had suffered only two hits, but one of them was in a very sensitive position.

In his combat report on the thirty-nine minute long encounter, Paul Zorner could only report a 'probable' as he and his crew had only seen the Boston disappear into the sea mist. However, a short time later a report appeared from an anti-aircraft battery on the island of Nordeney who had witnessed the whole engagement through an optical range finder. The crew of the battery also identified the bomber as a Boston, and had been able to track it until it was 150m from the surface of the sea. It had then disappeared into the mist. As it would have been impossible to recover at this height, from a vertical dive, they could only report its certain destruction. It is interesting to note however, that the only two-engined aircraft dispatched to Wilhelmshaven on this mission were Wellington bombers. Of the

As of 2 December 1942 Paul Zorner was stationed with 2./NJG 3 at Wittmundhafen. He is seen here in the cockpit of his Me110 carrying out pre-flight checks. (Zorner)

At Wittmundhafen with his crew in February 1943. (Zorner)

four such bombers lost, it would seem that Paul Zorner's victim was most likely to have been that piloted by Sgt J. Gauthier of 426 Squadron, based at Dishforth in Yorkshire.

On 16 March 1943, Paul Zorner was transferred to 3./NJG 3, and promoted to *Staffelkapitän*. This *Staffel* was based at Vechta in Northern Germany and, much to his relief, only flew the Bf110. By the time of this transfer he had six victories to his credit.

The spring of 1943 saw the first major US raids made during daylight hours. As the day fighter force on the Western Front was relatively small, part of the night fighter force was used to bolster their numbers. Those night fighter pilots that hadn't already scored more than ten victories were selected to fly against the US bombers:

> In these operations with the Bf110 there was only a slight opportunity for success. A formation of nine to twelve bombers had more than 100 guns, and they usually had to be attacked by only two Bf110s. In these circumstances the only attack that was feasible was from head-on where the defensive fire was least.
>
> For this tactic, however, the Bf110 was completely unsuitable, with a maximum speed of 460km per hour she was at most 40km per hour faster than the USAAF bombers. When we attacked from the front the fighter and the bomber approached each other at a speed of about 900km per hour. If immediately after the attack, the fighters made a tight turn to follow the bomber formation it took about thirty seconds. In this time the bombers were already 3.5km further on. To catch them up and overtake them to make the next head-on attack, therefore, took the fighter about fifteen minutes. The Bf110 had a maximum endurance of two and three-quarter hours, so the pilot could make at most three attacks before he had to break off the operation.

Wearing the Iron Cross First Class, awarded on 12 March 1943. Note that he also wears the Transport Pilot's Clasp in Silver above his left breast pocket. (Zorner)

Paul Zorner himself only flew two such daylight missions. The second of these occurred on 17 April and caused quite a stir at the time:

> I collected several hits in both my wings in the course of my second attack. Both engine radiators were leaking and banners of white smoke were forming behind them, the engines were overheating rapidly and I had to switch them both off. There was no airfield I could reach in a glide, so I would have to make a belly-landing in the open countryside. My Funker and I were not hurt. Now, on the day in question my own aircraft was unserviceable. Therefore the Kommandeur, Prinz zur Lippe-Weißenfeld had let me use his aircraft. He already had thirty-six victories, and the fin of his Bf110 therefore boasted thirty-six kill markings.
>
> My belly-landing took place in open countryside in the vicinity of Cloppenburg but the countryside wasn't completely open. Just about 100m from the spot where the Bf110 was lying on its belly was a sort of command bunker belonging to the Air Observation Corp. In any case, a large number of female Luftwaffe auxiliaries came streaming out of the bunker towards us. We were the focal point of their interest with thirty-six victory markings on our tail unit. Unfortunately we were unable to bask in the warmth of their interest for long, because the women had to go back to their bunker and we were taken back to Vechta by car.
>
> Somehow or other the story got around the young ladies that the pilot of the Bf110 and its thirty-six victory markings on its tail belonged together. When, about a year and a half later, I was awarded the Eichenlaub after fifty-eight victories, I received a poem from the crew of the bunker signed by a lot of the young ladies in which they recalled my belly-landing in April 1943. And, of the involuntary exaggeration of the thirty-six victory markings which had now been overtaken by reality. Only then did I realise what a lasting impression I must have made on at least some of the girls because they could still remember my name a year and a half later.

With no successes on either of the daylight missions, Paul returned to flying at night, but it was to be another ten weeks before his next success. However, from 29 June to 9 July, while based at St Trond, he accounted for three RAF bombers, two Wellingtons and a Lancaster respectively. Flight Sergeant Kleinschmidt piloted the first of these, a Wellington from 300 Squadron, with an all Polish crew. The aircraft was badly damaged during the encounter, so much so that it crashed at 02.22 hours, killing all on board. All three bombers were shot down over the Belgian mainland, each having just attacked the city of Cologne on their respective missions.

On 25 July 1943 Paul Zorner scored his tenth victory during a raid on Essen. Having been scrambled from Wittmundhafen at 23.26 hours, Paul was directed by his fighter control officer, *Oberleutnant* Janssen; who had already assisted him in six of his previous kills, to head on a westerly course. It was being reported that the bomber formations were heading east, which in turn led the controllers on the ground to believe that Hamburg would again be Bomber Command's target. However, on reaching the Friesian Island of Borkum, the bomber stream changed its course and headed south towards Essen. Paul recalls this night vividly:

> The sky was clear and there was good visibility above 1,000m, but unusually bright Northern Lights. My altitude was 6,600m and the altitude of the target was 6,000m. The

thought of having to approach the bomber out of the bright Northern Lights was very worrying. So I stayed at 6,600m until I was approximately 500m behind him. I throttled back both engines, lowered the landing gear and went down to 5,600m in a steep glide. The bomber appeared 300m ahead of me to the left against the dark background of the earth and rose against the brighter southern sky. I moved sideways under the bomber, until I was directly beneath it, I raised my aircraft and let him fly through my line of fire along its starboard wing. It started to burn immediately and the aircraft went down in a steep right spiral.

The Halifax, his tenth victory, crashed to the north-east of Groningen in Holland, its impact resulted in a large firework display as the green, red and white flares it was carrying burned brightly. Two minutes after the engagement with what had probably been a Pathfinder[9] aircraft, used to mark the intended target with flares, the starboard engine of his Bf110 started to burn and then stalled.

Having successfully extinguished the fire, Paul Zorner found that he couldn't set the pitch of the propeller to its glide setting. It soon became apparent to him that the aircraft wouldn't reach Wittmundhafen. With its port engine unable to cope with the extra workload the aircraft began to steadily lose height. Ordering his *Funker* to bale out, Paul jettisoned the canopy and waited for Heinrich Wilke to clear the aircraft. Watching Wilke tumble out of the cockpit and into the darkness, Paul Zorner frantically tried to exit the aircraft himself. But, in his own desperate attempt to get out, and with the aircraft diving vertically, his parachute got caught up on one of the support beams that strengthened the cockpit in the event of it overturning. Climbing back into the pilot's seat he was able to lower the flaps that he had previously forgotten to set, and bring the aircraft into a gentle glide. With the Bf110's airspeed now reduced he was able to bale out without further incident. Landing in a ditch at the side of a road, Paul was soon picked up by a passing motorcyclist and taken back to Wittmundhafen. His *Funker*, Wilke, had also managed to parachute to safety, and having spent the night in a water-logged meadow, had made his way to the nearest town. This was the only occasion during his entire combat career, and 272 missions, that Paul was forced to take to his parachute.

During the raid on Peenemünde on the night of 17/18 August 1943, Paul Zorner, now the *Staffelkäpitan* of 8/.NJG 3, achieved his eleventh and twelfth victories. Both machines were Lancasters and were shot down within ten minutes of each other.

Unfavourable weather conditions had delayed the take-off of *Oberleutnant* Zorner's *Staffel* from Kastrup in Denmark. This proved to be very fortuitous for them, as an earlier diversionary raid by Mosquitos, on Berlin, had already drawn many of those airborne German night fighter units away from Bomber Command's target.

When weather conditions had suitably improved, Paul Zorner was given the order to take-off, and he and his *Staffel* headed south. On clearing the storms he found the night sky was clear and illuminated by bright moonlight. While flying over the Baltic Sea en route to intercept the bomber stream, his *Funker* made radar contact with a target.

---

[9] This Halifax was probably LQ-M from 405 Squadron (PPF) flown by F/O M.E. Tomczak RCAF. All on board were killed except for F/O A.J. Sochowski who subsequently became a PoW.

Paul Zorner with his fiancée, Gerda, in May 1943. (Zorner)

With his bride, Gerda, following their marriage in Kaiserlautern on 11 October 1943. (Zorner)

The award certificate for the Ehrenpokal dated 31 August 1943, by which time Zorner had shot down a total of thirteen bombers. (Zorner)

Ich verleihe
dem

Oberleutnant
Paul Zorner
in Anerkennung seiner hervorragenden Tapferkeit
und der vorbildlichen Führung seiner
Nachtjagdfliegerstaffel

den Ehrenpokal
für besondere Leistung
im Luftkrieg

Hauptquartier des Ob. d. L., den 31. August 1943

Der Reichsminister der Luftfahrt
und Oberbefehlshaber der Luftwaffe

Göring

Reichsmarschall

Die erfolgte Verleihung wird beglaubigt
Der Chef des Luftwaffenpersonalamts

At an altitude of 4,400m Paul visually located a Lancaster and opened fire using the Bf110's forward-facing cannon. The badly damaged bomber fell from the sky but not before several parachutes were seen leaving the stricken aircraft. Minutes later, at 01.53 hours, it crashed into the icy waters of the Baltic Sea off the south-east coast of the island of Falster. After about ten minutes, while flying towards the research establishment at Peenemünde, Paul happened to glance down below his aircraft, only to see the silhouette of another Lancaster bomber pass directly beneath him. Instinctively he pressed home an immediate attack making effective use of the Messerschmitt's nose-mounted 20mm cannon. On being fired, the shells from the cannon must have struck either the bomber's fuel tanks or its bomb load, because having fired only one short burst, the Lancaster exploded in mid-air. What remained of this once magnificent aircraft crashed south of the Baltic Island of Rügen at 02.03 hours.

During a raid on Berlin, a further Lancaster fell to the guns of Paul Zorner on the night of the 22/23 November 1943. Having dropped its deadly cargo, the bomber was intercepted by Zorner over the German capital and shot down from an altitude of 6,500m. It was one of eleven Lancasters shot down from a total of twenty-six aircraft lost that night.

As November drew to a close, Zorner's Bf110G was fitted with a new and advanced type of radar known as *FuG 220 Lichtenstein SN-2*. The most important improvement of this particular model was that it was unaffected by the use of 'Window', or *Düppel* as it was known to the Germans. These strips of aluminium had been used to great effect by the RAF to jam and confuse German radar, and were first used on 24/25 July 1943, against the city of Hamburg – with devastating results. It was only to be a few short days before he would put this newly-acquired technology to good use.

At 18.44 hours on 2 December 1943, Paul Zorner's aircraft lumbered its way across the airfield at Luneberg and slowly rose into the air. With information received via his ground controller he was able to steer a course with a view of intercepting the incoming bomber stream. Half-an-hour later he spotted the silhouette of a Lancaster bomber on its way to bomb the German capital. Closing within 70m of the rear of the bomber, Paul fired one burst between its engines on the port wing. It immediately began to burn and within four minutes the Lancaster had crashed near Diepholz, approximately 90km to the west of Hanover.

Almost an hour after this action he made his way back into the airspace over Berlin. On looking out of the cockpit he could see that the capital was already on fire. Explosions from detonating bombs and the flak defences were clearly visible. Billowing smoke, brightly coloured flares from the target indicators, mixed with the glow of fires that were ravaging homes, factories and shops below could only have given him a small insight into the suffering and misery that the residents of the capital were now enduring.

From his starboard side Paul saw a Lancaster cross in front of him, apparently on its way from the target area, having already completed its bomb run. Manoeuvring in behind the British machine he attacked immediately. With a single burst he raked the Lancaster's port wing with cannon fire, setting it ablaze. This was enough to seal the bomber's fate and secure his fifteenth victory, which crashed to the south-west of Berlin.

By the time of his next mission on the night of 23/24 December, again over the darkened skies of Berlin, he had taken his tally of victories to sixteen by shooting down a Halifax to the north-west of Frankfurt three nights prior to this.

On being scrambled at 01.39 hours from Lüneburg airfield, Paul Zorner and his crew set a course to intercept the incoming bombers believed to be en route to raid Frankfurt for the second time in four days. It was to mark the beginning of a mission that would see this crew airborne for more than $3\frac{1}{2}$ hours, and having to fly in excess of 700 miles.

The bomber stream was plotted as it travelled across the German border from the south-east, but it soon became apparent though that the target wasn't Frankfurt as it continued its way eastward, deeper and deeper into the heartland of Germany. A little over an hour after take-off, Paul was able to identify a four-engined bomber as a Lancaster flying to the north of Frankfurt at a height of 5,500m. Matching the bomber's speed and height, he closed to within 100m of the rear of his intended victim and fired a long burst into its starboard wing. Drawing back into the darkness, he watched the Lancaster as its pilot put the aircraft into a dive in a desperate attempt to put out the fire that was now taking hold. When this failed, several parachutes were seen to blossom and then disappear into the dark night sky. The bomber then dived sharply crashing to the north of Frankfurt close to the town of Giessen. The entire encounter had lasted sixteen minutes, and during this time contact with the main force of the bomber stream had been lost.

With insufficient fuel to follow the bombers all the way to Berlin, Paul landed at Gütersloh and refuelled. As luck would have it, having bombed Berlin, the bomber stream headed west taking them close to Gütersloh. Within thirty-five minutes of having taken off for the second time that night, his *Funker*, Wilke, had a contact with the *SN-2,* and minutes later another Lancaster was spiralling down through the clouds.

His third and final victim that night was dispatched at 05.50 hours. The pilot of the Lancaster made things difficult for the German night fighter, who, on this occasion, had to make two attacks before the bomber finally succumbed to a sustained and withering burst of cannon fire. The starboard wing exploded and the remains of the bomber crashed at Cloppenburg, a tangled mess of twisted metal marking the final resting place of his nineteenth victory.

A further opportunity to score a multiple victory presented itself on the night of 5/6 January 1944, when Bomber Command attacked Stettin, the first major raid on this city since September 1941. Some 348 Lancasters and Halifaxes were dispatched to the target, which resulted in the destruction of over 500 homes and killed 244 people. Paul Zorner vividly remembers the mission as his wife, whom he had married in October 1943, was staying with him at Lüneburg over the Christmas and New Year period. This mission in particular highlighted the problems experienced night after night by the crews of the *Nachtjagd*. Not only those problems created by Bomber Command, but also those created by poor weather conditions and long-drawn-out flights across Germany:

> The weather that night was miserable. The cloud base was between 400 and 600m, visibility was not bad, but it was raining cats and dogs without interruption. Very late in the night heavy raids were reported to the north of Heligoland and heading east. We took off at 01.50 hours and we headed north-west past the Hamburg restricted area so that we wouldn't run into the fire of the heavy flak defences stationed there. At an altitude of almost 6,000m we broke through the ten-tenths cloud cover into a clear, starlit and, if I remember correctly, moonless sky.

Listening to the commentary from the ground controllers, it appeared to Paul Zorner that he had arrived rather late, so he immediately altered course and headed to the north-east. It was to be almost two hours before his *Funker* reported an *SN-2* contact.

> He [Wilke] talked me in towards it and soon I could make out directly ahead of me the four light blue exhaust flames of the engines. It was a bomber on its way to the target. Because of the prevailing weather conditions the only possible way to attack was from directly astern. I had to keep my nerve, get in close and aim accurately. I fired between his two starboard engines from a range of 100m. The wing began to burn fiercely at once and the aircraft vanished into the clouds in a wide spiral.

His attention was now drawn into the distance where the flashes from the flak defences and explosions from detonating bombs could clearly be seen. Checking his bearings it didn't take him long to figure out that Berlin was also being attacked. Bomber Command had in fact sent thirteen Mosquitos to the German capital as a diversionary tactic to keep the German night fighter force away from the main bomber stream. Paul Zorner continues the story:

> So we flew on towards Berlin, above which the clouds, illuminated by the fires, were beginning to glow red. Then my Funker had another radar contact. Ahead, but a little lower, I saw ahead of me against the light-coloured clouds another four-engined machine. I attacked from astern again, but I had been seen. The bomber began to take violent

evasive action and the rear gunner opened fire on us. As a result I was led into opening fire too early. Neither of us scored any hits. The same thing happened twice, three times and then four times. Now I approached the bomber from the right and above so that I could keep him in sight against the lighter clouds. From my experience I knew that our aircraft, with its camouflage paint work, was the hardest to see in this position. This time I was successful. I was able to approach to within about 100m of the bomber without being seen. A burst of fire between the two starboard engines resulted in an explosion in the wing, and in the aircraft crashing. It hit the ground at 03.51 hrs.

Having been in the air for two-and-a-half hours already, and with no more bomber contacts, Paul decided to fly back to Lüneburg airfield. With the aid of radio bearings from the airfield he was able to set a return course. It soon became apparent, however, that during the heat of battle he had drifted somewhat off his intended course. The Zorner crew was now further from Lüneburg than they had realised, and the blanket of cloud below was now becoming thicker and thicker. To make things worse the aircraft was low on fuel and it was thought that there wasn't enough left to reach Lüneburg. Therefore a substitute airfield would have to be found.

When the fuel warning light came on to indicate only five minutes' worth of fuel left, Paul was resigned to the fact that he and his crew would have to bale out. Miraculously, at the eleventh hour, lights from a small airfield came on immediately below them. Lowering the undercarriage right away he landed the aircraft without incident and taxied off the runway. Before the ground crew were able to signal to the pilot to switch off the engines they cut out of their own accord – the petrol tanks had run dry. This was not an uncommon problem. Many less fortunate crews were either forced to take to their parachutes or crash-land, often with dire results.

With confirmation of his twenty-first and twenty-second victories, further multiple kills followed. His most notable was achieved on the night of 20 January 1944, notable because Paul would achieve his first night-time victories using *Schräge Musik*. His aircraft, a Bf110G, had been fitted with this new weapon system since the beginning of December 1943. However, the twin cannons had to be installed by the crews themselves and were supplied in the form of a conversion kit. Fitting the cannons was itself not a problem but adjusting and synchronising the sights were. With the new armament fitted to the aircraft Paul attempted to use it on 20 December 1943, and on 6 January 1944. But each time he squeezed the triggers he saw the shells explode harmlessly above the bomber indicating that the target had been missed. Understandably frustrated by this he met with *Hauptmann* Rudolf Schoenert, the man universally recognised as the innovator of *Schräge Musik* and at that time the *Kommandeur* of NJGr.10. Schoenert's response was to send Paul Zorner, based at Lüneburg, a master armourer who showed the crews how to synchronise the new weapon system. This was achieved by looking up through the reflector sight as the trigger was squeezed, and watching the puff of smoke caused by the detonating ammunition. By adjusting the sights manually the aim was to converge the puff of smoke at a specific point along the sights thus synchronising them at the required range. His first opportunity to test the accuracy of *Schräge Musik* wasn't long in coming.

On the night in question, 20 January 1944, Bomber Command dispatched 769 aircraft to the German capital. Having abandoned the usual direct route to the target, the bomber stream flew in over the North Sea well to the north of the Dutch mainland. Paul Zorner recalls the operation:

> At that time I was taking part in a course for prospective Group Commanders at Werneuchen. The bombers' route to the target was if I remember correctly, over the North Sea followed by a southerly heading towards Berlin. It was a clear night, visibility was good and there was scattered cloud. We took off from Werneuchen at 18.29 hours, flew towards the bombers and climbed to 6,000m. It was after almost an hour that my Funker picked up the first contacts on his radar, but they were much higher. So we climbed, and at about 19.20 hours we had a target at 6,800m. At 19.26 hours I caught sight of a bomber in front of me heading south, and I identified it as a Halifax. Below me there was a large gap in the cloud – an ideal position for an attack from below with Schräge Musik. I moved below the bomber and aimed at the two port engines. A short burst, and the wing began to burn. I moved to one side and waited to see what would happen. The fire in the bomber grew, and eventually we saw several parachutes open below the aircraft. The bomber went into a vertical dive and finally crashed at 19.31 hours well to the north of Berlin.
>
> In Berlin we could see bombs exploding, so we headed there. Shortly afterwards, when we were flying over a bright layer of cloud, I saw, without getting a radar contact, a bomber some distance beneath us against this cloud layer. In this situation there could be no question of an attack from below. I therefore attacked from astern, and the bomber began to take evasive action. I had to make four attacks before he finally began to burn. Quite remarkably there was no return fire from the bomber, despite my having made four attacks. At least, I didn't see any defensive fire, and there was no damage to my machine. The burning aircraft went down in a broad spiral. We didn't see any parachutes. It hit the ground at 19.45 hours, also far to the north of the target. It is probable that in my first attack I hit the fuselage of the aircraft and put the rear gunner out of action straight away. We didn't find any more targets, and we landed back at Werneuchen at 21.05 hours.

Over the next four weeks *Oberleutnant* Zorner shot down a further six Lancasters, increasing his personal score to thirty. On the night of 15 February he shot down a Lancaster to the west of the island of Rügen and a second to the north-west of Berlin. 4 more were to follow in the early hours of 20 February during Bomber Command's raid on Leipzig, when 79 aircraft were lost from a total of 823. At this stage of the war, it was the highest loss of aircraft inflicted on Bomber Command by the German defences.

The most successful night of Paul Zorner's career took place just four days later on the night of 24/25 February 1944. The target was a new one for Bomber Command, the ball-bearing factories at Schweinfurt in central Germany, which had been bombed the previous day by the Americans. For this raid Air Marshal Harris decided to split his bomber force in two, each wave being separated by an interval of two hours.

With confused and contradictory reports of numerous bombers heading towards the *Reich*, it was not clear to Paul Zorner what the intended target was to be, and he therefore expected several nuisance raids during the course of the evening. He finally took off from Lüneburg at 20.09 hours when it became apparent that a strong force was advancing over Belgium and Northern France towards Southern Germany. He vividly recalls the encounter:

The air commentary could be heard clearly, and my Funker reported continuously on the course and location of the head of the bomber stream. From the air commentary, in which no hint was given of the target, we deduced that the target would be a long way south. We flew along to the east of the Ruhr at 5,500m and finally turned directly south. It was a dark night, and as far as I remember there were only a few clouds in the sky, and the visibility was relatively good. The bomber stream seemed to change its southerly course to an easterly one and we began to hope we hadn't taken off in vain. Finally we saw the first burning aircraft going down ahead of us. We had been in the air for two hours when my Funker, Heinrich Wilke, had his first contact on the SN-2, a target crossing right to left in front of us. He lost it, but it made us change course further to the east. A few minutes later, when we were in the area south west of Stuttgart, Wilke picked up another contact and directed me towards it. At 22.12 hours I saw, left of me and a little higher, a four-engined bomber. I went down a little lower and took my aircraft astern and below the bomber, a Lancaster. I intended to attack with my Schräge Musik. With my first attack I saw the explosive shells above me, but with no effect on the bomber. So I decided to attack again, this time with 'Spray Fire' – that is, I wouldn't fire one exact burst but fly my aircraft in such a way that a long burst of fire would be located in and around the bomber in a sort of funnel shape. The result came about unexpectedly quickly. The bomber began to burn in both wings, and we were able to move off to one side and watch. The bomber went into a flat turn to the left, then into a steeper dive, finally going down vertically south-west of Stuttgart. There was a fierce fire and a number of explosions. The bomber had been on its way to the target, so it still had its bombs and a lot of fuel on board.

Meanwhile my Funker had picked up a new target on the SN-2. At 22.20 hours I picked up at the same height and just ahead of me the silhouette of a four-engined aircraft. I found myself so close behind the bomber that I only had to throttle back and ease my aircraft to the starboard to have his port wing in my sights. A short burst from about 80m between the engines, and his left wing began to burn fiercely. He too went down in a left-hand spiral and the impact point was lit up bright red by the fireball.

Only three minutes later I saw four small exhaust flames in front of me. I was right behind the aircraft, and I could feel the turbulence of his airscrews. I went a little lower, positioned myself a small distance to the right and pulled in towards him. These were the tensest seconds of any attack. Every time one has to keep one's nerve, go in still closer and risk the other one firing first and accurately, so that one was shot down. I always tried to fire from as close as possible between the first and second engines on either side. I hit him in the starboard wing from about 80m astern. There was only a weak fire, therefore I fired into the same wing a second time, and a big flame erupted. To my surprise the aircraft went into a steep dive and crashed to the ground at 22.30 hours.

Having been airborne for two-and-a-half hours, Paul Zorner landed at Echterdingen situated to the south of Stuttgart, where he was able to refuel and re-arm. Walking into the operations room he learnt that Schweinfurt had been attacked, but that the general air situation was still very confused. The bomber stream was tracked flying west on its homeward journey, but there was also a new incoming flight being tracked flying over Belgium and Luxembourg. Within half an hour of landing, his aircraft was again ready for take-off. Believing that a further attack was imminent he took off at 23.50 hours, and headed directly for the incoming bomber stream. Half an hour later while flying at an altitude of 6,000m, radar contact was made with a target which was flying towards him but at a higher altitude. After climbing to 6,700m he saw ahead of him, and off to the right, a lone bomber:

> This time I attacked from the same height, and in doing so I had an uneasy feeling. I therefore opened fire from about 120m and aimed at the rear turret, but I didn't see any hits. The bomber began to take evasive action, but there was no return fire. I quickly caught up with him a little, and hit him with another burst in the right wing from about 120m. In a fraction of a second he burst fiercely into flames. He went down vertically and crashed at 00.35 hours north-west of Stuttgart.

Listening in to the running commentary from the ground controller, Paul Zorner headed for Schweinfurt, which also appeared to be the target for the second wave of bombers. He set a course on a zigzag heading in an attempt to catch up with the end of the bomber stream:

> At 00.43 hours my Funker reported a contact to me below, but in the direction we were flying. I throttled my engine right back and did a tight 360° turn. When I was at 5,500m I was once more sitting behind an aircraft. My Funker talked me in and I recognised a Lancaster. As there was no cloud beneath us I decided to attack with Schräge Musik. The first burst of fire showed no result. Seemingly my gunsight still wasn't properly adjusted. In the bomber it seemed certain that they hadn't seen us because it calmly flew straight on. I flew about 100m beneath him, pulled my aircraft up a little, fired, and let the wing of the bomber pass through my sight. The wing began to burn with a steady flame. I moved over to the right a short distance away at the same height, so that the bomber crew couldn't see us through the flames, and I watched. The bomber flew on, gliding calmly; the fire in the aircraft didn't go out, but it didn't grow any stronger either. At last we saw some parachutes, and only then did the bomber begin to dive. It came down to the north of Stuttgart.

After flying for another hour, and having had no further contacts, the Zorner crew landed at Langendiebach to the north-east of Hanau. As the aircraft touched down, their most successful mission came to a close.

With five victories that night his total now stood at thirty-five and recognition for his achievements soon followed. He was promoted to *Hauptmann* on 1 March 1944, and almost three weeks later on 20 March he received the German Cross in Gold.

On 22 March, over 800 aircraft were dispatched to attack Frankfurt. During this raid two further Lancasters fell to the upward-firing guns of Paul Zorner. Both aircraft were shot down in single attacks; cannon shells tore through each of their starboard wings and ignited the fuel tanks contained within. The first, which dived vertically as a result of the attack, crashed to the north of the target. The second followed thirty minutes later, crashing to the south-west of Frankfurt from an altitude of 5,800m. Although the German defences accounted for thirty-three aircraft that night, they were unable to prevent a large amount of damage being caused to the city. Many of Frankfurt's historic buildings were destroyed. It is reported that about half of the city's population were without water, electricity and gas. Almost 1,000 people were killed and a further 120,000 made homeless.

His thirty-eighth victory came on the night of 24 March and proved to be one of his most difficult. The target was Berlin. It proved to be a successful night for the German defenders with a total of seventy-two bombers destroyed, it is reported that fifty of these were shot down by flak while the remaining losses were inflicted by the *Nachtjagd*.

While flying at 6,700m, Zorner's *Funker*, Heinrich Wilke, reported a contact on the *SN-2* at 22.52 hours. Two minutes later Paul made visual contact with the ominous silhouette of a Lancaster bomber. Very carefully he positioned himself underneath the bomber and fired a burst into the port wing. Nothing happened. Looking up into the reflector sight he repositioned his aircraft and fired two more bursts, both of which missed. He watched incredulously as the 20mm shells exploded harmlessly behind and above the Lancaster. By now the tension in his aircraft was mounting – surely somebody within the bomber must have seen them by now. But again nothing happened, and the bomber flew on unperturbed. Having come to the conclusion that his *Schräge Musik* was not properly aligned Paul throttled back. He pulled in behind the Lancaster and opened fire at a distance of 100m using his forward-firing cannons. After two further prolonged bursts into the port wing it began to burn fiercely, and seconds later it began to plummet towards the ground. Just four minutes later it crashed and exploded in a huge fireball.

Paul Zorner increased his personal tally to forty-one on 26 March. He accounted for one third of Bomber Command's losses that night by shooting down three Lancasters which had been dispatched to raid Essen.

Four days later he was awarded the Night Fighter Clasp in Gold, followed on 5 April with a transfer to *Nachtjagdgeschwader* 5, as the *Gruppenkommandeur* of the third *Gruppe*, stationed at Mainz-Finthen near Frankfurt.

His forty-second victory occurred in the early hours of 21 April 1944, and was one that only a select few night fighters ever achieved; the destruction of an RAF Mosquito. Paul Zorner recalls this rare encounter and his subsequent victory:

> In general the Mosquito, because of its high speed, was thought to be invulnerable to attack. And as a British intruder there was a danger to our Night Fighters at take-off and landing at their operational bases, she was greatly feared! Very few of this type of aircraft had been shot down. My success could be attributed to pure chance.
>
> If I remember correctly the RAF flew in over the north of Holland and later turned south-west to attack Cologne. That night the Nachtjagd High Command estimated that there would be an attack on north Germany, so that we at Mainz were not expected to be in action. We were not scrambled until the bombs began to fall on Cologne. My own take-off was delayed for technical reasons. As a result I didn't get airborne until very late,

01.39 hours, and the attack was already under way. Perhaps I still had time to get a straggler. Indeed my Funker got a contact on a single target at about 02.42 hours. It seemed to be heading steadily north-west. My Funker talked me in and we stayed in a layer of cloud, which was certainly not more than 200m thick. At 02.50 hours I saw a shadow in front of me. I closed in further and from the rear I identified a twin-engined aircraft, which seemed to be a Ju88 and was on a westerly heading. A Ju88 could only be one of our Night Fighters. But for him the war was over for tonight. Where was he going on a westerly heading near Brussels? So I went in closer and when the range was about 50m I saw that it wasn't a Ju88 and that his port airscrew was not turning. He was flying on one engine. It could only be an aircraft from the other side, whose pilot was trying to get home on one engine. Quite obviously he didn't suspect anything, because he was flying quite calmly on his way. So I went even closer, aimed at the good engine and fired, He went down immediately. The aircraft, which was out of necessity trimmed to compensate for the lack of power on the left, tipped over his starboard wing and went into a dive and disappeared into the haze. We circled in the area for a little while, and after about four minutes we saw below us something flash and then a fire. There was a report the next morning of the destruction of a Mosquito in the area to the south-east of Antwerp.

Two Mosquitos were reported lost that night, both of which were on Serrate patrols in support of the raid on Cologne. The first of these, Mosquito, HJ644, of No. 239 Squadron, crashed between Arnhem and Amsterdam, killing the pilot, S/Ldr Kinchin and his navigator, F/Lt Sellors.

The second Mosquito, DD616, was from No. 169 Squadron, operating out of Little Snoring, Norfolk. The aircraft, crewed by F/Lt Morgan and F/Sgt Bentley is the machine believed to have been shot down by Paul Zorner south-east of Antwerp. Both the pilot and navigator escaped injury when the aircraft crashed in Belgium.

In the early hours of 23 April Paul shot down an unidentified four-engined bomber to the south-west of Aachen. Closing to a range of just 80m he raked the bomber's port wing from astern with cannon fire. The machine simply exploded.

Five days later on 28 April, Bomber Command sent a force of 322 Lancasters to destroy armament factories at Friedrichshafen as it manufactured engines and gearboxes for tanks. Diversionary attacks were made which were successful in causing confusion throughout the ground stations that controlled the German night fighters. Although no Bomber Command aircraft were lost on their inward-bound journey, the night fighter force was able to reorganise themselves and caught the bomber force while they were over the target. 18 of the Lancasters were shot down, 3 of them by Paul Zorner in a little over an hour, taking his tally to 46.

Almost four months earlier, Paul Zorner had achieved his twenty-fifth victory; this in the past had usually been enough to secure the award of the Knight's Cross. Now, on 9 June 1944, he finally received the decoration from the hands of General Schmid, the commander of *XII. Fliegerkorps*. This was in recognition of his forty-eighth kill, accomplished after shooting down two more Lancasters on 1 and 3 June respectively. Paul Zorner vividly recalls his feelings as he accepted this prestigious award:

On 9 June 1944, after having achieved his forty-eighth victory, Paul Zorner was awarded the Knight's Cross. Twenty-five victories had usually been enough to secure the award but, as the war progressed, the number of 'kills' required to win this prestigious medal rose steadily. (Zorner)

Above everything else, the development of the war led me to have mixed feelings. In October 1941 I volunteered for the Nachtjagd because I wanted to protect my homeland from air attacks. In the summer of 1944 the German cities were already extensively destroyed. As I was awarded the Ritterkreuz we were deployed in a defensive role against bombing attacks in the area north of Paris, as preparation for the Allied invasion. So I was no longer defending my homeland!

Two days after the award ceremony, on 11 June, 432 bombers comprising of Lancasters, Halifaxes and 19 Mosquitoes, were tasked to bomb railway targets at Acheres, Dreux, Orleans and Versailles in support of the recent Normandy invasion.

Once the bomber stream had been detected by ground radar, Paul Zorner's *Gruppe* were scrambled to intercept this force from their new airfield at Laon-Athies. Having got airborne without incident, aircraft of III./NJG5 successfully located part of the bomber stream to the south-west of Dreux.

Heinrich Wilke quickly made a contact on his radar set and guided Paul Zorner towards a contact that turned out to be a lone Halifax. Manoeuvring carefully and positioning himself directly behind the bomber, Paul closed the distance to just 70m before opening fire. Accurate cannon fire tore through the Halifax, which tipped over and went down vertically. To his utter amazement those rounds that missed this Halifax struck a second Halifax 300m away which he hadn't previously been aware of. This second machine banked slowly over on its port wing and went down in a left-hand spin. Minutes later, through the almost impenetrable darkness, Paul identified the ghostly silhouette of a third Halifax which he attacked this time using his *Schräge Musik*. Looking up into the reflector sight he squeezed the trigger and watched the cannon shells dance across both wings as they exploded on impact. Pulling back into the relative safety of the dark, Paul watched the damaged aircraft spiral away towards the ground. Within eight minutes, three Halifax bombers lay burning to the south-west of Dreux. According to official records only three Halifaxes were shot down that night – *Hauptmann* Zorner had accounted for them all.

A little over thirty minutes later, having flown a course to Chartres after witnessing the detonations of bombs and their subsequent fires, Heinrich Wilke made another contact with an RAF bomber flying at an altitude of 2,400m. As there was no cloud and the ground was dark, Paul pushed the control column forward, and very slightly increased speed until he was 150m directly below his target. With the dark backdrop of the ground he had very little chance of being seen by the Lancaster's ever vigilant machine-gunners. The fire from his *Schräge Musik* tore through the void separating the two aircraft and into the bomber's starboard wing starting a large fire. The stricken machine went into a glide which quickly became a steep dive, it crashed two minutes later several kilometres to the north of Chartres. With its final resting place marked on the map, Paul Zorner decided to return to Laon-Athies, having secured his forty-ninth to fifty-second victories.

Two days later on 13 June 1944, the Germans launched the first of their 'Retaliation' weapons, the V-1. The first of these exploded near Gravesend and within a fortnight around 2,000 further 'Flying Bombs' had been launched at southern England. To counter this new threat, beginning on the night of the 16/17 June, the RAF began bombing the launch sites situated on the *Pas de Calais*.

Whiling away the time before the next mission.

(Zorner)

One such raid took place on 24/25 June, with Bomber Command sending a force of 739 aircraft, consisting of 535 Lancasters, 165 Halifaxes, and 39 Mosquitos. It was reported to have been a clear moonlit night over the V-1 sites; these conditions not only made it ideal for the bombers on their bomb runs, but also for the German night fighters defending the area.

Paul made his first contact with the incoming bomber stream at 00.30 hours, unable to identify the make of the machine, he positioned himself 100m behind it. He slowly raised the nose of the Bf110 until the starboard wing of the target filled his gun sights. Gripping the control column firmly he squeezed the triggers which fired the forward facing cannon and machine-guns. Under such a sustained hail of gunfire the result was inevitible. The bomber went down in a gentle glide out of which it never recovered, finally crashing to the east of Boulogne. A second success that night; and his fifty-fourth victory, was an unidentified four-engined bomber. This time, carefully positioning himself 200m underneath the RAF machine, and using *Schräge Musik*, he riddled its starboard wing with cannon fire. The doomed bomber carried on its straight and level course for a short time before it went down steeply in an almost vertical dive. It exploded in the air with a terrific force at 00.50 hours, resulting in a huge fireball. The remains crashed north-west of Etaples close to the Channel coast.

Further victories followed, a Lancaster was shot down on 1 July 1944, for his fifty-fifth victory, and three more were added on 24/25 July when Stuttgart was attacked. This was the first of three raids on the city over a five-day period, during which time much of the centre of Stuttgart was destroyed.

On 17 September 1944 in recognition of his achievements, *Hauptmann* Paul Zorner became the 588th recipient of the Oak Leaves to the Knight's Cross. But with the war going badly for Germany at this time there was the inevitable delay in receiving the decoration just as there had been with the Knight's Cross. He describes his frustration:

> With the award of the *Eichenlaub* it took just as long. I shot down my fiftieth to fifty-first victories on 11 June but it was three months later on the 17 September when I was awarded them. This time it took even longer until I was actually presented with the medal which happened on 2 December 1944, and was personally awarded by Göring at the Air Ministry in Berlin.

In less than a month Paul was transferred from III./NJG 5, and made *Kommandeur* of II./NJG 100. This was an independent *Gruppe*, which was directly subordinate to the 7th *Jagddivision* and stationed at Novy-Dvor, on the Austria/Czechoslovakia border. The *Gruppe* was equipped with fifty-three of the latest models of the Junkers 88, and a total of 630 personnel. From February 1945, the *Gruppe* was transferred to Wien/Seyring situated to the north-east of Vienna.

Further jubilation came the way of the Zorner crew when *Feldwebel* Heinrich Wilke, the *Funker* for all Paul's fifty-eight victories, was finally given recognition for his outstanding bravery, with the awarding of the Knight's Cross on 25 November, one of only a handful of *Funkers* to be so decorated.

Paul Zorner, now a *Major*, achieved his fifty-ninth and final victory in January 1945 when the US Airforce attacked Graz. Incoming enemy aircraft were reported approaching

```
Datum:                    194     Datum:                    194
um:                  Uhr         um:                  Uhr
von:                              an:
durch:                           durch:
                                 Rolle:

Vermerke:

Fernschreiben

+ - FRR  LBRL   4071   19/9  1515 =

AN HERRN  HAUPTMANN PAUL    ZORNER, KOMMANDEUR =
ROEM 3./ N. J. G.  5  LUEBECK - BLANKENSEE =
IN DANKBARER  WUERDIGUNG IHRES HELDENHAFTEN EINSATZES  IM
KAMPF  FUER DIE ZUKUNFT   UNSERES  VOLKES VERLEIHE ICH IHNEN
ALS   588. SOLDATEN DER  DEUTSCHEN WEHRMACHT DAS
- EICHENLAUB -- ZUM RITTERKREUZ  DES  EISERNEN KREUZES  =
ADOLF HITLER


  HERZLICHE GLUECKWUENSCHE .=
  DIE FERNSCHREIBSTELLE ++
```

On 17 September 1944 a telegram from the Führer's Headquarters arrived informing Hauptmann Zorner that he had been awarded the Oak Leaves to the Knight's Cross. (Zorner)

from the south and heading towards Vienna. Although he had some fifty-three aircraft at his disposal, only thirty-five of them were technically fit for operations, and of those only four could be brought up to operational readiness. This was further complicated by the lack of fuel, an ominous sign that the systematic bombing of Germany's fuel industry was having a devastating effect on the Luftwaffe's ability to operate. His *Gruppe* was ordered to scramble a single Ju88. As it had been some time since he had flown operationally Paul decided to fly himself. Tracking any incoming bombers in this theatre of the war was made very difficult, as there were no longer any ground radar systems in place, such as *Freya* or *Würzburg*. A great deal of reliance was therefore placed on ground-based radio monitoring organisations, which in itself was rather hit and miss. After some considerable time in the air, and having already flown past Vienna, his *Funker* had a contact at the maximum range of the *SN-2* radar. Flying at full throttle Paul was able to close the distance to the target quite quickly. He recounts his last victory of the war:

> As there was no cloud beneath me I remained lower and positioned myself under the bomber. From the tail unit I identified it as a Liberator. I fired into the starboard wing between the two engines with *Schräge Musik*. The wing began to burn within, at most, three seconds. I had just pulled off to starboard when the bomber became a huge ball of fire from which burning fragments were raining down to the ground. After sometime we got a radio contact with the operations room at Novy Dvoragain and after a break of months we were able to report a success.

Two days after a crash landing at Paderborn airfield on 5 October 1944, Oberstleutnant Helmut Lent died of his injuries. At the time of his death Lent was the highest scoring night fighter pilot with 102 victories. Six highly decorated officers from the Nachtjagd escorted his casket, one of who was Paul Zorner (far left). (Zorner)

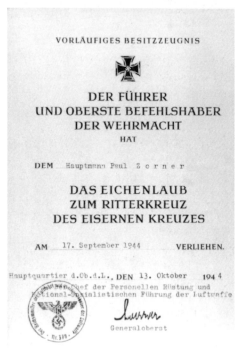

VORLÄUFIGES BESITZZEUGNIS

DER FÜHRER
UND OBERSTE BEFEHLSHABER
DER WEHRMACHT
HAT

DEM Hauptmann Paul Z o r n e r

DAS EICHENLAUB
ZUM RITTERKREUZ
DES EISERNEN KREUZES

AM 17. September 1944 VERLIEHEN.

Hauptquartier d.Ob.d.L., DEN 13. Oktober 1944

Right: The preliminary certificate for the Oak Leaves to the Knight's Cross. *Left:* Major Zorner wearing the Oak Leaves to the Knight's Cross. He became the 588th member of the Wehrmacht to receive this decoration. (Zorner)

Paul Zorner with his wife, Gerda, and their
daughter, Uta, in February 1945. (Zorner)

The war drew inexorably towards its climax. Outnumbered, out-gunned and with dwindling resources, the pilots and their crews fought on bravely. Their efforts however were to no avail.

On 8 May 1945, with the war in Europe now officially over, Paul Zorner attempted to evacuate himself and about eighty of his personnel from Karlsbad and Marienbad in the north-west of Czechoslovakia. He reached the American frontline but only he and his interpreter were allowed through. Refusing to leave his men, he decided to remain with them. For over a week they camped in a nearby field, watched over by American sentries.

Waking early on the morning of the 17 May, Paul found that the American soldiers had disappeared and to his utter horror Russian troops had replaced them. Over the following days the German prisoners were marched about 190km without food across Teplitz-Schönau and Dresden to Hoyerswerda in Saxony, about 55km north-east of Dresden. Arriving at the camp, Paul was separated from the rest of his men and placed in a smaller stockade within the main camp along with 2,000 other officers.

Frustratingly, each day he witnessed the continual release of soldiers from the main camp while the officers were told on a daily basis that it would soon be their turn. While they waited they passed the monotonous hours playing cards and holding lectures, while surviving on a meagre diet of bitter-tasting fish meal soup and bread.

At the beginning of October, those internees that remained were suddenly transported to the south Caucasus Mountains in Southern Russia. Six weeks later, with the journey completed, Paul Zorner along with 500 other officers were separated and then housed in a camp situated some 600m up in the mountains. The remaining 1,500 officers were taken

Prison camp 2/518 at Tkibuli, near Kutaisi in the Caucasus. The building on the far left was the officer's quarters, in the middle were the living quarters, and on the far right were the latrines. (Zorner)

to a second camp 300m higher up in the same mountain range. Any remaining hope he had of being released quickly finally evaporated. His future looked very uncertain.

Apart from a few native Georgians who lived there the only other contact with the outside world came from Russian civilians who in the past had committed petty criminal offences, and had been transported south in order to serve their sentences. These prisoners were allowed to travel within a forty mile radius around the camp as long as they completed their allocated work, for which they received some form of monetary payment.

Many aspects of camp life, its daily running and organisation were left to the prisoners to arrange. Paul Zorner, as a highly decorated officer was given the responsibility for the workshops, kitchens, and more importantly to keep peace and order in the camp. He describes the cramped conditions under which he and the other prisoners tried to live:

> The camp itself consisted of an accommodation block with twenty rooms in two storeys, a single storey 'office building', a 'housekeeping building' and a 'latrine'. The rooms in the accommodation block were about 4m by 3m in area and contained nothing except a wooden framework along one of the longer walls upon which were mounted, at about 0.5m and 1.8m height, layers of boards about 2m across. In front of them was a corridor barely a metre wide. In eighteen of these twenty rooms about 500 prisoners of war were accommodated, 22 men to a room. On the bed-racks each man had an area to lie on smaller than 2 by 0.4m. We could only sleep on one side, and we could only turn from side to side by doing so all at the same time. In the remaining two rooms of the accommodation block a 'sick quarters' had been set up. The rooms in the office building

were of the same size. In two of them the German 'Leadership Team' and the Battalion orderly room were located. One room was allocated as a repair centre for a tailor and a cobbler and as a 'clothing room'. The remaining five rooms were also occupied by men. In the 'housekeeping building' there was a room with a large boiler. There was the necessary kitchen equipment and a place for firewood. A second room served as a store for foodstuffs. At first the latrine comprised of only a hole in the ground with a long plank of wood across it.

After being in the camp for about a month, the prisoners were divided up into work parties, often having to endure a march of approximately 5 or 6km each morning along a railway line, stepping from sleeper to sleeper until they reached their place of work. Already weakened as a result of only being fed 0.5l of thin cabbage soup and 600g of bread a day, the prisoners were then forced to work in a quarry for eight hours. It wasn't surprising then that their physical condition soon began to deteriorate. Many still wore their original uniforms, which by now were hanging off their thin and drawn bodies. Most had had their prized boots stolen, and now wore foot-shaped wooden boards with straps fixed to them as a primitive form of sandal.

In February 1946, the Russians changed the internal running of the camp and Paul found himself in one of the 'Quarry Brigades'. He describes the type of work he and his companions were expected to undertake:

Of all the work parties, this one had the hardest labour to perform. Although this was certainly intended as a punishment for my 'wrong doing', it didn't basically make a lot of

A rare period of celebration among the prisoners as they celebrate the birthday of one of the inmates. (Zorner)

difference to me. As a pilot I had received the highest food rations in the Wehrmacht right up to the capitulation. In the quarry brigade we received the heaviest worker's rations, 600g of bread extra a day. We had to bore into huge limestone blocks of 40 to 50m^3 in size. The holes were then filled with explosives by a Russian foreman and exploded. We then had to carry the pieces to a slide, on which they slid down into a storage area. From there they were taken away by another work Kommando and used as ballast for the foundations of buildings.

By November, with their work now finished, 100 of the strongest 'stone breakers' were sent to the upper camp, where the prisoners were working in the worst possible conditions in deep mines. Conditions were dreadful. Almost every week accidents occurred which often resulted in the deaths of those involved. Paul found himself, until the end of 1946, labouring in these coal mines on the night shift, working from 22.00 to 06.00 hours.

This work was supposed to have been completed by the end of the year, but by the beginning of January 1947 the quota was increased in order to build up stocks. On hearing this news Paul Zorner refused to work any further. He had heard that even in Russia, prisoners of war with the rank of *Major* or above could not be forced to work.

His refusal to work brought him immediate unwanted attention from the Russian secret police, the NKVD. The Russian officer stood in front of Paul, face-to-face, noses almost touching, and then he simply began shouting and screaming abuse at the former German pilot. Seeing that this had no effect whatsoever, and with Paul still refusing to return to the coal mine, the Russian officer had him locked in the 'cooler' overnight. The following

After three years of captivity, in 1948, this picture was sent to his family back in Germany. (Zorner)

morning the NKVD officer tried a different approach. He tried to explain in a friendly manner that in the Peasants' and Workers' paradise everyone had to work, otherwise he was a parasite living off his comrades. Although indignant at being spoken to in such a manner Paul explained that despite the fact he wouldn't return to the mines he was prepared to work with a Silesian polisher in the carpenter's brigade. The NKVD officer begrudgingly agreed to the request. With a moral victory under his belt Paul Zorner returned to work.

With a change of Camp Commandant in April 1946, conditions began to slowly improve with the prisoners receiving the food they were entitled to. The ill-treatment from the guards, which had previously been rare, stopped altogether.

By September he was allowed for the first time to write a postcard consisting of no more than twenty-five words to his wife which she received just before Christmas 1946. Towards the end of 1947 this restriction was lifted and he was able to send letters, and from the spring of 1948 the prisoners were allowed to receive packages from their families. It was at this time that the first whisperings were heard of an agreement among the Allies, which would allow the repatriation of all German prisoners of war by the end of 1948.

Continuing his work as a carpenter, Paul waited patiently for events to unfold which would surely signal his release and that of his fellow countrymen. When 1948 came and went, and with no sign of freedom in sight, he decided to try and organise his own repatriation, but for this he would need to improve his spoken Russian.

In March 1949, a storeman was needed with some knowledge of the Russian language to work on a small building site and act as an interpreter. Paul was given the job and he began to formulate an escape plan that would take him across the border to Turkey. Circumstances however, overtook him.

There was a sudden announcement that all officers from the rank of *Major* and above were to collect their belongings and be ready to leave. Excitement quickly spread throughout the camp. Their hope was further raised when the Commandant informed those prisoners fortunate enough to be leaving that they were to be taken to Kiev and released.

Arriving in Kiev, Paul Zorner found himself accommodated with other German prisoners of war, all of whom were staff officers and men from former specialist units, such as counter-espionage and so on. To their horror and amazement, military tribunals were held and many of these men were tried in 'Kangaroo' courts. At the conclusion of the trials some of the prisoners were sentenced to terms of further imprisonment, varying between ten and twenty-five years' hard labour.

At the beginning of December 1949, those prisoners, including Paul Zorner, that hadn't been sentenced were deloused, given new clothes, and told that they should ready themselves for release. On 19 December, Paul and his remaining countrymen were put into goods wagons equipped with bunks and transported to Brest-Litovsk. Arriving on the 23 December, they were all ordered out and their numbers checked and rechecked. It was then back on to the train. After a long and anxious wait the train set off in the direction of the Russian-Polish border. Here he recalls those last nerve-racking days as their homeland drew closer and closer, the atmosphere in the goods wagon was growing more and more tense. After almost five years in captivity they were almost free:

After five long years of internment a gaunt looking Paul Zorner is finally reunited with his wife and daughter, summer 1950. (Zorner)

After several months of recuperation, the signs of recovery from his enforced Russian captivity are apparent. (Zorner)

Spring 1954. After studying engineering at Stuttgart University Paul Zorner went on to have a successful career in the chemical and plastics industry. (Zorner)

When we got there, we were ordered, 'All out and fall in in front of the wagons!' We were then counted. At last we got back in again and waited a considerable time. Then the train began to move – but backwards! At that moment, for the first time and only time in my fifty-five months of captivity, I cried. Our mistrust of the Soviet system, which we simply couldn't understand, was so great that we considered it completely possible that we were now on the way back to the Caucasus or to Siberia.

Throughout the following night we remained in the Brest-Litovsk railway station. It was Christmas Eve 1949. I don't think that any German occupant of that train slept. Then the morning came, it was bitterly cold and once again we had to climb out, we were counted and we climbed back into the wagons. At last we set off towards the west. At the border we stopped, unknown uniforms appeared, they must have been Polish: get out again, be counted, and get back in again. Now the Russian guards disappeared and the train set off again. At last we breathed freely. We didn't know what it was like in Poland, that is true, but Russia was behind us.

On 29 December we arrived in Frankfurt/Oder. We got out of the goods wagons, and heard German sounds around us again at last! We parted from our comrades who were staying in the GDR and we were driven to a normal train. We were greeted very warmly and then disinfected with a cloud of powder. We were given a few marks pocket money, rations for the journey and a railway ticket to the nearest station. I had to travel on to Ulm to an American unit, but I wasn't processed until 1 January. On 2 January, I had to travel further to Tuttlingen, south of Stuttgart, in the French zone, because I wanted to go to Kaiserslauten so that I could obtain my discharge certificate. On 3 January, at last,

I got my discharge certificate and a railway ticket to Kaiserslauten. I could go, and I was free! Then I travelled via Stuttgart and at six o'clock on the morning of 4 January 1950, I was at home with my wife and child. Now the war was over for me, too.

After a short period of recovery Paul began practical training in a local machine company, and he combined this with a mechanical engineering course at the Technical University in Stuttgart. With his training complete he commenced a new career in the field of refrigeration engineering.

In January 1956, with a view to restarting his flying career, he joined the new *Bundes*Luftwaffe. However, he was no longer considered fit enough to fly jet aircraft and was offered instead an opportunity to remain as an engineer. Understandably he didn't want to remain there if he couldn't fly, so, in May 1957 Paul returned to industry. He worked initially in the field of Cryogenics and then later in the reconstruction and maintenance service within the chemical industry.

By the time Paul finally retired in 1981, he had become chief engineer for one of the Hoechst factories situated near Frankfurt, producing plastics. He now lives quietly in retirement with his wife, Gerda, in Homburg.

Appendix I

German Medals and Awards

Pilot's Badge. Instituted on 12 August 1935 and worn on the left breast of the tunic. (Hoffmann)

Iron Cross Second Class. Instituted on 1 September 1939. Its ribbon was usually worn through the second button hole of the tunic. Approximately 2,300,000 were awarded. (Ted Gardener)

Iron Cross First Class. Instituted on 1 September 1939 and worn at the centre of the left breast pocket of the tunic. (Greiner)

Ehrenpokal. Instituted on 27 February 1940, some 58,000 of these goblets were awarded up to 5 July 1944. (author's collection)

German Cross in Gold. Instituted on 28 September 1941 and worn on the right breast pocket of the recipient's tunic. (author's collection)

Night Fighter Clasp. Instituted on 30 January 1941. There were three designations of clasp: Bronze for 20 operational flights, Silver for 60 and Gold for 110. (Greiner)

Wound Badge. Instituted on 1 September 1939. Three classes were awarded: Black for one and two wounds, Silver was awarded for sustaining three or four wounds and Gold for more than five. (Greiner)

Night Fighter Clasp with Pendant. As the war progressed and the number of operational flights grew steadily pendants were issued. The example here represents a total of 250 operational flights. Later on in the war this version was replaced with a box, which contained the number of operational flights flown, for example 300, 400 and so on. Usually worn above the left breast pocket. (Greiner)

Knight's Cross. Instituted on 1 September 1939. This highly sought award was worn around the neck and was only awarded to between 7,000 and 7,500 members of the Wehrmacht. (Hoffmann)

Oak Leaves to the Knight's Cross. Instituted on 3 June 1940 and attached to the Knight's Cross by means of a clasp. Approximately 880 were awarded during the war. (Gardener)

Swords and Oak Leaves to the Knight's Cross. Instituted on 21 June 1941, only a total of 159 were awarded. (Greiner)

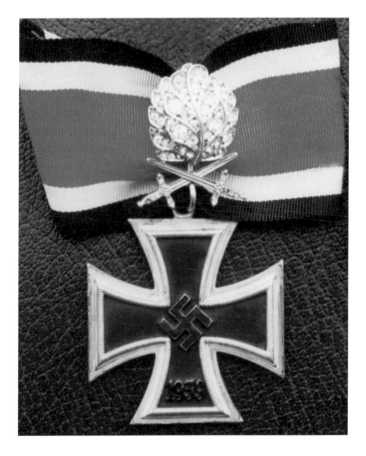

Diamonds, Swords and Oak Leaves to the Knight's Cross. Instituted on 15 July 1941. At the time of its introduction the Diamonds were the highest award the German Wehrmacht had to offer, only 27 of its combatants were bestowed with it. (Greiner)

Appendix II

Wolf Falck Statistics

Aerial Victories

No.	Date	Time	Location	Aircraft Type
1	5.9.39	06.40	Dalikow, Poland	PZL P.23 bomber
2	11.9.39	16.05	8km SE of Biala-Podlaska	Fokker F IX
3	11.9.39	16.10	12km SW of Biala-Podlaska	Single-engined reconnaissance aircraft
4	18.12.39	14.40	19km SW of Heligoland	Wellington IA
5	10.1.40	12.57	North Sea Planquadrat 565	Blenheim IV Planquadrat 565
6	17.2.40	16.10	North Sea Planquadrat ID	Blenheim IV
7	9.4.40	06.38	Vaerlöse, Denmark	Fokker D.XXI

Dates of Promotion

1.10.34	*Leutnant*
1.4.36	*Oberleutnant*
9.39	*Hauptmann*
1.7.40	*Major*
1.1.43	*Oberstleutnant*
1.7.43	*Oberst*

Dates of Awards

18.4.35	Pilot's Badge
13.9.39	Iron Cross Second Class
10.10.39	Sudeten Commemoration Medal with Swords
30.1.40	Iron Cross First Class
7.10.40	Knight's Cross
2.7.41	Flying Clasp in Silver
17.2.43	Pilot's Badge of the Royal Bulgarian Air Force
12.6.43	Virtute Aeronautica.
No. 967	Honorary Pilot's Badge of the Royal Romanian Air Force

Appendix III

Georg Hermann Greiner Statistics

Aerial Victories

No.	Date	Time	Location	Aircraft Type
1	26.6.42	06.00	NW Holland	Wellington
2	6.10.42	-	Leeuwarden, Holland	Halifax
3	-		3.43	Near Rastatt, Germany Short Stirling
4	26.5.43	-	Leeuwarden, Holland	Lancaster
5	26.5.43	-	Leeuwarden, Holland	Lancaster
6	6.7.43	-	Küster, near Leeuwarden, Holland	Short Stirling (Minelayer)
7	25.7.43	-	Terschilling, NW of Leeuwarden, Holland	Halifax
8	3.8.43	-	Holland	Lancaster
9	3.8.43	-	Holland	Wellington
10	24.8.43	-	Over Berlin	Halifax
11	23.9.43	-	Over Hannover	Lancaster
12	23.9.43	-	Over Hannover	Lancaster
13	27.9.43	-	-	Halifax
14	15.1.44	-	St Dizier, France	Lancaster
15	30.1.44	13.00	Osnabrück, Germany	B-17
16	10.2.44	12.25	Osnabrück, Germany	B-17
17	15.2.44	22.59	St Dizier, France	Lancaster
18	6.3.44	12.46	Osnabrück, Germany	B-17
19	6.3.44	15.53	Osnabrück, Germany	B-24
20	23.4.44	01.34	Düsseldorf, Germany	Halifax
21	25.4.44	02.25	Antwerp, Belgium	Lancaster
22	28.4.44	01.41	St Trond, Belgium	Lancaster
23	28.4.44	02.12	St Trond, Belgium	Halifax
24	2.5.44	00.28	Brussels, Belgium	Halifax
25	2.5.44	00.36	Brussels, Belgium	Halifax
26	9.5.44	04.11	Courtrai, Belgium	Halifax
27	12.5.44	00.27	Löwen, Belgium	Halifax
28	13.5.44	01.12	Hasselt, Belgium	Lancaster
29	25.5.44	00.29	Aachen, Germany	Lancaster
30	28.5.44	02.28	Antwerp, Belgium	Halifax
31	28.5.44	02.39	Antwerp, Belgium	Halifax
32	11.6.44	01.25	Paris, France	Halifax

33	16.6.44	00.54	Lille, France	Lancaster
34	5.7.44	02.05	Dieppe, France	Halifax
35	21.7.44	-	-	Lancaster
36	21.7.44	-	-	Lancaster
37	12.8.44	00.29	Frankfurt, Germany	Lancaster
38	22.9.44	22.36	Mönchengladbach, Germany	Halifax
39	22.9.44	23.28	Mönchengladbach, Germany	Lancaster
40	24.9.44	21.55	Münster, Germany	Halifax
41	4.11.44	19.21	Between Duisburg and Essen, Germany	Halifax
42	4.11.44	19.35	Between Duisburg and Essen, Germany	Halifax
43	5.1.45	19.12	Hannover, Germany	Lancaster
44	5.1.45	19.15	Hannover, Germany	Lancaster
45	5.1.45	19.18	Hannover, Germany	Lancaster
46	5.1.45	19.22	Hannover, Germany	Halifax
47	21.2.45	23.21	Neuss, Germany	Halifax
48	21.2.45	23.40	Neuss, Germany	Halifax
49	3.3.45	21.57	Dortmund, Germany	Lancaster
50	3.3.45	22.08	Dortmund, Germany	Lancaster

Dates of Promotion

-	*Leutnant*
20.4.42	*Oberleutnant*
15.4.44	*Staffelkapitän* 11./NJG 1
1.6.44	*Hauptmann*
1.11.44	*Gruppenkommandeur* IV./NJG 1

Dates of Awards

25.6.42	Iron Cross Second Class
1.10.42	Night fighter Clasp in Bronze
1.6.43	Iron Cross First Class
4.9.43	Night fighter Clasp in Silver
26.12.43	Honour Goblet
16.2.44	Night fighter Clasp in Gold
29.3.44	German Cross in Gold
27.7.44	Knight's Cross
17.4.45	Oak Leaves to the Knight's Cross
20.4.45	Night fighter Clasp in Gold with Pendant (200 missions)

51	3.3.45	22.12	Dortmund, Germany	Lancaster

Appendix IV

Werner Hoffmann Statistics

Aerial Victories

No.	Date	Time	Location	Aircraft Type
1	26.6.42	02.26	Frel, 6km SE of Heide	Lockheed Hudson
2	26.6.42	03.24	North Sea, 6km north of Büsum	Whitley V
3	21.4.43	00.45	Near Eggesin, Germany	Halifax
4	21.4.43	00.50	Near Borken, Germany	Halifax
5	30.5.43	01.45	-	Halifax
6	25.6.43	01.21	Near Erkelenz, Germany	Lancaster
7	25.6.43	01.51	Near Brasel, Belgium	Wellington
8	29.6.43	02.18	Near Leopoldsburg, Belgium	Short Stirling
9	4.9.43	00.32	North of Berlin	Lancaster
10	7.9.43	00.24	East of Munich	Halifax
11	7.9.43	00.45	North of Munich	Halifax
12	27.9.43	23.18	Hanover	Lancaster
13	18.10.43	20.25	Hanover	Halifax
14	22.10.43	21.14	Kassel	Lancaster
15	22.10.43	21.32	Bückeburg	Lancaster
16	23.11.43	20.08	Berlin	Halifax
17	2.12.43	20.23	Berlin	Lancaster
18	2.12.43	20.34	Berlin	Lancaster
19	2.1.44	03.06	Berlin	Lancaster
20	20.1.44	19.20	Berlin EE9	Lancaster
21	29.1.44	03.12	Berlin DF8	Halifax
22	29.1.44	03.27	Berlin FH5	Halifax
23	29.1.44	03.55	Berlin FH5	Halifax
24	30.1.44	20.15	Berlin	Lancaster
25	30.1.44	20.36	Berlin	Lancaster
26	15.2.44	20.48	Rostock TD7	Halifax
27	20.2.44	02.51	Brunswick GB9	Lancaster
28	20.2.44	03.17	Genthin-Stendal, Germany	Halifax
29	4.5.44	00.36	Mailly-Le-Camp, France	Four-engined bomber
30	4.5.44	00.37	Mailly-Le-Camp, France	Lancaster
31	3.6.44	01.24	27km South of Evreux, France	Four-engined bomber
32	28.6.44	03.50	Paris	Four-engined bomber
33	29.6.44	00.58	Area of radio beacon 'Willi' Map Ref: TH	Four-engined bomber

34	8.7.44	01.31	Area of radio beacon 'Benno' Map Ref: TD-UD	Lancaster
35	8.7.44	01.40	RC9-RD	Lancaster
36	8.7.44	01.50	RG	Lancaster
37	13.7.44	02.12	CL3-CL6-CM1 to 4	Lancaster
38	13.7.44	02.18	CL2/CL5	Lancaster
39	15.7.44	02.01	CL2-4	Lancaster
40	30.8.44	01.37	RA	Four-engined bomber
41	14.12.44	16.54	Libau, Latvia	DB-3-F
42	20.12.44	17.19	East of Libau	PS 84
43	20.12.44	18.09	East of Libau	DB-3-F
44	20.12.44	18.28	East of Libau	DB-3-F
45	6.1.45	21.12	Danzig	Halifax
46	14.2.45	22.00	Danzig	Boeing
47	14.2.45	22.11	Radio beacon 'Anton'	Lancaster
48	16.3.45	21.18	UU	Lancaster
49	16.3.45	21.26	TB	Halifax
50	16.3.45	21.30	TB-6 or TC-1-4	Lancaster

Werner Hoffmann is also credited with a day victory, a Spitfire, achieved over the beaches of Dunkirk on 24 May 1940.

Dates of Promotion

4.12.36	*Fahnenjunker*
1.6.37	*Gefreiter*
1.8.37	*Unteroffizier*
1.12.37	*Fähnrich*
1.9.38	*Oberfähnrich*
1.1.39	*Leutnant*
1.8.40	*Oberleutnant*
1.2.43	*Hauptmann*
1.6.44	*Major*
1.6.44	*Gruppenkommandeur* of I./NJG 5

Dates of Awards

2.6.38	Pilot's Badge
1.10.38	Commemorative Medal (entry into the Sudetenland)
15.6.40	Iron Cross Second Class
19.6.40	Wound Badge in Black
10.7.40	Iron Cross First Class
21.5.41	Night Fighter Clasp in Bronze
16.2.42	Night Fighter Clasp in Silver
8.7.43	Night Fighter Clasp in Gold
15.11.43	German Cross in Gold
26.12.43	Honour Goblet
4.5.44	Knight's Cross

Appendix V

Peter Spoden Statistics

Aerial Victories

No.	Date	Time	Location	Aircraft Type
1	18.8.43	01.55	Hanshagen-Greifswald	Lancaster
2	24.8.43	01.10	Berlin	Stirling
3	24.8.43	01.20	Berlin	Four-engined bomber
4	23.11.43	20.02	40km west of Berlin	Lancaster
5	14.1.44	19.30	Near Braunschweig	Four-engined bomber
6	14.1.44	19.35	Near Braunschweig	Four-engined bomber
7	27.1.44	20.27	30km west of Berlin	Four-engined bomber
8	27.1.44	20.36	20 m west of Berlin	Four-engined bomber
9	30.1.44	20.29	Stettin. AZ 206-44	Four-engined bomber
10	21.7.44	23.22	20km NW of Vienna	Wellington
11	13.8.44	00.26	40km SW of Darmstadt	Four-engined bomber
12	26.8.44	01.12	35km NW of Rüsselsheim	Four-engined bomber
13	12.9.44	00.12	20km NW of Darmstadt	Lancaster
14	12.9.44	00.18	20-30km NW of Darmstadt	Lancaster
15	4.12.44	19.33	20-25km SW of Heilbronn	Lancaster
16	4.12.44	19.38	25-30km SW of Heilbronn	Lancaster
17	4.12.44	19.42	30-35km SW of Heilbronn	Lancaster
18	22.12.44	18.59	20-40km NW of FF Graf	Four-engined bomber
19	1.2.45	19.34	25km SW of Karlsruhe	Liberator
20	21.2.45	20.40	30km SW of Worms	Lancaster
21	23.2.45	20.11	Pforzheim-Karlsruhe	Four-engined bomber
22	23.2.45	20.14	30km SW of Pforzheim	Lancaster
23	7.3.45	22.06	Dessau	Four-engined bomber
24	7.3.45	22.29	50-60km SW of Dessau	Four-engined bomber

Dates of Promotion

1.3.41	*Fahnenjunker-Gefreiter*
1.6.41	*Fahnenjunker-Unteroffizier*
1.10.41	*Fähnrich*
1.2.42	*Leutnant*
1.12.44	*Oberleutnant*
19.3.45	*Gruppenkommandeur of I./NJG 6*
20.4.45	*Hauptmann*

Dates of Awards

20.8.43	Iron Cross Second Class
26.8.43	Wound Badge in Black
15.11.43	Iron Cross First Class
13.1.44	Night Fighter Clasp in Bronze
8.7.44	Night Fighter Clasp in Silver
5.10.44	Honour Goblet
3.1.45	Wound Badge in Silver
2.45	German Cross in Gold

Appendix VI

Paul Zorner Statistics

Aerial Victories

No.	Date	Time	Location	Aircraft Type
1	17.1.43	21.54	North Sea, 45km NW of Juist	Halifax
2	11.2.43	20.44★	North Sea, 40km WNW of Borkum	Lancaster
3	19.2.43	20.34★	North Sea, 12km north of Norderney	Boston
4	27.2.43	20.46★	North Sea, 30km NNW of Schirmannikoog	Stirling
5	7.3.43	20.50★	North Sea, 12km NE of Norderney	Wellington (Minelayer)
6	14.3.43	03.51★	North of Norderney	Wellington
7	29.6.43	02.20★	15km SE of Antwerp, Belgium	Wellington
8	4.7.43	01.45★	10km SW of St Trond, Belgium	Wellington
9	9.7.43	02.20★	30km west of Malmedy, Belgium	Lancaster
10	25.7.43	23.54★	10km NE of Groningen, Belgium	Halifax
11	18.8.43	01.53★	Baltic Sea, SE of Falster	Halifax
12	18.8.43	02.03★	Baltic Sea, south of Rügen	Lancaster
13	23.11.43	20.05★	East of Berlin	Lancaster
14	2.12.43	19.20	FS-5 Diepholz	Lancaster
15	2.12.43	20.26	SSW of Berlin	Lancaster
16	20.12.43	-	NW of Frankfurt	Halifax
17	24.12.43	02.50	NE of Frankfurt	Lancaster
18	24.12.43	05.39	South of Diepholz	Lancaster
19	24.12.43	05.56	Cloppenburg	Lancaster
20	3.1.44	-	Luckenwalde	Lancaster
21	6.1.44	-	NW of Stettin	Lancaster
22	6.1.44	-	NW of Stettin	Lancaster
23	20.1.44	-	North of Berlin	Lancaster
24	20.1.44	-	North of Berlin	Lancaster
25	15.2.44	-	Baltic Sea, West of Rügen	Lancaster
26	15.2.44	-	NW of Berlin	Lancaster
27	20.2.44	03.02	North of Hannover	Lancaster
28	20.2.44	03.15	Wesendorf, Germany	Lancaster
29	20.2.44	03.22	Burg/Gardelegen, Germany	Lancaster
30	20.2.44	03.32	South of Briest, Germany	Lancaster
31	24.2.44	22.13	SW of Stuttgart	Lancaster
32	24.2.44	22.21	SW of Stuttgart	Lancaster
33	24.2.44	22.27	South of Stuttgart	Lancaster

34	25.2.44	00.23	NW of Stuttgart	Lancaster
35	25.2.44	00.44	North of Stuttgart	Lancaster
36	22.3.44	21.42	North of Frankfurt	Lancaster
37	22.3.44	22.16	SW of Frankfurt	Lancaster
38	24.3.44	22.53	LF Xantippe	Lancaster
39	26.3.44	22.01	North of Oberhausen, Germany	Lancaster
40	26.3.44	23.03	West of St Trond,	Lancaster
41	26.3.44	23.12	SW of Brussels, Belgium	Lancaster
42	21.4.44	03.00	SE of Antwerp, Belgium	Mosquito
43	23.4.44	01.03	SW of Aachen	Four-engined bomber
44	28.4.44	01.19	South of Nancy, France	Lancaster
45	28.4.44	01.43	SW of Strasbourg, France	Lancaster
46	28.4.44	02.09	NW of Friedrichshafen	Lancaster
47	1.6.44	02.30	30km WNW of Tergnier, France	Lancaster
48	3.6.44	01.19	30km WNW of Evreux, France	Lancaster
49	11.6.44	00.58	SW of Dreux, France	Halifax
50	11.6.44	00.58	SW of Dreux, France	Halifax
51	11.6.44	01.06	SW of Dreux, France	Halifax
52	11.6.44	01.41	NW of Chartres, France	Lancaster
53	25.6.44	00.32	East of Boulogne	Four-engined bomber
54	25.6.44	00.48	NW of Etaples, France.	Four-engined bomber.
55	30.6.44	01.21	15km SW of Bourges, France	Lancaster
56	25.7.44	02.23	West of Strasbourg, France	Four-engined bomber
57	25.7.44	02.33	NW of Strasbourg, France	Four-engined bomber
58	25.7.44	02.53	NW of St Dizier	Four-engined bomber
59	1.45	01.30	SSE of Graz, Austria	Liberator

★ Time the aircraft was observed hitting the ground.

Dates of Promotion

1.11.39	*Fähnrich*
1.1.40	*Oberfähnrich*
1.4.40	*Leutnant*
1.4.42	*Oberleutnant*
1.3.44	*Hauptmann*
5.4.44	*Gruppenkommandeur* of III./NJG 5
13.10.44	*Gruppenkommandeur* of II./NJG 100
1.12.44	*Major*

Dates of Awards

9.6.41	Iron Cross Second Class
21.8.41	Transport Pilot's Clasp in Bronze
22.10.41	Transport Pilot's Clasp in Silver
12.3.43	Iron Cross First Class
31.8.43	Honour Goblet
20.3.44	German Cross in Gold
30.3.44	Night Fighter Clasp in Gold
9.6.44	Knight's Cross
17.9.44	Oak Leaves to the Knight's Cross

Appendix VII

Top Night Fighter Pilots

Name	Victories	Unit/s	Award	Died
Maj Schnaufer, Heinz	121	NJG 1,4	RK+Br	13.7.50
Oberst Lent, Helmut	102 (+8 day)	NJG 1,2,3	RK+Br	7.10.44
Maj Prinz zu Sayn-Wittgenstein	83	NJG 2,3,5	RK+S	22.1.44
Oberst Streib, Werner	67 (+1 day)	NJG 1	RK+S	15.6.86
Hptm Meurer, Manfred	65	NJG 1	RK+E	22.1.44
Oberst Radusch, Günther	65	NJG 1,2,3,5	RK+E	29.7.88
Maj Schoenert, Rudolf	65	NJG 1,2,5,100	RK+E	30.11.85
Hptm Rökker, Heinz	63 (+1 day)	NJG 2	RK+E	
Maj Zorner, Paul	59	NJG 2,3,5,100	RK+E	
Hptm Becker, Martin	58	NJG 3,4,6	RK+E	
Maj Herget, Wilhelm	58 (+15 day)	NJG 3,4	RK+E	27.3.74
Hptm Raht, Gerhard	58	NJG 2,3	RK+E	11.177
Oblt Francsi, Gustav	56	NJG 100	RK	
Hptm Kraft, Josef	56	NJG 1,4,5,6	RK+E	
Hptm Strüning, Heinz	56	NJG 1,2	RK+E	24.12.44
Oblt Welter, Kurt	56 (+7 day)	NJG 11,300	RK+E	7.3.49
Maj Frank, Hans-Dieter	55	NJG 1	RK+E	27.9.43
Ofw Vinke, Heinz	54	NJG 1	RK+E	26.2.44
Hptm Geiger, August	54	NJG 1	RK+E	29/30.9.43
Maj Prinz zur Lippe-Weißenfeld	51	NJG 1,3,5	RK+E	12.3.44
Maj Hoffmann, Werner	50 (+1 day)	NJG 3,5	RK	
Ofw Kollack, Reinhard	49	NJG 1,4	RK	6.2.80
Hptm Greiner, Georg	47 (+4 day)	NJG 1	RK+E	
Otl Lütje, Herbert	47 (+3 day)	NJG 1,6	RK+E	18.1.67
Hptm Hager, Johannes	47 (+1 day)	NJG 1	RK	

Award Abbreviations

Br	Diamonds
S	Swords
E	Oak leaves
RK	Knight's Cross

Rank Abbreviations

Otl	*Oberstleutnant*
Maj	*Major*
Hptm	*Hauptmann*
Oblt	*Oberleutnant*
Lt	*Leutnant*
Ofw	*Oberfeldwebel*

Appendix VIII

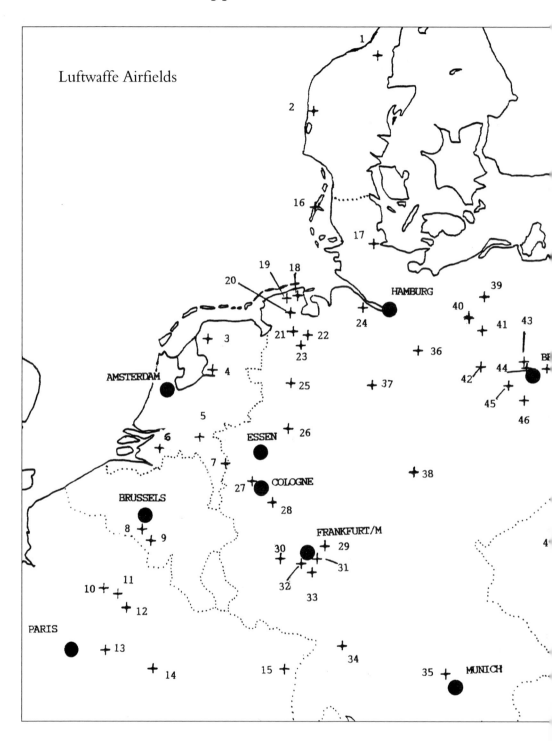

Luftwaffe Airfields

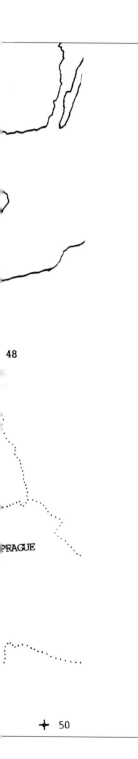

Key

Denmark:
1 Aalborg
2 Grove

Holland:
3 Leeuwarden
4 Deelen
5 Eindhoven
6 Gilze-Rijen
7 Venlo

Belgium:
8 St Trond
9 Florennes

France:
10 Tergnier
11 Athies/Laon
12 Juvincourt
13 Coulommiers
14 St Dizier
15 Hagenau

Germany (north):
16 Westerland
17 Schleswig
18 Jever
19 Wittmundhafen
20 Marx
21 Zwischenahn
22 Oldenburg
23 Vechta
24 Stade
25 Rheine

The Ruhr area:
26 Münster/Handorf
27 Köln/Butzweilerhof
28 Bonn/Hangelar

Germany (south):
29 Langdiebach
30 Mainz/Finthen
31 Zellhausen
32 Rhein/Main
33 Darmstadt
34 Echterdingen
35 Schleissheim

Germany (central):
36 Lüneburg
37 Wunsdorf
38 Erfurt/Bindersleben

Germany (east):
39 Rechlin
40 Parchim
41 Neuruppin
42 Stendal
43 Döberitz
44 Staaaken
45 Brandenberg/Briest
46 Jüterbog
47 Werneuchen
48 Königsberg
49 Prague/Ruzyn
50 Wien/Schwechat

Appendix IX

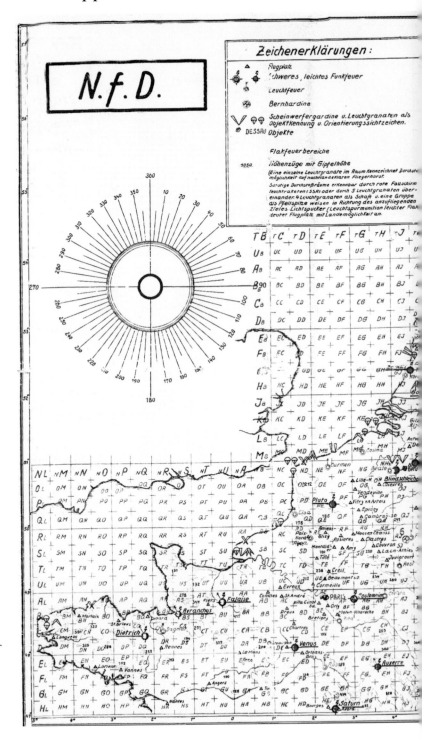

Night Fighters navigational map showing how the occupied areas of Western Europe were broken down into specific areas known as *planquadrates*, each of which was allocated two reference letters in order to identify its exact location.

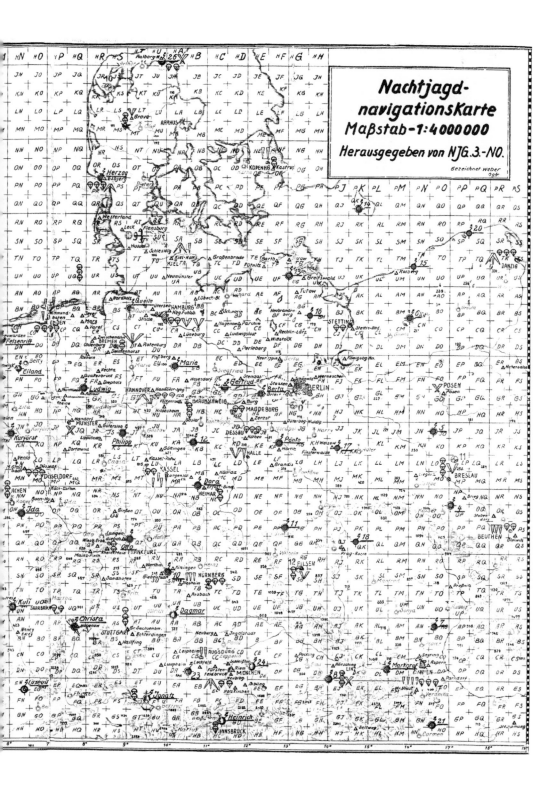

Nachtjagd-
navigationsKarte
Maßstab-1:4000000
Herausgegeben von NJG.3.-NO.

Gezeichnet Weber
294

Glossary

Abitur	Equivalent of Higher School Certificate or A levels
Abschuss	'Shootdown' – an aerial victory
Adler	Eagle
Alarmstart	Scramble
Blitzkrieg	'Lightning War'
Bodenplatte	Base plate
Bordfunker	Radar/radio operator
Bordmechaniker	Air Mechanic/Flight Engineer. When required, used as a rear-gunner
Deutsches Kreuz (DK)	German Cross awarded in gold and silver
Dunkel Nachtjagd	Radar controlled night fighting without the use of searchlights
Düppel	Aluminium coated paper strips used by the RAF to jam the German radar. Known by the British as 'Window'
Ehrenpokal (EP)	Goblet of honour
Eichenlaub (EL)	Oakleaves. The first higher grade of the Knight's Cross
Ergänzungsgruppe	Supplementary training group
Ergänzungsstaffel	Supplementary training squadron
Experte	A fighter 'Ace'
Fahnenjunker	Officer Cadet
Fähnrich	Rank equivalent to that of an RAF Warrant Officer
Fasan	Pheasant. Code word used when enemy activity expected
Flakscheinwerfer	Searchlight Battery
Flieger	Airman
Fliegerdivision	Air Division
Fliegerhorst	Airfield
Fliegerkorps	Air Corps
Flugzeugführer	Pilot
Freie Jagd	'Free Hunt'
Freya	Early German ground radar
Frontflugspange	Front Line Clasp awarded in bronze, silver and gold
Führer	Leader
Funker	Radio/Radar Operator
Gefechtsstand	Operations Room

Gefreiter	Rank equivalent to that of an RAF aircraftman
Gemeinschaft	Association
Generalmajor	Major-General
Geschwader	Operational unit of the Luftwaffe, usually consisted of three or more *Gruppen*
Geschwaderkommodore	The officer commanding a *Geschwader*
Gruppe	Operational unit of the Luftwaffe, usually consisted of three *Staffeln*
Gruppenkommandeur	The officer commanding a *Gruppe*
Gymnasium	Grammar school
Hauptmann	Rank equivalent to that of an RAF Flight Lieutenant or Army Captain
Helle Nachtjagd	Interception of an enemy aircraft using searchlights. Literal translation being 'light night fighting'
Himmelbett	Code word for a system of close-control night fighting. Literal translation 'four-poster bed'
Hitlerjugend	Hitler Youth
Horrido	Verbal exclamation to announce a 'Kill'
Jagddivision	Fighter Division
Jagdflieger	Fighter Pilot
Jägerleitoffizier	Fighter Control Officer
Kampfgeschwader	Bomber unit (KG)
Kapitän	The officer commanding a *Staffel*
Katschmarek	Slang term for a 'Wingman'
Kauz	Owl
Kette	Flight of three aircraft
Kommandeur	Commander. The officer commanding a *Gruppe*
Korps	Corps
Leutnant	Rank equivalent to that of an RAF Pilot Officer
Lichtenstein	An early air intercept radar used by the *Nachtjagd*
Luftflotte	Air Fleet
Luftkriegsschule	Air Warfare School
Luftwaffe	German Air Force
Major	Rank equivalent to that of RAF Squadron Leader
Moskito	Mosquito
Nachtjagd	Night hunting/fighting. The name by which the German night fighter force was known
Nachtjagddivision	Night fighter Division
Nachtjagdgeschwader (NJG)	Night fighter *Geschwader*
Nachtjäger	Night fighter pilot or aircraft
Oberfeldwebel	Rank equivalent to that of RAF Flight Sergeant
Obergefreiter	Rank equivalent to that of RAF Leading Aircraftman
Oberleutnant	Rank equivalent to that of RAF Flying Officer
Oberschule	High school

Oberst	Rank equivalent to that of RAF Group Captain
Oberstleutnant	Rank equivalent to that of RAF Wing Commander
Offizier	Officer
Planquadrat	A grid reference square for navigation
Pulk	An American heavy bomber formation – a combat box
Raum	*Himmelbett* control area
Reichsarbeitdienst	Reich Labour Service
Reichsmarschall	Rank held only by Hermann Göring
Reichsverteidigung	Air defence of the *Third Reich*
Ritterkreuz (RK)	The Knight's Cross to the Iron Cross
Ritterkreuzträger	Holder of the Knight's Cross
Rotte	Flight of two aircraft
Rottenflieger	Wingman, i.e. the second man in a *Rotte*
Rottenführer	Leader of a flight of two aircraft
Sau	Sow or boar
Schräge Musik	German code word for the upward firing cannon fitted in the roof/canopy of the night fighter's aircraft
Schwarm	Flight of aircraft consisting usually of no more than three machines
Schwerter (S)	Swords. The second higher grade of the Knight's Cross
Sieg Heil!	Used by the night fighter pilots to announce a 'Kill'
Sitzkreig	Phoney War
Stab	Staff
Staffel	Usually consisted of nine aircraft. The basic operational flying unit of the Luftwaffe
Staffelführer	Temporary or probationary officer commanding a *Staffel*
Staffelkapitän	Officer commanding a *Staffel*
Stieglitz	Goldfinch. A pre-war biplane used as a training aircraft
Sturmstaffel	Attack/Assault *Staffel*
Unteroffizier	Rank equivalent to that of RAF Corporal
Vaterland	Fatherland
Verwundetenabzeichen	Wound badge, awarded in black, silver and gold
Viermot	Four-engined aircraft
Volksschule	Elementary school
Volkssturm	Territorial Army. Usually consisted of those who were unfit, too young or too old to join the regular armed forces. Used in the last months of the war in the defence of the *Reich*
Wehrmacht	The combined German armed forces
Wilde Sau	Wild Boar. Code word given to the freelance interception of RAF bombers, usually over the target area
Würzburg	Later type of ground radar used originally by German searchlights and anti-aircraft units
Würzburg Riese	Giant Würzburg. Improved version of the Würzburg

	control radar used in the *Himmelbett* control system
Zahm	Tame
Zahme Sau	Tame Boar. Code word given for freelance interception within the bomber stream
Zerstörer	Destroyer name given to long range and ground attack fighter aircraft
Zerstörergeschwader (ZG)	Destroyer *Geschwader*
Zerstörergruppe	Destroyer *Gruppe*

Bibliography

Aders, Gebhard (1978) *History of the German Night Fighter Force 1917-1945*, Jane's Publishing Company London 1978

Bekker, Cajus (1994) *The* Luftwaffe *War Diaries*, Da Capo Press Inc

Boiten, Theo (1997) *Nachtjagd*, The Crowood Press Ltd

Bowman, Martin W. and Cushing, Tom (1996) *Confounding The Reich*, Patrick Stephens Ltd

Chorley, William R. (1997) *Bomber Command Losses*, Midland Counties Publications

Davies, Brian L (1995) *Uniforms and Insignia of the* Luftwaffe *1933-1940*, Arms and Armour

Ethell, Jeffrey and Price, Alfred (1981) *Target Berlin*, Jane's Publishing Ltd

Held, Werner and Nauroth, Holger (1991) *Bf110 Over All Fronts*, Schiffer Publishing Ltd

Hinchliffe, Peter (1999) *Schnaufer: Ace of Diamonds*, Tempus Publishing Ltd

Hinchliffe, Peter (1996) *The Other Battle*, Airlife Publishing Ltd

Ishoven, Armand Van (1985) *Messerschmitt Bf110 At War*, Ian Allan Ltd

Jagerblatt (Various Dates) 'Offizielles Organ der Gemeinschaft der Jagdflieger e.V.'

Ketley, Barry and Rolfe, Mark (1996) Luftwaffe *Fledglings 1935-1945*, Hikoki Publications

Kock, Werner (1996) *Das Kriegstagebuch Des Nachtjagdgeschwader 6,* Wittmund

Lucas, Laddie (1989) *Thanks For The Memory*, Stanley Paul and Co. Ltd

Middlebrook, William R and Everitt, Chris (1996) *The Bomber Command War Diaries*, Midland Publishing Ltd

Middlebrook, Martin (1984) *The Battle of Hamburg*, Penguin Books Ltd

Middlebrook, Martin (1990) *The Berlin Raids*, Penguin Books Ltd

Middlebrook, Martin (1986) *The Nuremberg Raid*, Penguin Books Ltd

Middlebrook, Martin (1988)*The Peenemünde Raid*, Penguin Books Ltd

Mombeek, Eric, with Smith, J.R. and Creek, E.D. (1999) *Jagdwaffe Volume 1*, Classic Publications

Obermaier, Ernst (1989) *Die Ritterkreuzträger Der* Luftwaffe *1939-1945 Volume 1*, Verlag Dieter Hoffmann, Mainz

Shirer, William L. (1977) *The Rise and Fall of the Third Reich*, Book Club Associates